Getting Started

Level III CFA® Exam

Welcome

As the VP of Advanced Designations at Kaplan Schweser, I am pleased to have the opportunity to help you prepare for the CFA® exam. Getting an early start on your study program is important for you to sufficiently **prepare**, **practice**, and **perform** on exam day. Proper planning will allow you to set aside enough time to master the Learning Outcome Statements (LOS) in the Level III curriculum.

Now that you've received your SchweserNotes™, here's how to get started:

Step 1: Access Your Online Tools

Visit **www.schweser.com** and log in to your online account using the button located in the top navigation bar. After logging in, select the appropriate level and proceed to the dashboard where you can access your online products.

Step 2: Create a Study Plan

Create a study plan with the **Study Calendar** (located on the Schweser dashboard) and familiarize yourself with your financial calculator. Check out our calculator videos in the **Candidate Resource Library** (also found on the dashboard).

Step 3: Prepare and Practice

Read your SchweserNotes™ Volumes 1–5

At the end of each reading, you can answer the Concept Checker questions for better understanding of the curriculum.

Attend a Weekly Class

Attend live classes online or take part in our live classroom courses in select cities around the world. Our expert faculty will guide you through the curriculum with a structured approach to help you prepare for the CFA® exam. The Schweser **On-Demand Video Lectures**, in combination with the **Weekly Class**, offer a blended learning approach that covers every LOS in the CFA curriculum.

Practice with SchweserPro™ QBank

Maximize your retention of important concepts by answering questions in the **SchweserPro™ QBank** and taking several **Practice Exams**. Use **Schweser's QuickSheet** for continuous review on the go. (Visit **www.schweser.com/cfa** to order.)

Step 4: Attend a 3-Day, 5-Day, or WindsorWeek™ Review Workshop

Schweser's late-season review workshops are designed to drive home the CFA® material, which is critical for CFA exam success. Review key concepts in every topic, **perform** by working through demonstration problems, and **practice** your exam techniques.

Step 5: Perform

Take a **Live** or **Live Online Schweser Mock Exam** to ensure you are ready to **perform** on the actual CFA® exam. Put your skills and knowledge to the test and gain confidence before the exam.

Again, thank you for trusting Kaplan Schweser with your CFA exam preparation!

Sincerely,

Derek Burkett

Derek Burkett, CFA, FRM, CAIA

VP, Advanced Designations, Kaplan Schweser

——— The Kaplan Way ———

Prepare
Acquire new knowledge through demonstration and examples.

Practice
Apply new knowledge through simulation and practice.

Perform
Evaluate mastery of new knowledge and identify achieved outcomes.

Visit our website, www.schweser.com/cfa-free-resources, to view all the free materials we have to help you prepare.

 Question of the Day

 Kaplan Schweser Adaptive CFA® Review Mobile App

How to Pass Videos

Contact us for questions about your study package, upgrading your package, purchasing additional study materials, or for additional information:

888.325.5072 (U.S.) | +1 608.779.8327 (Int'l.)

staff@schweser.com | www.schweser.com/cfa

BOOK 2 – PRIVATE WEALTH MANAGEMENT AND INSTITUTIONAL INVESTORS

SCHWESERNOTES™ 2018 LEVEL III CFA® BOOK 2: PRIVATE WEALTH
MANAGEMENT AND INSTITUTIONAL INVESTORS

©2017 Kaplan, Inc. All rights reserved.

Published in 2017 by Kaplan, Inc.

Printed in the United States of America.

ISBN: 978-1-4754-6038-4

READINGS AND LEARNING OUTCOME STATEMENTS

READINGS

The following material is a review of the Private Wealth Management and Institutional Investors principles designed to address the learning outcome statements set forth by CFA Institute.

STUDY SESSION 4

Reading Assignments

Private Wealth Management (1), CFA Program 2018 Curriculum, Volume 2, Level III

STUDY SESSION 5

Reading Assignments

Private Wealth Management (2), CFA Program 2018 Curriculum, Volume 2, Level III

STUDY SESSION 6

Reading Assignments

Portfolio Management for Institutional Investors, CFA Program 2018 Curriculum, Volume 2, Level III

LEARNING OUTCOME STATEMENTS (LOS)

The CFA Institute learning outcome statements are listed in the following. These are repeated in each topic review. However, the order may have been changed in order to get a better fit with the flow of the review.

STUDY SESSION 4

The topical coverage corresponds with the following CFA Institute assigned reading:

8. **Managing Individual Investor Portfolios**
The candidate should be able to:
   a. discuss how source of wealth, measure of wealth, and stage of life affect an individual investors' risk tolerance. (page 2)
   b. explain the role of situational and psychological profiling in understanding an individual investor's attitude toward risk. (page 2)
   c. explain the influence of investor psychology on risk tolerance and investment choices. (page 5)
   d. explain potential benefits, for both clients and investment advisers, of having a formal investment policy statement. (page 6)
   e. explain the process involved in creating an investment policy statement. (page 7)
   f. distinguish between required return and desired return and explain how these affect the individual investor's investment policy. (page 8)
   g. explain how to set risk and return objectives for individual investor portfolios. (page 8)
   h. discuss the effects that ability and willingness to take risk have on risk tolerance. (page 8)
   i. discuss the major constraint categories included in an individual investor's investment policy statement. (page 14)
   j. Prepare and justify an investment policy statement for an individual investor. (page 19)
   k. determine the strategic asset allocation that is most appropriate for an individual investor's specific investment objectives and constraints. (page 27)
   l. compare Monte Carlo and traditional deterministic approaches to retirement planning and explain the advantages of a Monte Carlo approach. (page 30)

The topical coverage corresponds with the following CFA Institute assigned reading:

9. **Taxes and Private Wealth Management in a Global Context**
The candidate should be able to:
   a. compare basic global taxation regimes as they relate to the taxation of dividend income, interest income, realized capital gains, and unrealized capital gains. (page 40)
   b. determine the effects of different types of taxes and tax regimes on future wealth accumulation. (page 43)
   c. explain how investment return and investment horizon affect the tax impact associated with an investment. (page 43)
   d. discuss the tax profiles of different types of investment accounts and explain their effects on after-tax returns and future accumulations. (page 54)
   e. explain how taxes affect investment risk. (page 58)
   f. discuss the relation between after-tax returns and different types of investor trading behavior. (page 60)

©2017 Kaplan, Inc.

g. explain tax loss harvesting and highest-in/first-out (HIFO) tax lot accounting. (page 62)

h. demonstrate how taxes and asset location relate to mean–variance optimization. (page 66)

The topical coverage corresponds with the following CFA Institute assigned reading:

10. Estate Planning in a Global Context

The candidate should be able to:

a. discuss the purpose of estate planning and explain the basic concepts of domestic estate planning, including estates, wills, and probate. (page 79)

b. explain the two principal forms of wealth transfer taxes and discuss effects of important non-tax issues, such as legal system, forced heirship, and marital property regime. (page 80)

c. determine a family's core capital and excess capital, based on mortality probabilities and Monte Carlo analysis. (page 83)

d. evaluate the relative after-tax value of lifetime gifts and testamentary bequests. (page 88)

e. explain the estate planning benefit of making lifetime gifts when gift taxes are paid by the donor, rather than the recipient. (page 88)

f. evaluate the after-tax benefits of basic estate planning strategies, including generation skipping, spousal exemptions, valuation discounts, and charitable gifts. (page 91)

g. explain the basic structure of a trust and discuss the differences between revocable and irrevocable trusts. (page 93)

h. explain how life insurance can be a tax-efficient means of wealth transfer. (page 95)

i. discuss the two principal systems (source jurisdiction and residence jurisdiction) for establishing a country's tax jurisdiction. (page 95)

j. discuss the possible income and estate tax consequences of foreign situated assets and foreign-sourced income. (page 95)

k. evaluate a client's tax liability under each of three basic methods (credit, exemption, and deduction) that a country may use to provide relief from double taxation. (page 96)

l. discuss how increasing international transparency and information exchange among tax authorities affect international estate planning. (page 98)

STUDY SESSION 5

The topical coverage corresponds with the following CFA Institute assigned reading:

11. Concentrated Single-Asset Positions

The candidate should be able to:

a. explain investment risks associated with a concentrated position in a single asset and discuss the appropriateness of reducing such risks. (page 107)

b. describe typical objectives in managing concentrated positions. (page 109)

c. discuss tax consequences and illiquidity as considerations affecting the management of concentrated positions in publicly traded common shares, privately held businesses, and real estate. (page 109)

d. discuss capital market and institutional constraints on an investor's ability to reduce a concentrated position. (page 110)

e. discuss psychological considerations that may make an investor reluctant to reduce his or her exposure to a concentrated position. (page 111)

f. describe advisers' use of goal-based planning in managing concentrated positions. (page 111)

g. explain uses of asset location and wealth transfers in managing concentrated positions. (page 113)

h. describe strategies for managing concentrated positions in publicly traded common shares. (page 116)

i. discuss tax considerations in the choice of hedging strategy. (page 119)

j. describe strategies for managing concentrated positions in privately held businesses. (page 120)

k. describe strategies for managing concentrated positions in real estate. (page 124)

l. evaluate and recommend techniques for tax efficiently managing the risks of concentrated positions in publicly traded common stock, privately held businesses, and real estate. (page 125)

The topical coverage corresponds with the following CFA Institute assigned reading:

12. **Risk Management for Individuals**
The candidate should be able to:

a. compare the characteristics of human capital and financial capital as components of an individual's total wealth. (page 140)

b. discuss the relationships among human capital, financial capital, and net wealth. (page 142)

c. discuss the financial stages of life for an individual. (page 142)

d. describe an economic (holistic) balance sheet. (page 143)

e. discuss risks (earnings, premature death, longevity, property, liability, and health risks) in relation to human and financial capital. (page 145)

f. describe types of insurance relevant to personal financial planning. (page 146)

g. describe the basic elements of a life insurance policy and how insurers price a life insurance policy. (page 147)

h. discuss the use of annuities in personal financial planning. (page 152)

i. discuss the relative advantages and disadvantages of fixed and variable annuities. (page 154)

j. analyze and critique an insurance program. (page 157)

k. discuss how asset allocation policy may be influenced by the risk characteristics of human capital. (page 159)

l. recommend and justify appropriate strategies for asset allocation and risk reduction when given an investor profile of key inputs. (page 161)

STUDY SESSION 6

The topical coverage corresponds with the following CFA Institute assigned reading:

13. **Managing Institutional Investor Portfolios**
The candidate should be able to:

a. contrast a defined-benefit plan to a defined-contribution plan and discuss the advantages and disadvantages of each from the perspectives of the employee and the employer. (page 173)

b. discuss investment objectives and constraints for defined-benefit plans. (page 173)

c. evaluate pension fund risk tolerance when risk is considered from the perspective of the 1) plan surplus, 2) sponsor financial status and profitability, 3) sponsor and pension fund common risk exposures, 4) plan features, and 5) workforce characteristics. (page 174)

d. Prepare an investment policy statement for a defined-benefit plan. (page 175)

e. evaluate the risk management considerations in investing pension plan assets. (page 177)

f. Prepare an investment policy statement for a participant directed defined-contribution plan. (page 177)

g. discuss hybrid pension plans (e.g., cash balance plans) and employee stock ownership plans. (page 178)

h. distinguish among various types of foundations, with respect to their description, purpose, and source of funds. (page 179)

i. compare the investment objectives and constraints of foundations, endowments, insurance companies, and banks. (page 180 and page 194)

j. discuss the factors that determine investment policy for pension funds, foundations, endowments, life and non-life insurance companies, and banks. (page 194)

k. Prepare an investment policy statement for a foundation, an endowment, an insurance company, and a bank. (page 180 and page 194)

l. contrast investment companies, commodity pools, and hedge funds to other types of institutional investors. (page 193)

m. compare the asset/liability management needs of pension funds, foundations, endowments, insurance companies, and banks. (page 192)

n. compare the investment objectives and constraints of institutional investors given relevant data, such as descriptions of their financial circumstances and attitudes toward risk. (page 194)

Managing Individual Investor Portfolios[1]

Exam Focus

The morning exam has traditionally been heavily weighted toward investment policy statement (IPS) questions for individuals and institutions.

To answer IPS questions successfully, you must:

1. Be familiar with and understand a large number of potential issues that might apply in a given situation. These are covered in the SchweserNotes and in the CFA readings. There is no substitute for reading the material.

2. Carefully read and understand the facts of the case to determine which issues from #1 above are relevant. Because each case is unique, you cannot expect to pass just by repeating what you saw as the answer to a previous question. CFA Institute says that the Level III exam is unique in requiring a high level of judgment and it is these questions where that most comes into play. You will have the opportunity to practice this as you go forward in the Schweser material.

3. Recognize that there is a process at work in constructing an IPS and doing a strategic asset allocation (SAA). The CFA material provides examples of the output from this process and discusses the inputs but does not focus on the construction process. However, the exam has required candidates to construct an IPS and then use it. We focus on this in our material.

4. The last stage is to construct a written answer that reflects #1, #2, and #3. This has not been required on other levels of the exam. The morning session is generally referred to as *essay*; however, the more precise term is *constructed response*. The key points that should appear in your answer have been decided, and your answer is evaluated strictly in terms of how well it makes and supports those points in coherent fashion. Practice writing an effective constructed response answer many times before the exam.

5. A significant percentage of Level III candidates find this section frustrating because it does not meet their personal sense of consistency. Past answers are quite consistent on the main, important issues (with a few exceptions, we will discuss these). But they also include a range of random, unimportant comments. The random comments are frustrating to candidates who try to repeat what they have seen in past answers. Try to move past that and learn what is expected. Up to now, the CFA exam

---

1. Terminology used throughout this topic review is industry convention as presented in Reading 8 of the 2018 Level III CFA exam curriculum.

process has primarily focused on precise mathematical techniques. The Level III material will continue to draw on those skills. However, this exam will likely test your ability to find what another trained professional would have been expected to find and write, when confronted with sometimes contradictory issues.

The next pages will lay out a variety of issues with which you are expected to be familiar. They may or may not be relevant to a given portfolio question. The exam will likely test the ability to determine what is relevant to a particular case and then apply it.

INVESTOR PROFILING AND RISK TOLERANCE

LOS 8.a: Discuss how source of wealth, measure of wealth, and stage of life affect an individual investors' risk tolerance.

LOS 8.b: Explain the role of situational and psychological profiling in understanding an individual investor's attitude toward risk.

CFA® Program Curriculum, Volume 2, page 162

Due to the variety of individual circumstances, the adviser may utilize *situational profiling* as a starting point in understanding the client and his needs. Situational profiling begins with determining the investor's source of wealth, measure of perceived wealth versus needs, and stage of life. These can provide insight into the individual's risk tolerance and return objectives.

Source of Wealth

Generally, wealth is created either *actively* through entrepreneurial activities or *passively. Passive wealth might come from* inheritance, windfall, or through long, secure employment and conservative investment. The manner in which an individual has accumulated wealth provides clues about his psychological makeup and his *willingness* to take risk.

Active wealth creation. Wealth that has been accumulated through *entrepreneurial activity* may be the result of considerable risk taking. Thus, an individual classified as an entrepreneur could exhibit a significant willingness to take risk. Keep in mind, however, that entrepreneurs might be willing to accept *business risk* because they feel in control of the firm and their futures. The method of wealth acquisition can lead to different attitudes toward *investment risk.*

The bottom line is that when someone is classified as an entrepreneur, it may indicate an above-average willingness to tolerate risk. You must, however, be careful to look for statements and/or actions that confirm the assumption or might indicate otherwise. Willingness can be indicated by both statements and actions.

Passive wealth creation. Wealth acquired through windfall or inheritance could indicate a lack of knowledge related to and discomfort with making investment decisions. These individuals may have below-average *willingness* to tolerate risk. Due to their lack of investment experience, these investors generally have little confidence in their abilities to regain their wealth should they experience significant losses and thus can have a strong desire to protect it.

An individual who has accumulated wealth through conservative consumption and savings over a lifetime of secure employment has probably demonstrated a policy of delayed consumption and careful, low-risk investments. This individual has demonstrated a desire for long-term financial security and would be classified as having below-average willingness to take risk.

Measure of Wealth

Generally, there is a positive correlation between a client's *perception* of wealth and his willingness to take investment risk. If an investor perceives his wealth as small, he will have low risk tolerance and wish to hold only low-volatility investments. The opposite is of course true for an individual who perceives his wealth as large.

Stage of Life

According to conventional wisdom, investors in the earlier stages of life have the ability to add to their portfolios through employment-related income and have time to recover from short-term market downturns. They are able to tolerate greater portfolio volatility and take risk.

Life stages are a progression and the normal progression is:

- *Foundation* phase when individuals are seeking to accumulate wealth through a job and savings, seeking education, or building a business. Their long time horizon can allow considerable risk taking. However, they often have little financial wealth to risk, and this may reduce ability to take risk. On the other hand, those who inherit wealth can often assume high risk given their long time horizon. The conclusion will depend on the specifics of the investor's circumstances.
- *Accumulation* phase when earnings or business success rise and financial assets can be accumulated. Financial demands, such as buying a house or educating children, may also rise. This could be a time of maximum savings and wealth accumulation with a higher ability to bear risk.
- *Maintenance* phase, which often means retirement. Preserving wealth and living off the portfolio return often become important. The ability to bear risk will be declining but is probably not low. Life expectancy can be long, with a need to maintain purchasing power. Being too conservative could lead to a decline in standard of living.
- *Distribution* stage means assets exceed any reasonable level of need for the individual and a process of distributing assets to others can begin. This might involve gifts now or making plans for distribution at death. For the wealthy, financial objectives may extend beyond their death so that the time horizon remains long and ability to bear risk could remain high, depending on the overall situation.

This progression is not always linear. Setbacks or windfalls along the way could move someone ahead or back, regardless of the simple passage of time.

Professor's Note: These are generalities that have to be considered in the context of all the case information. A retired individual with very low needs relative to wealth can have high ability to take risk. An elderly client with significant wealth and goals to pass this on to future generations may choose a significantly more aggressive portfolio allocation than would be implied by naively considering stage of life.

TRADITIONAL FINANCE VS. BEHAVIORAL FINANCE

Traditional finance (i.e., modern portfolio theory) assumes investors exhibit three characteristics:

1. *Risk aversion.* Investors minimize risk for a given level of return or maximize return for a given level of risk and measure risk as volatility.

2. *Rational expectations.* Investors' forecasts are unbiased and accurately reflect all relevant information pertaining to asset valuation.

3. *Asset integration.* Investors consider the correlation of a potential investment with their existing portfolios. They focus on the impact of adding a new asset on the return and risk of the total portfolio.

Based on these assumptions, it can be expected asset prices will reflect economic factors, and portfolios can be constructed holistically—this means by looking at weighted average returns and risk calculations that rely on covariance (and correlation).

In contrast, **behavioral finance** assumes other factors may also be relevant. Decision models also need to consider:

Professor's Note: Consider this a cursory review of terms that are better covered in other Study Sessions.

1. *Loss aversion* occurs when the framing of a decision as a gain or loss affects the decision. For example, given a choice between (1) a small known loss of $800 and (2) a 50/50 chance of losing $1,600 or $0 (which is, on average, losing $800), individuals choose uncertainty and choose the 50/50. But rephrase this as gains and they choose certainty. For example (1) a small known gain of $800 or (2) a 50/50 chance of gaining $1,600 or $0 (which is, on average, gaining $800), individuals choose certainty and take the sure $800. Phrased as a gain, they take certainty, which is consistent with traditional finance. Phrased as a loss, they take uncertainty, hoping to avoid a loss, hence the term *loss aversion*.

2. *Biased expectations* are a cognitive error that can occur from overconfidence in predicting the future. Some examples include assuming the results of the average manager will be those of a particular manager, excessively focusing on outlier events, and mistakenly letting one asset represent another asset.

3. *Asset segregation* occurs when investors view assets in isolation and do not consider the effect of correlation with other assets. As a result:
   - Asset prices will reflect both underlying economics and the investor's subjective feelings.
   - Portfolio construction will be segmented by layers with each layer reflecting the priority of its goals to that investor. Assets will be selected by layer.

INVESTOR PSYCHOLOGY AND PERSONALITY TYPES

LOS 8.c: Explain the influence of investor psychology on risk tolerance and investment choices.

CFA® Program Curriculum, Volume 2, page 166

Behavioral models indicate that the investment valuation and decision process incorporates more than the traditional fundamental financial variables seen in portfolio theory. Behavioral finance assumes investors also include individual preferences based on personal tastes and experiences. That is, individuals value personal and investment characteristics that may or may not be considered in traditional finance valuation processes.

Additionally, individuals tend to construct portfolios one asset at a time rather than using a diversified portfolio (i.e., asset integration) approach. Wealth creation is determined not from an overall portfolio perspective but by making investment decisions that relate to specific goals (e.g., pyramiding).

Investor attitudes are affected by numerous personal factors, including socioeconomic background, experiences, wealth, and even frame of mind. Through the use of questionnaires that focus on non-investment-related questions concerning personal attitudes and decision making, investors can be categorized within broad *personality types*.

The personality typing questionnaire should be considered only a first step. The results of the questionnaire should be used as a starting point in determining the client's risk tolerance and attitude toward and understanding of investment decision making. Having a better understanding of the client helps the manager anticipate the client's concerns, structure a discussion of the client's investment program in terms the client will understand, and construct a relevant IPS.

Personality Types

Four very general categories of attitude and style result from this type of questionnaire and may provide indications into investment-related behavior. Through the questionnaire process, investors can be classified as *cautious, methodical, individualistic,* or *spontaneous.*

Cautious investors are risk averse and base decisions on feelings. They prefer safe, low-volatility investments with little potential for loss. They do not like making their own investment decisions but are difficult to advise and will sometimes even avoid professional help. Their inability to make decisions can lead to missed investment opportunities. Once they have made investment decisions, their portfolios exhibit low turnover. Look for individuals who minimize risk and have trouble making decisions.

Methodical investors are risk averse and base decisions on thinking. They diligently research markets, industries, and firms to gather investment information. Their investment decisions tend to be conservative and, because they base decisions on facts, they rarely form emotional attachments to investments. They continually seek confirmation of their investment decisions, so they are constantly on the lookout for better information. Look for individuals who are conservative, gather lots of data, and look for more information.

Individualistic investors are less risk averse and base decisions on thinking. They do their own research and are very confident in their ability to make investment decisions. When faced with seemingly contradictory information, they will devote the time needed to reconcile the differences. Individualistic investors tend to have confidence in their ability to achieve their long-term investment objectives. Look for individuals who are confident and make their own decisions.

Spontaneous investors are less risk averse and base decisions on feelings. They constantly adjust their portfolios in response to changing market conditions. They fear that failing to respond to changing market conditions will negatively impact their portfolios. They acknowledge their lack of investment expertise but at the same time tend to doubt investment advice. Their reactions to changing investment trends combined with a tendency to over-manage their portfolios leads to high turnover. Portfolio performance is diminished by high trading costs. Look for individuals who have high portfolio turnover, chase fads, and continually want to do something.

THE INVESTMENT POLICY STATEMENT

LOS 8.d: Explain potential benefits, for both clients and investment advisers, of having a formal investment policy statement.

CFA® Program Curriculum, Volume 2, page 171

> **For the Exam:** We now turn to the construction process for an investment policy statement (IPS). An IPS can range from a simple 1-page document prepared by the investment manager to a large book prepared by other experts retained by the client. For purposes of the exam, the IPS focus is on the Objectives and Constraints (O&C) section. For the exam, the terms *IPS* and *O&C* may be used interchangeably, though technically O&C is just part of IPS. Strategic asset allocation (SAA) may or may not be a part of the IPS. Some authors suggest it is, others do not include it in the IPS itself but treat it as a separate step. The exam generally treats it as a separate step.

The investment policy statement (IPS), in fact the entire process of developing the IPS, is valuable for both the client and the investment adviser. Ultimately the IPS must be internally consistent with the return and risk objectives, reasonable given the prevailing capital market conditions, and consistent with the client's constraints. However, it is more reasonable to approach the construction in parts. The IPS will include the financial objectives of the client (the O in O&C) as well as the constraints (the C).

For the *client*, the benefits of the IPS include:

- The IPS identifies and documents investment objectives and constraints.
- The IPS is dynamic, allowing changes in objectives and/or constraints in response to changing client circumstances or capital market conditions.
- The IPS is easily understood, providing the client with the ability to bring in new managers or change managers without disruption of the investment process.
- Developing the IPS should be an educational experience for the client.
    - Clients learn more about themselves and investment decision making.
    - They are better able to understand the manager's investment recommendations.

For the *adviser*, the benefits include:

- Greater knowledge of the client.
- Guidance for investment decision making.
- Guidance for resolution of disputes.
    - Signed documentation that can be used to support the manager's investment decisions as well as the manager's denials of client investment requests.

LOS 8.e: Explain the process involved in creating an investment policy statement.

CFA® Program Curriculum, Volume 2, page 172

For the Exam: A typical IPS starts with two objectives: return, then risk. Next it will discuss the five constraints: time horizon, taxes, liquidity, legal, and unique. An easy way to remember this is RRTTLLU (Return, Risk, Time horizon, Taxes, Liquidity, Legal, Unique).

However, the order of presentation is not the same as the construction process. The exam question may ask for RRTTLLU or it may ask for the constraints (TTLLU) and then R and R, or for only some of the items. To construct the IPS, you should think through the case facts presented, the material from the reading assignments, and how they affect the constraints (TTLLU). This will largely lead you to the correct assessment of the risk and return objective. Ultimately, the risk and return have to be compatible. However, if you think in terms of appropriate risk setting the appropriate return, you will make fewer mistakes.

- As you determine the client's objectives and constraints, be sure to address each separately using the information in the case. *Objectives:* required return and risk tolerance. Constraints: time horizon, tax considerations, liquidity needs, legal and regulatory concerns, and unique circumstances.
- If a follow-on question asks for the SAA, it is important that you check the consistency of the asset classes and overall SAA with the objectives and constraints of the IPS.

The wrong approach to answering exam questions can lead to wasted time and costly mistakes. When approaching an essay question:

- Pay attention to the minutes assigned to the question. The minutes are part of the instructions. If a question is assigned 2 minutes you should give a brief answer. But if the same question were given 8 minutes, the answer starts the same but you should go into considerably more detail, as it is worth 4 times the points. This falls under the heading of showing good judgment.

- Then read over the question *before* you start reading the story to know what you need to address. As you read, underline anything you were taught would be relevant. In an IPS question, almost everything will be relevant and the story can run for a page or more. All of the wordy parts matter, including modifiers like "a lot" or "very," as well as notes like "I'm surprised," et cetera.

- Practice making small notes in the margin that you can understand so you do not forget to work all the relevant information into your answer, such as which specific facts are going to affect each R, each T, each L, and U.

- Think before you write, reread the actual question, and then start to answer it, being sure to answer each specific item requested.

The overall process for creating an IPS is much the same for individual and institutional clients. You will see some differences as you move along in the material. The most prominent is that willingness to bear risk is generally not an issue in institutional portfolios. It is presumed such portfolios can focus on the objective issue of ability to bear risk.

CLIENT OBJECTIVES

LOS 8.f: Distinguish between required return and desired return and explain how these affect the individual investor's investment policy.

LOS 8.g: Explain how to set risk and return objectives for individual investor portfolios.

LOS 8.h: Discuss the effects that ability and willingness to take risk have on risk tolerance.

CFA® Program Curriculum, Volume 2, pages 172 and 174

The Return Objective

Ultimately, the return and risk objective have to be consistent with reasonable capital market expectations as well as the client constraints. If there are inconsistencies, they must be resolved by working with the client.

For the Exam: Major inconsistencies, such as unrealistic return objectives, are not common in exam questions. If there were issues in the question data that were inconsistent, you should clearly point them out in your answer. These would have to be based on data from the question and not your own personal opinions. For example in the typical IPS question, you are not given capital market data, so you would not use your own opinions on capital market expectations to answer the question. Despite this, you are expected to be familiar with the recent exam questions. If a client makes very extreme statements like wanting a 15% per year return with low risk, you would point out that this is not reasonable.

This leads some candidates to demand the exact numeric division point between reasonable and unreasonable. Unless such divisions are provided in the reading assignments, they do not exist. You need to be able to recognize highly unreasonable return objectives even if there is no specific division point provided. It is pointless to demand things that are not covered in the curriculum.

Often the return can be divided into a required and desired component. The division depends on what is important to that client and the facts presented. Required return is what is necessary to meet high-priority or critical goals to that client. They might include living expenses, children's education, health care, et cetera. Desired return goals will likewise depend on the client but might be things like buying a second home, world travel, et cetera.

Some managers distinguish return between income and growth sources. This is considered in the CFA material to be suboptimal to a total return approach. Total return does not distinguish return from dividends, interest, or realized or unrealized price change. As long as a sufficient return is earned over the long run, funds can be available to meet the return needs.

The return objective will also specify whether it is nominal (including inflation) or real and pretax or after-tax.

For the Exam: The treatment of inflation and taxes in the current reading assignments and past exam questions is not consistent and has caused considerable confusion.

To illustrate, consider a client in a 30% tax bracket with $1,000,000, needing a $30,000 after-tax distribution at the end of the year with that amount growing at an estimated 2% inflation rate in perpetuity.

Current CFA Readings Approach:

1. First calculate the real, after-tax return: 30 / 1,000 = 3.00%.

2. Then add inflation for the nominal, after-tax return: 3.00% + 2.00% = 5.00%.

3. Last gross up for taxes to calculate the nominal, pretax return: 5.00% / (1 – 0.30) = 7.14%.

This approach is consistent with the readings on taxation and an assumption that 100% of return is subject to taxation at a single, effective tax rate each year. In other words, no sheltering or tax deferral is available. It is the conservative approach in that it calculates the highest nominal, pretax return.

Issues with Old Exam Questions: Some very old exam questions first gross up the real, after-tax return of 3% for taxes and calculates the real, pretax return: 3.00% / (1 − 0.30) = 4.29%. Inflation is then added for a nominal, pretax return of: 4.29% + 2.00% = 6.29%. This approach is not particularly logical because it implicitly assumes that any return due to inflation is never taxed. In other words, the 4.29% is fully taxed each year but the 2.0% is never taxed. If you did this on your personal tax return, it would, at best, be disallowed and, at worst, you could go to jail. You cannot exclude the effects of inflation from taxable income.

Schweser Current Exam Recommendations: Read the question very closely and follow the directions given in the question. Expect current questions to provide specific directions to follow. If the question says anything like "assume accrual taxation at a specified tax rate," "be conservative," or "assume the relevant tax rate is (and gives a number)", then apply the method discussed earlier under the Current CFA Readings Approach and add inflation before tax gross up.

If the case specifically says that tax sheltering methods are expected to reduce taxable income by an amount equivalent to the level of inflation, then inflation would be excluded from grossing up as in the old exam questions. This is not irrational as the taxation readings make it clear there are methods that can effectively reduce the level of income subject to taxes.

Spreadsheet modeling can be a desirable way to analyze return needs over multiple years if the necessary computer tools are available. (They are not available on exam day, but the output could be used.)

Example: Use of spreadsheet output on the exam

Client #107 has a portfolio valued at $1,100,000 and wants to increase the value to $1,200,000 in 5 years. An analysis of the client's non-portfolio inflows and outflows shows the client will need $15,000 from the portfolio in one year and this amount is estimated to rise by 3% inflation per year. What is the client's calculated return need?

Answer:

Required Distribution in	Nominal Distribution
1 year	CF1 = $15,000
2 years	CF2 = $15,000 × 1.03 = $15,450
3 years	CF3 = $15,000 × 1.03^2 = $15,914
4 years	CF4 = $15,000 × 1.03^3 = $16,391
5 years	CF5 = $15,000 × 1.03^4 = $16,883$ $16,883 + $1,200,000 = $1,216,883 year 5 distribution

With a $1,100,000 beginning value (CFo = −1,100,000), the IRR required return is 3.15%.

Note: If you do not remember how to do an IRR calculation given multiple year cash flows, you could review your SchweserNotes from Level I or your calculator instruction manual. Such skill is presumed for the exam.

It is tempting to treat this as an annuity question with 1,200,000 as a FV and 15,000 as a PMT. That will not work because the 1,200,000 is a nominal number and 15,000 is a real number that has to be inflated to reflect the effects of future inflation.

For the Exam: You should approach answering the return objective in stages:

The first step would be to list the objectives the client wants the portfolio to achieve. These could be primary goals like maintain standard of living at the current level of $100,000, grow the portfolio to some projected value, et cetera. If there are desired but less critical goals, list those as well. It will be easier not to try and make any calculations yet.

Second, quantify the investable asset base and the numeric need. For example, the question might ask for the return target next year. The investable base will be the current value of the portfolio and the need is the amount that needs to be generated this year. Questions can also be more complicated and test your time value of money skills. If the question asks for the return in the first year of retirement and retirement will start in three years, you will have to project what the portfolio will be worth in three years and what the return need will be three years from now using the information provided in the question. Hint: If you think you need to make up a number as an assumption to make a calculation, reread the information carefully. There will be information to guide you. Anything is possible but there has not been a question where you had to make up your own assumption for a calculation. It would be very hard for such a question to be graded.

Ownership of a personal residence is something that will be noted in the IPS, usually under unique. But it is not part of investable assets and should not be included in that number.

Last, calculate a percentage return by dividing the return need by investable base.

While this may sound simple, you must be careful to include all relevant facts in the calculation and answer the question as it was asked. The question might specify pretax or after-tax, nominal or real. Generally, the exam is asking for the return for the next year, and you should assume this unless directed otherwise. However the exam has asked questions that specified a future year or over a multiyear time period.

The Risk Objective

This objective should address both the client's *ability* and *willingness* to take risk. The client's ability to take risk is determined objectively, while willingness to take risk is a far more subjective, emotional matter.

Ability to take risk. When we talk about ability to take risk, we are talking about the ability of the portfolio to sustain losses without putting the client's goals in jeopardy; we are talking about how much volatility the portfolio can withstand and still meet the client's required expenditures. Ability to take risk is significantly affected by the investor's time horizon and the size of the expenditures relative to the portfolio.

Generally, if expenditures are small relative to the client's portfolio, the client has an increased ability to take risk. The portfolio can experience significant losses and continue to meet the expenditures. Likewise, if the time horizon is considered long, conventional wisdom states that the portfolio has more time to recover from poor short-term performance. All else equal, as the time horizon increases, the client's ability to take risk increases.

If the expenditures are large relative to the size of the portfolio, the loss the portfolio can sustain and still continue to meet required expenditures is significantly reduced. The client has reduced ability to take risk.

Another consideration is the importance of goals. To determine the importance of a goal, consider the consequences of not meeting it. For example, goals related to maintaining the client's current lifestyle, achieving a desired future lifestyle, providing for loved ones, et cetera are usually classified as *critical*. Those related to acquiring luxury items, taking lavish vacations, et cetera might be important but they are usually considered secondary.

The importance of required expenditures and the ability to take risk are inversely related. All else equal, as the importance of an expense increases, the more we have to ensure it is met. We have to protect against portfolio losses that could place it in jeopardy. Our ability to take risk is thus reduced, and we have to structure the portfolio with low expected risk.

If a spending goal or amount can be changed, the client has *flexibility*. For example, assume we have built a lavish retirement lifestyle into the client's planning. If the annual retirement spending can be safely reduced without causing much concern to the client, this flexibility provides the client with an increased ability to take risk. In determining flexibility, look for the ability to eliminate or reduce spending, eliminate or change the amounts of bequests or charitable donations, add to or increase annual income, et cetera.

If the client is still working or has other assets, then this would increase the ability to take risk, as asset value that is lost can potentially be replaced. Liquidity needs could also be a factor that reduces ability if they require large amounts of the portfolio to be distributed and significantly reduce the available assets.

Willingness to take risk. The client's willingness to take risk is subjective and determined through an analysis of her *psychological* profile. There is no hard-and-fast rule for judging willingness to tolerate risk, so you have to look for statements or evidence in the client's actions.

Clients sometimes indicate their *willingness* to take risk in their statements. These statements usually take the form of disallowing risky investments or specific statements about risk itself. Either type of statement could indicate that the client focuses on risk and has a reduced willingness to take risk.

You could see misleading statements about risk, however, especially when the client assesses his own risk tolerance. Rather than accept the client's statement, you should always look for confirming or contradicting evidence. On one past exam, for example, a client stated that he had *average* risk tolerance. Reading further, we found that the client had a very large investment portfolio, considerable annual income, and a long time horizon. He also regularly invested in what we would consider high-risk investments. From his point of view, he had average risk tolerance but he was average only when compared to his peer group of wealthy investors. He actually had above-average ability and willingness to take risk.

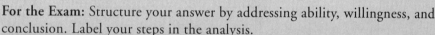

For the Exam: Structure your answer by addressing ability, willingness, and conclusion. Label your steps in the analysis.

Ability to bear risk is decreased by:

- Shorter time horizon.
- Large critical goals in relation to the size of the portfolio.
- High liquidity needs.
- Goals that cannot be deferred.
- Situations where the portfolio is the sole source of support or an inability to replace losses in value.

Willingness to bear risk is determined by statements the client makes or by actions or by life experiences.

Your conclusion should generally go with the more conservative of the two. If there is a conflict between the two, it should definitely be pointed out. Occasionally, a past answer has taken an average of the two if there was not a serious conflict in them. Going with the more conservative is generally best and be sure to state that you have done this.

Like the return objective, the risk objective should be as specific, relevant to the client, and as measurable as possible. Past questions have often specified a maximum shortfall risk, usually defined as E(R) – 2 standard deviations. In such cases, you must list this in your answer. It has been listed both under willingness or the overall risk tolerance conclusion so either should be acceptable. Watch for a question that includes a statement like max shortfall of losing 15% defined as E(R) – 3 standard deviations. Go with what is in the question and not what you saw in an old question.

INDIVIDUAL INVESTOR CONSTRAINTS

LOS 8.i: Discuss the major constraint categories included in an individual investor's investment policy statement.

CFA® Program Curriculum, Volume 2, page 176

For the Exam: Constraints are important because they generally have a significant effect on the risk and return objectives. Conceptually you should think through the constraints before doing the objectives. For the most part, the constraints require you to organize and record the information given in the story in a relevant fashion. If you feel the need to make lengthy calculations in the constraints, it is probably more appropriate to wait and do so in the return objective.

A typical question might require you to address all five constraints in ten minutes. You should give a brief factual answer, listing each constraint and support your statement with relevant facts from the story. If there are no issues on a particular constraint, list the constraint and say so. Leaving it blank is wrong.

Alternatively, a question may only ask you to address specific constraints and might assign more minutes. In this case, only address what was requested and be sure to provide more detail in your answer.

There are five constraints: (1) time horizon, (2) tax considerations, (3) liquidity, (4) legal and regulatory factors, and (5) unique circumstances.

Time Horizon

Time horizon is often important because it affects ability to bear risk. In the most basic terms, an individual's time horizon is the expected remaining years of life. It is the total number of years the portfolio will be managed to meet the investor's objectives and constraints. While there are no precise definitions in the reading assignments, 15 years or more is typically considered long term and short term usually three years or less. In addition, many time horizons are *multistage*.

ST < 3 years

A stage in the time horizon is indicated any time the individual experiences or expects to experience a change in circumstances or objectives significant enough to require evaluating the IPS and reallocating the portfolio. Consider the following time horizon statement for a 50-year-old individual planning to retire at age 60:

The individual has a long-term time horizon with two stages: 10 years to retirement and retirement of 20–25 years.

In this case, as in most, retirement means a significant change in circumstances for the individual. Prior to retirement, the individual likely met most if not all living and other expenses with her salary, maybe even managing to save (add to the portfolio).

At retirement and with the subsequent loss of salary, the individual will have to rely solely on the portfolio to meet any liquidity needs, including living expenses, travel and entertainment expenses, gifts to family or charity, et cetera. Changes in the client's circumstances are significant enough to warrant reallocating the portfolio according to a new set of objectives and constraints.

> **For the Exam:** When completing the time horizon section of the IPS, remember the following:
>
> - State the number of stages in the time horizon, the main objective of each stage, and the number of years in each stage, if identifiable.
> - Look for stages defined by people other than the client. For example, a client may be entitled to a large future inheritance or retirement plan payout that will significantly change her circumstances.
> - You could see a client with significant wealth whose concern has been refocused from meeting living expenses to maximizing bequests to heirs (i.e., maximizing the value of the portfolio). Because the focus includes a time period after the client's expected life, the time horizon could be stated as multi-generational.
> - The time horizon you see on the exam is often long term. Note: there is no reason there could not be a client who is of advanced age or is terminally ill and has a short-term, single-stage horizon.

Tax Considerations

Taxation is a global issue and must be taken into account when formulating an investment policy for an individual. Some general classifications of taxes are as follows:

- *Income tax.* Taxes paid, usually annually, on any form of income (e.g., wage, rental, dividend, interest).
- *Capital gains tax.* Taxes incurred on the appreciation at the sale of an asset that has increased in value.
- *Wealth transfer tax.* Taxes paid on the total value of assets transferred to another individual through inheritance, gifts, et cetera.
- *Personal property tax.* Taxes paid on value of an asset (e.g., automobiles, real estate).

The effects of taxes must be considered when determining the investment strategy for any taxable investor. Capital gains taxes, for example, affect the realized selling price of an asset regardless of when it is sold. Annual taxes reduce the value of the portfolio every year and thus affect the final multi-period value of the portfolio through a reduction in annual compounding.

The following strategies are used to reduce the adverse impact of taxes:

- **Tax deferral.** Minimize the potentially compounding effect of taxes by paying them at the end of the investment holding period. Strategies that fall under this category focus on long-term capital gains, low turnover, and *loss harvesting* (i.e., reduce net taxable gains by recognizing portfolio gains and losses simultaneously).
- **Tax avoidance.** Invest in tax-free securities. Special savings accounts and tax-free municipal bonds are examples of investment securities that generate tax-free returns.
- **Tax reduction.** Invest in securities that require less direct tax payment. Capital gains may be taxed at a lower rate than income, so securities that generate returns mainly as price appreciation offer the investor a lower effective tax rate. Annual taxes should be reduced through loss harvesting, when available.
- **Wealth transfer taxes.** The client can minimize transfer taxes by planning the transfer of wealth to others without utilizing a sale. Often these strategies are quite specific to the jurisdiction in which the investor resides. Considering the timing of the transfers is also important. For example, if wealth is transferred at death, taxes will have been deferred as long as possible. On the other hand, transferring wealth prior to death (i.e., an early transfer) might be optimal if the recipient's tax rate is lower than the tax rate of the donor.

> **For the Exam:** A charterholder is not considered to be a tax expert. You will most typically need to just state the relevant tax situation and rates as given in the question data. You are expected to be able to make calculations to convert between pre- and after-tax as needed and other items specifically covered in the curriculum. Generally any detailed calculations related to taxes should be done in the return objective section. Maximizing after-tax return is the typical objective of most taxable investors. If there are complex tax issues, point out the need to seek qualified advice.

Liquidity

Liquidity can be important in affecting ability to bear risk and in details of the return calculation or SAA. Depending on the situation, liquidity can have a number of meanings and interpretations. In a portfolio context, it means the ability to meet anticipated and unanticipated cash needs.

The liquidity of assets and of a resulting portfolio is a function of the transaction costs to liquidate and price volatility of the assets. High costs and a lengthy time to complete the sale make for lower liquidity. Higher price volatility makes for less liquidity as it increases the probability the asset would be sold for a low value.

Clients' needs for liquidity include:

- Ongoing, anticipated needs for distributions such as living expenses.

- Emergency reserves for unanticipated distributions could be appropriate if client specific and agreed to in advance. Otherwise they create a "cash drag" on portfolio return by continually holding assets in lower return cash equivalents. Holding three months to one year of the annual distribution in cash reserves could be reasonable if agreed to in advance.
- One-time or infrequent negative liquidity events requiring irregular distributions should be noted. Be as specific as possible as to when and how much is needed.
- Positive liquidity inflows not due to the portfolio assets should also be noted.
- Illiquid assets, such as those restricted from sale or those on which a large tax bill would be due on sale, should be noted.
- The client's ownership of a home is generally an illiquid asset and could be noted here. Alternatively it is often recorded under unique.

For the Exam:

- The need for ongoing distributions should be disclosed and analyzed in calculating the return objective. Some past answers also list it under the liquidity constraint and the recommended course is to also show it there.
- A one-time or a couple of times liquidity distribution event should be listed here, specifying how much and when to the extent possible. If it will occur immediately or soon (say in the next year), it should also be deducted from the investable base of assets before calculating the necessary return. Alternatively, something like a specified annual distribution to meet college for four years would be treated as a time horizon stage with the distribution as part of the return need during that stage.
- Emergency cash reserves should not be listed unless given specific reason in the question data. They create unnecessary cash drag. They should be listed here if specifically requested and then provided for by holding the appropriate cash equivalent asset in the SAA. Occasionally a past exam answer has, for no reason, included a small emergency reserve, such as three months' living expenses, even if not specifically requested. This is probably okay as long as it is small. It is better not to do so unless specifics of the question make it appropriate.
- Holdings of illiquid assets that are restricted from sale should be noted here. Alternatively, they could be noted under unique. Assets with a low cost basis where the sale would trigger a large tax bill could be listed here as less liquid due to the large bill that would be incurred on the sale. The tax constraint is probably the more logical place to record them or under unique.

Legal and Regulatory Factors

The legal and regulatory constraints that apply to individuals typically relate to tax relief and wealth transfer. The specific constraints vary greatly across jurisdictions and typically call for legal advice.

The most common legal constraints facing individual clients on previous Level III exams have related to personal trusts and foundations. Trusts are formed as legal devices for transferring personal wealth to future generations. In forming a trust, the grantor files documents and transfers assets to the trust. When the trust is *revocable*, the grantor retains ownership and control over the trust assets and is responsible for taxes on any income or capital gains. The grantor often remains as trustee and either manages the trust assets personally or hires a manager.

In an *irrevocable* trust, the grantor confers ownership of the assets to the trust, which is managed by a professional trustee. The assets are considered immediately transferred to future generations and thus can be subject to wealth transfer taxes, such as gift taxes. The trust is a taxable entity, much like an individual, so it will file tax returns and pay any taxes related to the trust assets. The individual who originally funded the trust no longer has control of the assets and is not taxed on them.

Family foundations are another vehicle, similar to the irrevocable trust, used to transfer family assets to future generations. Family members frequently remain as managers of the foundation's assets. Several forms of foundations are discussed in Study Session 5, Portfolio Management for Institutional Investors.

> **For the Exam:** Much like taxes, you are not presumed to be a legal or regulatory expert beyond what is specifically taught in the curriculum. When completing the legal and regulatory constraint section of the IPS, remember the following:
>
> - If there are no noticeable legal concerns, state there are none beyond your normal ethical responsibilities under the Code and Standards.
> - If the client has or desires a trust, mention that the manager must follow the trust document. Some types of trusts specify paying all income to the income beneficiaries during their lifetimes and then distributing assets to remaindermen at the death of the income beneficiaries. This can require the manager to balance the competing interests (income versus capital appreciation) of the two groups. You should mention this if it comes up.
> - Mention any other legal or regulatory issues brought up in the story.
> - If any complex legal issues associated with trusts or other matters are brought up, only answer based on what is taught and state that you will seek qualified expert advice.

Unique Circumstances

This is a catch-all category for anything that can affect the management of the client's assets and not covered in the other constraints. Items that have appeared on past exams and should be mentioned in this section of the constraints include the following:

- Special investment concerns (e.g., socially responsible investing).
- Special instructions (e.g., gradually liquidate a holding over a period of time).
- Restrictions on the sale of assets (e.g., a large holding of a single stock).
- Asset classes the client specifically forbids or limits based on past experience (i.e., position limits on asset classes or totally disallowed asset classes).
- Assets held outside the investable portfolio (e.g., a primary or secondary residence).
- Desired bequests (e.g., the client intends to leave his home or a given amount of wealth to children, other individuals, or charity).
- Desired objectives not attainable due to time horizon or current wealth.

For the Exam: When completing the client's unique circumstances constraint, remember the following:

- Don't leave it blank. Say none or list anything important that did not fit in the above constraints.
- On some past exams, the client's portfolio included a large amount of stock in a company founded by the client or relatives. This could be listed under unique circumstances.
- Other common unique circumstances to mention are investor-imposed limits on asset classes or even a total disallowance of some investment classes.
- Home ownership can be covered by listing it under unique. If the client has indicated what happens to the home at the client's death, write it down.

THE INVESTMENT POLICY STATEMENT (IPS)

LOS 8.j: Prepare and justify an investment policy statement for an individual investor.

CFA® Program Curriculum, Volume 2, page 186

Four examples are provided to illustrate these concepts in exam like questions. The nature of constructed response questions makes it impossible to ever define the exact wording of what is acceptable. You will be graded on whether you answer the question asked in a way consistent with what is taught in the curriculum. These examples illustrate a range of how questions can be asked and how they can be answered in acceptable fashion in the time allotted. You should begin to adjust your thinking process to align with them.

Example 1:

William Elam recently inherited $750,000 in cash from his father's estate and has come to Alan Schneider, CFA, for investment advice. Both William and his wife Elizabeth are 30 years old. William is employed as a factory worker and has an annual salary of $50,000. Although he receives total health care coverage for himself and his family, he makes no contributions to his firm's defined benefit pension plan and is not yet vested in any of the company's other retirement benefits. Elizabeth is an early childhood teacher with a salary of $38,000. She has only very recently opened a tax-deferred 403(b) retirement savings account. Their four children are ages six, five, four, and three. They have a small savings account, no investments other than Elizabeth's meager retirement account, and credit card debt of $20,000.

When interviewed, William made the following statements to Schneider:

- With a family of six, our combined salaries just meet our living expenses. It would be safe to assume that both our salaries and expenses will grow only at the rate of inflation.
- We do not intend to use our new wealth to improve our current lifestyle, but we may want to consider setting up a trust fund in the future for our children.
- We would like the portfolio to at least earn enough each year to maintain its current value in real terms and then to help fund our retirement.
- We also want to use our portfolio to send our kids to college and maybe pay for future luxuries, like a new home and travel.
- I would like to trade securities like my friend, Keith, who is an experienced and successful investor. He told me that he holds stocks for no more than a month. After that, if he hasn't made a profit, he sells them.
- Everyone I know is buying technology stocks, so I feel we should also.
- My mother has the same portfolio she had a year ago. I can't imagine how you can make any real money that way. Besides, she hasn't taken advantage of any of the latest hot stocks.

A. **Evaluate** the Elams' situational profile according to the following:

    i.   Source of wealth.
    ii. Measure of wealth.
    iii. Stage of life.

6 minutes

Answer:

i.   Source of wealth. The Elams have gained wealth passively through inheritance. This is associated with lower risk tolerance as they have no experience with risk taking. 2 points

ii. Measure of wealth. William seems to perceive his wealth as considerable. He compares himself to a friend who he sees as rich, which leads William to see himself taking considerable risk. 2 points

iii. Stage of life. Elam and his wife are both 30 years old and in the foundation phase. This gives them a long time horizon which increases ability to take risk. 2 points

Note: The answers given are specific in making appropriate references to the story and reasonable for the point value. They may even go slightly beyond what was asked by pointing out the implications for the risk objective.

B. **Classify** William as one of the following investor types. **Justify** your classification.

    i.   Cautious investor.
    ii. Methodical investor.
    iii. Spontaneous investor.
    iv. Individualistic investor.

2 minutes

Answer:

William is spontaneous. His statements related to holding technology stocks (and not missing a good investment), frequent trading, and his mother's trading inactivity support this.

C. **Formulate** the objectives and constraints for the Elams. **No calculations are required.**

20 minutes

① salary.
② Inheritens

② Measure.

Investment Objectives and Constraints for the Elams		
Objectives	Return	The objectives are: • Maintain the real value of the portfolio. • Provide for retirement. • Pay for the children's college (ages six, five, four, and three). • If possible, buy a new home and travel. With only $750,000, it may be difficult to do all this. 5 points
	Risk	**Ability:** Higher due to long time horizon at age 30 but lower as their needs look high versus wealth; they have minimal other wealth; they have debts and are unable to save. **Willingness:** William's statements indicate an above-average willingness to tolerate risk though he appears unsophisticated and not very knowledgeable regarding risk taking. **Overall:** Average risk tolerance or lower is most appropriate given their ability factors. 5 points Note: This was an open-ended question to cover the O&C. Nevertheless, a predetermined point value will be applied by section. Label your answer by section and use specific facts to support your answer as possible. The amount of detail in the answer is reasonable for the facts and point value. Often there will be conflicting issues in the question and you will be graded for properly enumerating and recognizing them.
Constraints	Time horizon	Overall long and multistage, as they are both 30. • The first stage is until the children enter college. Their ages are six, five, four, and three. • The second stage is while the children are in college. • The third stage is up until retirement. • The fourth stage is during retirement.
	Taxes	The Elams are taxable investors. We need their tax rate.
	Liquidity	$20,000 is needed to pay off credit card debt. A small emergency cash fund would be appropriate, as they have no savings.
	Legal and regulatory	None beyond normal duties to client. If they wish to pursue a trust for the children, qualified advice will be needed.
	Unique circumstances	Their wealth is sudden and inherited and William at least seems to have simplistic ideas of risk and return.

Professor's Note: The details throughout the answer are reasonable. If you knew what you were doing it could be easily written in 40–50% of the allotted time, which gives you sufficient time to read the story and plan your answer.

Another trained professional reading this O&C would have a good understanding of the client's situation. That makes it a good answer.

Example 2: Single-year required return calculation

Bonnie DuBois, a 60-year-old U.S. citizen, has just retired after a 35-year career in the fashion industry. Through a modest lifestyle, disciplined saving, and the help of a financial adviser, she has accumulated a $2,000,000 diversified portfolio. Over the last several years, the portfolio allocation has been gradually adjusted to only domestic large-cap stocks and bonds. She holds only investments she has thoroughly researched and continually looks for better, more definitive information.

DuBois's house has been paid off for several years and she does not intend to purchase another house. She has always led a modest lifestyle and intends to continue doing so. During her retirement, she will help support her son Barry, his wife Betty, and their three children (ages 14, 12, and 10). Barry's and Betty's combined salaries barely meet their living expenses.

DuBois estimates she will need $60,000 after-tax in her first year of retirement and likes to keep 6 months of her living expenses on hand. She plans to continue supporting her son and his family by providing them with $30,000 after-tax over the coming year. Both figures are expected to increase each year at the general rate of inflation of 3%. She has informed Barry that at her death her portfolio will be gifted to a local museum with instructions to pay Barry and Betty a lifetime $20,000 annuity. In addition to meeting spending needs, she wishes to maintain the real value of her portfolio. DuBois is in the 25% marginal tax bracket.

A. **Evaluate** DuBois's *situational profile* according to the following:

  i.   Source of wealth.
  ii. Measure of wealth. perception
  iii. Stage of life.

6 minutes

Answer:

i.   Source of wealth. Gradually accumulating wealth over a long career is indicative of a client with a conservative nature and average to below-average willingness to take risk. 2 points

ii. Measure of wealth. DuBois has made no specific indication of her view on her wealth, but the decision to retire and maintain a moderate lifestyle plus patient accumulation of assets, suggests she sees her wealth as adequate but not excessive, indicative of moderate risk tolerance. 2 points

iii. Stage of life. She is in the maintenance (retirement) phase of living off her portfolio and thinking ahead to the distribution in annual gifts to her son's family and then disposition at death. This long-term view suggests moderate risk. 2 points

B. **Classify** DuBois as one of the following investor types. **Justify** your classification.

   i. Cautious investor.

   ii. Methodical investor.

   iii. Spontaneous investor.

2 minutes

Answer:

DuBois is a methodical investor. She has a conservative nature, researches investments carefully, and is constantly on the lookout for new and better information. 2 points

C. In the following template, **formulate** DuBois's:

   i. Return objective and calculate the required after-tax return over the coming year.

4 minutes

   ii. Risk objective (willingness, ability, and overall).

4 minutes

   iii. Constraints.

10 minutes

For the Exam: Before you read the story, you should have looked at the questions and looked ahead at the template to be thinking about the time and space you will use for your answer. These are part of the instructions. While the answer is presented as requested, you could have filled in the constraints, then risk then return. In many ways that better reflects the logic of constructing the answer.

Investment Objectives and Constraints for DuBois		

Objectives

Return

Maintain her real standard of living ($60,000) and support her son and his family ($30,000). Both are after-tax real numbers.

Beyond her death the estate goes to a local museum with a lifetime annuity for the son and family of $20,000.

Need after-tax $60,000 + $30,000 = $90,000
Investable base is $2,000,000
Required real after-tax is 90 / 2,000 = 4.5%
Required nominal after-tax is 4.5% + 3% = 7.5%

4 points

Risk

Overall, her risk objective is average.

Ability to tolerate risk is average, as she just retired with assets to support herself. It is her sole source of support. She needs inflation protection. Her time horizon is rather long, as she is only 60 and she is thinking of gifts beyond her lifetime.

Willingness is not specifically addressed but is also average, as she has been a long-term investor, gradually accumulating assets. She has been moving toward only domestic large-cap stocks and bonds.

Note: It would have been reasonable to suggest somewhat below average but it would not be reasonable, given her time horizon and need for inflation protection, to say very low risk.

Constraints

Time horizon

DuBois has a long-term, single-stage time horizon of 20–25 years or more given her age of 60.

Note: You could mention the goals at her death but they are not particularly relevant and she has not asked for advice on those issues.

Taxes

She is in a 25% marginal tax bracket.

Liquidity

None beyond a 6-month cash reserve. We should clarify if this is 60,000 / 2 or 90,000 / 2.
- Hold a 6-month cash reserve. It is unclear if this is 1/2 of 60,000 or of 90,000.
- Meet ongoing distribution needs.

Legal and regulatory

We have our general responsibilities to the client. Expert legal and tax advice regarding her annual gifts to son and plans after death are appropriate.

Unique circumstances

The annual payment to DuBois's son's family and the desire to leave the portfolio to a museum could be listed here.

or

None, if these were covered elsewhere.

10 points total, 2 per constraint

Example 3:

It is now five years later. DuBois's son and his wife have both received significant promotions so that they no longer require annual support from DuBois. DuBois is meeting with her financial adviser, Begren Knutsen, to determine if and how her IPS should be altered. Because she no longer needs to provide the annual financial help to her son, DuBois will instead plan bequests. She specifies the portion of the portfolio allocated to equities should use only domestic stocks.

DuBois's portfolio has remained at $2,000,000. She and Knutsen estimate her time horizon at 20 years, at which time she plans to leave a bequest of $1,200,000 in today's dollars to her son and to the museum ($2,400,000 total). She also plans to withdraw $75,000 per year, after tax, to cover her living expenses. She has already paid this year's expenses, so the first of the 20 $75,000 withdrawals will be in one year.

A. Has her portfolio met the previous objectives?

2 minutes

B. How have the following items changed?

    i.   Risk Objective
    ii. Liquidity
    iii. Time Horizon

9 minutes

C. **Calculate** her new return objective.

4 minutes

Answer:

A. The $2,000,000 nominal value has not changed. She has not kept up with inflation, so the original objectives were not met. Presumably the distributions requested have been made.

2 points

B. i. There is no indication of change in willingness but ability has been affected. Her time horizon is shorter, as she is five years older, but ability is higher as she is thinking even more about after-death bequests, a longer horizon. She still needs inflation protection during her life and total annual need is down, as she is no longer supporting her son. Lower need versus wealth raises ability. A conclusion of no net change is appropriate.

Note: This is one of the outlier questions where the amount to say is a bit excessive for the point value. That does happen on occasion. Just go through the items you were taught to look for, and in this case acknowledge they have moved in conflicting directions. Only mentioning she is older would be an incomplete answer.

ii. No significant change. A 6-month reserve is now $75,000 / 2.

iii. Her time horizon is shorter, as five years have passed, and a 20-year planning horizon has been decided.

3 points per item for a total of 9 points

C. Her return target is 20 payments of $75,000 in real terms starting in 1 year and a terminal real value of $2.4 million.

20 N; 75,000 PMT; 2,400,000 FV; –2,000,000 PV; CPT I/Y = 4.39%

In nominal terms she must earn 4.39% + 3% estimated inflation for 7.39% after tax.

4 points

STRATEGIC ASSET ALLOCATION

LOS 8.k: Determine the strategic asset allocation that is most appropriate for an individual investor's specific investment objectives and constraints.

CFA® Program Curriculum, Volume 2, page 188

A strategic asset allocation is the mix of portfolio asset classes that could meet the portfolio objectives of return and risk while being consistent with the constraints. For a taxable investor, the returns should be after-tax and consider all current and future tax implications. These will be further discussed in a subsequent reading assignment.

When given a choice of several portfolios, a process of elimination can be used to discard unacceptable portfolios.

For the Exam: This topic will be covered in multiple Study Sessions and is regularly tested as part of a broader IPS question. It is an example of heuristic rules and could be referred to as process of elimination or experience-based approach. It is a taught process and not a random collection of ideas. In particular the use of risk/return analysis is used as a last step and only if needed. Often you never get to that step and if used too early, it can lead to the wrong answer.

Summarizing the various points you should commonly consider, you should eliminate portfolios that:

- Violate constraints such as:
  - Excess cash equivalents (cash drag).
  - Insufficient cash equivalents to meet appropriate liquidity needs.
  - Hold or fail to hold assets specified in the constraints. For example, retain at least 10% in tech stocks.
- Violate the specified risk objective, such as max shortfall risk or standard deviation.
- Generate insufficient return. Note if you rely on this one and calculated return incorrectly, you are in trouble. In addition, there have been questions where you were instructed not to consider return. Also be sure to use after-tax return if appropriate.
- Have inappropriate asset classes or weightings even if not an outright constraint violation.
  - The taught rule of thumb is 60/40 for the average investor. This means 60% in equity like assets that offer appreciation over time and 40% in income-producing assets that lack that long-term appreciation (i.e., bonds and cash equivalents). High- (low-) risk investors should scale up (or down) the equity type asset weight.
  - Ignoring home ownership. The home is not per se a portfolio asset but it should not be ignored. If a home of substantial value is owned, it does create real estate exposure and makes additional real estate allocations less appropriate.
- Fail to address a concentration issue, such as stock of a former employer or low basis inherited stock. The SAA should indicate the desired allocation. Whether it would actually be sold is a separate issue to be addressed later when considering cost versus benefit.
- At this point, a return to risk ranking, such as Sharpe ratio, could be appropriate if needed for the final selection.

To answer these types of questions, first review the client's O&C. Next, carefully review any specific directions in the question and quickly eliminate portfolios that have clear violations of the O&C. Then make any necessary calculations if needed, such as after-tax return, shortfall risk, Sharpe ratio, et cetera. Be careful with the calculations; you generally have no reason to get to all of them. You would have already been down to one portfolio and should have already stopped.

Example 4:

Possible portfolio asset allocations for DuBois are shown in Exhibit 1. Based solely on the objectives and constraints from DuBois's IPS in Example 2, **select** the *most appropriate asset* allocation for DuBois and **justify** your selection with *three* reasons in the following template. For each allocation not selected, **state** *one* reason why it was rejected.

Exhibit 1: Alternative Portfolio Allocations

	Asset Class Weights (%)			
Asset Class	A	B	C	D
Cash	20	5	5	10
Domestic large-cap equities	35	40	15	10
Domestic small-cap equities	25	10	15	10
Domestic government bonds	5	20	15	10
Domestic corporate bonds	0	20	15	10
Direct real estate	0	0	20	10
Global bond fund	0	5	0	10
Global equity fund	15	0	0	10
Private equity fund	0	0	10	10
Fund of funds hedge fund	0	0	5	10
Total	100	100	100	100
Expected after-tax return (%)	8.0	7.7	8.4	8.1
Expected standard deviation (%)	12.5	10.1	13.0	12.7

Template for Example 4

Most Appropriate	Three Justifications
B	1. Meets return requirement of 7.39%. 2. 5% cash meets the liquidity needs. 3. Only domestic stock per client direction. **Additional justifications:** 4. 50% equity fits a moderately conservative risk objective.

Inappropriate	One Justification
A	1. Too much cash at 20%. **Additional justification:** 2. 75% allocation to equity is high for moderate risk. 3. Holds non-domestic equity.
C	1. 20% allocation to direct real estate is excessive given the home ownership. **Additional justifications:** 2. Private equity, hedge fund, and real estate create a large illiquid position and may be too risky for her situation.
D	1. Excess cash holdings. **Additional justifications:** 2. Additional 10% in real estate is excessive. 3. Includes non-domestic equity. 4. This looks like naive diversification and not effective diversification.

THE MONTE CARLO APPROACH TO RETIREMENT PLANNING

LOS 8.l: Compare Monte Carlo and traditional deterministic approaches to retirement planning and explain the advantages of a Monte Carlo approach.

CFA® Program Curriculum, Volume 2, page 196

The previous Example 3 for DuBois is a good illustration of traditional, deterministic, steady-state, linear return analysis. But that single required return number is not representative of the actual volatile returns of markets and provides no insight into risk. Even when a standard deviation for the selected portfolio is included, it means little to the typical investor.

The development of inexpensive computers and commercially available software provide access to more powerful tools, such as Monte Carlo simulation. Both traditional and Monte Carlo analysis starts with inputs such as:

- Time horizon to retirement and length of retirement.
- Investors' income and savings, assets, and tax status.
- Interest rates, asset returns, inflation, et cetera.

The traditional approach then calculates a single, constant, required return. In Monte Carlo simulation, each of the variables is also given a probability distribution to allow for real world uncertainty. A single timeline path is then generated, showing what could happen over time to the portfolio. This is repeated to generate perhaps 10,000 path outcomes consistent with the assumed probability distributions.

Monte Carlo simulation is very flexible and the advantages include the following:

- It considers path dependency. A simple path dependency was considered at Level II in analyzing a mortgage-backed security (MBS), specifically, that the level of prepayments and cash flow at any future point depend on both the level of rates at that point and the prior history of rates, prepayments, and cash flow up to that point. Simulations of portfolio performance can be more complex. For example, consider an investor requiring a GBP25,000 per year withdrawal for living from a portfolio of GBP500,000. But suppose very poor markets lead to a decline in the portfolio of 50%. The fixed withdrawal need now becomes a much larger portion of the portfolio. Even if the markets recover, the diminished portfolio is smaller if the withdrawal comes at a low point. This could permanently diminish the living standard of the investor due to the random decline in the market. Path dependency could also consider issues, such as the interaction of changing inflation on the portfolio values and on the investor's withdrawal needs.
- It can more clearly display tradeoffs of risk and return. The 10,000 paths can be ranked from best to worst to assess the probability of any given outcome as well as how much better or worse it could it get.
- Properly modeled tax analysis, which considers the actual tax rates of the investor as well as tax location of the assets (held in taxable or tax-deferred locations), can be assessed. How the tax burden changes with market returns and withdrawals could be considered.

- A clearer understanding of short-term and long-term risk can be gained. For example, reducing the holdings of risky stock would reduce the short-term variability of the portfolio but increase the long-term risk of not having sufficient assets.
- It is superior in assessing multi-period effects. Traditional analysis projects portfolio return as a simple weighted average of the asset returns, geometrically compounded. Risk (variance) is the traditional formula taught in the CFA curriculum. Monte Carlo simulation can better model the real stochastic process where return over time depends not only on the starting value of the period but also on the additions or withdrawals to the portfolio at each future period.
- Points along the timeline can be considered to answer questions, such as, "Do savings need to be increased?" "Can I retire earlier?" "Must I retire later?"

Like any complex model, it is only as good as the inputs. Poor or simplistic inputs or modeling can create poor results. Disadvantages include:

- Simplistic use of historical data, such as expected returns, for the inputs. Returns change and have a major effect on projected future values of the portfolio.
- Models that simulate the return of asset classes but not the actual assets held. Simulating the return of the Wilshire 5000 when a fund with fees will be held could significantly overstate the future value or time period over which distributions can be sustained. Real assets have expenses.
- Tax modeling that is simplistic and not tailored to the investor's situation.

Like any complex model, there are pros and cons, but it is superior to the traditional single-return analysis.

For the Exam: There will be several other readings that also discuss Monte Carlo simulation. You do not know how to actually do it, so the likely questions would focus on the pros and cons or a simple overview of how it works. The above material covers those well.

A later reading will show you the output of such models and how to utilize the output—another reasonable question.

KEY CONCEPTS

LOS 8.a
Sources of Wealth

Active wealth creation through risking financial capital (such as an entrepreneur) is associated with higher *willingness to take risk*.

Passive wealth accumulation (such as an inheritance or saving over time) does not demonstrate the same willingness.

Measures of Wealth

High *perceived wealth* is associated with higher *willingness to take risk*.

Stage of Life

In general, an inverse relationship exists between age and risk tolerance. Younger investors (foundation phase) typically have higher *ability to take risk*.

Investors in mid-career (accumulation phase) still have a long time horizon, and *ability to take risk* generally remains high.

Investors approaching and then in retirement (maintenance and then distribution phases) have a declining time horizon and may see a reduction in *ability to take risk*.

LOS 8.b
Situational profiling places individuals into categories according to stage of life or economic circumstances. Situational profiling is only a first step in understanding an individual's preferences, economic situation, goals, and desires. The starting points for situational profiling include investigating an investor's sources of wealth, measures of wealth, and stage of life.

LOS 8.c
Behavioral models may assist the manager in understanding the client. Modeling often starts with a client questionnaire and then categorizes the client along two dimensions:
- Higher versus lower risk tolerance.
- Decision process (based more on objective thinking or subjective feeling).

LOS 8.d
Benefits to the Client
- Objectives and constraints are considered in formulating investment decisions that benefit the client.
- The process is dynamic and allows changes in circumstances to be incorporated.
- A well-written IPS represents the long-term objectives of the investor.
- Subsequent managers should be able to implement decisions congruent with the individual's goals.

Benefits to the Adviser
- The IPS can be consulted for clarification as to the appropriateness of specific investment decisions.
- Most IPSs contain a stated review process, indicate dispute resolutions, and identify potential problems.

LOS 8.e
- Determine and evaluate the investor's risk and return objectives. Planning return expectations should take place concurrently with risk tolerance discussions.
- Determine portfolio constraints.
- Define the appropriate investment strategy based upon an analysis of objectives, constraints, and market expectations.
- Determine the proper asset allocation to meet the investor's objectives and constraints. An SAA is sometimes included.

LOS 8.f
Required expenditures are mandatory objectives and, along with the value of the investable portfolio, are used to calculate the client's required return. Desired expenditures are non-primary goals, such as buying a vacation home, taking lavish vacations, and the like, that are not considered when calculating the total investable portfolio or required return.

LOS 8.g
All else equal, portfolio size versus needs, total wealth versus needs, time horizon, and ability to take risk are positively related. Goal importance, level of spending needs, and ability to take risk are negatively related. Flexibility can increase the ability to take risk. Willingness to take risk is subjective. Explicit statements, client actions, and situational profiling are used to indicate the client's willingness to take risk.

LOS 8.h
The overall risk tolerance conclusion generally goes with the lower of ability or willingness to take risk. Any discrepancy between the two should be noted. If ability is exceedingly large compared to willingness it's possible to average the two, but this is unusual. Deferring to the more conservative measure is the preferred method.

LOS 8.i
Client constraints include time horizon, taxes, liquidity needs, legal and regulatory considerations, and unique circumstances.

Time horizon: The total time period over which the portfolio will be managed to meet the investor's objectives and constraints. A stage in the time horizon is indicated any time the individual experiences or expects to experience a change in circumstances significant enough to require evaluating the IPS and reallocating the portfolio. This can include retirement and major expenses such as college costs, expected inheritance, et cetera.

Tax considerations: General classifications of taxes include income tax, capital gains tax, transfer tax, and wealth or personal property tax. Strategies used to reduce the adverse impact of taxes include tax deferral, tax avoidance, tax reduction, and transferring wealth to others without utilizing a sale.

Liquidity: Spending needs that will be met by the investment portfolio (i.e., do not consider spending needs that will be met by salary or other income sources). Assume the client will use current income from the portfolio and/or liquidate assets as necessary to meet spending needs.

Legal and regulatory factors: Typically relate to tax relief and wealth transfer. The specific constraints vary greatly across jurisdictions and usually call for legal advice.

Unique circumstances: Special investment concerns; special instructions; restrictions on the sale of assets; asset classes the client specifically forbids or limits based on past experience; and assets held outside the investable portfolio, such as a primary or secondary residence, bequests, and desired objectives not attainable due to time horizon or current wealth.

LOS 8.j
The investment policy statement (IPS) is a document that is developed as the result of a client interview to determine their risk (ability and willingness) and return objectives and the five constraints, which consist of the time horizon, unique circumstances, taxes, legal and regulatory, and liquidity constraints. An asset allocation for the client's portfolio is then determined and implemented, monitored, and subsequently revised as needed depending on changes in the client's circumstances as reflected in a periodic review of the client's IPS.

LOS 8.k
A strategic asset allocation (SAA) can be selected using a process of elimination. Asset mixes that do not meet required return, exceed allowable risk, or violate constraints are eliminated. Allocations with either excess or insufficient cash are eliminated. If more than one acceptable SAA remains, then diversification can be considered following the generalization that an average risk investor would be allocated 60% to equity (growth) type assets and 40% to bond (fixed income) type assets. If necessary for a final selection, then the SAA with higher return to risk is selected.

Throughout the process the simplest decisions that are most directly related to the case facts are used first until one SAA remains.

LOS 8.l

Deterministic planning techniques use single values for economic and financial variables. For instance, expected rates of return, inflation, and interest rates are assigned single point estimates and then used in a modeling framework to estimate assets available for the retirement period. Although useful in formulating expected investment outcome at the retirement stage of life, the deterministic estimation process generates only a single number. Investors do not have the capability of evaluating probabilities of that expected value occurring.

Monte Carlo techniques take into account distributions and associated probabilities for input variables and generate a probabilistic forecast of retirement period values. Instead of seeing one single outcome, the investor can see a range of possibilities for the future.

- Probabilistic forecasts give both the client and manager a better indication of the risk/return tradeoff in investment decisions.
- Monte Carlo simulations explicitly show the tradeoffs of short-term risks and the risks of not meeting goals.
- Monte Carlo is better able to incorporate tax nuances.
- Monte Carlo can better model the complications associated with future returns by more effectively incorporating the compounding effect of reinvestment.

CONCEPT CHECKERS

1.   Situational profiling is a first step at determining investor attitudes towards risk. **Describe** a situational profile according to:
        i.   Source of wealth.

        ii. Measure of wealth.

        iii. Stage of life.

2.   **Describe** investor characteristics often associated with the following personality types:
        i.   Cautious investor.

        ii. Methodical investor.

        iii. Spontaneous investor.

        iv. Individualistic investor.

3.   **Explain** differences between *required returns* and *desired returns*. **Discuss** how each relates to an individual investor's risk tolerance.

4.   **Describe** ability and willingness to take risk. **Explain** how an investor might resolve inconsistencies between the two.

5. **Describe** the process of elimination when determining an appropriate asset allocation for an individual investor.

6. According to principles of the behavioral finance investment framework, loss aversion would *most likely* lead an investor to:
   A. fully adjust expectations to new information as it arrives.
   B. prefer to take a small loss rather than take a risk with a potential but not certain larger loss.
   C. prefer to take a risk with a potential but not certain larger loss than take a certain small loss.

7. With respect to benefits of an IPS, which of the following statements is *most accurate*?
   A. An adviser can benefit because the IPS is dynamic and can accommodate changing conditions.
   B. A client can benefit because the IPS can clarify points for decision making and for resolving disputes.
   C. An adviser can benefit because the IPS can clarify points for decision making and for resolving disputes.

For more questions related to this topic review, log in to your Schweser online account and launch SchweserPro™ QBank; and for video instruction covering each LOS in this topic review, log in to your Schweser online account and launch the OnDemand video lectures, if you have purchased these products.

ANSWERS – CONCEPT CHECKERS

1. i. Information related to source of wealth describes how an investor accumulated wealth. At one end of the spectrum is wealth acquired through active means (e.g., entrepreneurial activities). This indicates knowledge and experience with risk-taking activities. The other end of the spectrum is wealth acquired through passive means (e.g., inheritance or long-term employment in a stable corporation). The latter may indicate an investor with less knowledge and experience of risk-taking activities.

   ii. The key to understanding measures of wealth relates to how an investor perceives his level of wealth. The perception of wealth may be in relation to funds required to sustain lifestyle activities. If a portfolio is perceived as small, risk tolerance may be low. If a portfolio is perceived as large, risk tolerance may be high.

   iii. Stage of life descriptions indicate where an investor is in relation to the life cycle. Life expectancy is a large factor in connecting stage of life to risk tolerance. Due to a long time horizon, young investors often have a high tolerance for risk. Older investors, however, may have a diminished risk tolerance.

2. i. Cautious investors are the most risk averse. They tend to take long periods of time to make decisions and often invest in only the safest securities.

   ii. Methodical investors spend long periods of time evaluating security characteristics. They expend a large amount of effort on their analytical capabilities but are confident when making investment decisions. Portfolios tend to be somewhat conservative.

   iii. Spontaneous investors pay little attention to valuation issues. They are more concerned with creating a portfolio that holds the latest "hot" investment idea. Due to their nature, spontaneous investors' portfolios exhibit high turnover and volatility.

   iv. Individualistic investors are very confident in making independent investment decisions. They are less risk averse than methodical investors.

3. Required returns are those returns associated with critical or primary investor goals. Desired returns are associated with secondary goals. Both must be consistent with the risk tolerance exhibited by the investor.

4. Ability to take risk is associated with time horizon, size of investment portfolio, and investor goals. If time horizon is short, size of portfolio is small, and goals are critical, ability to take risk is low. Willingness to take risk is a much more subjective measure. Personal knowledge and experiences affect an investor's willingness to take risk. Often the financial services professional will need to educate the client on the basics of risk and return in order to reconcile any difference between the client's willingness and ability to accept risk.

5. Eliminate portfolios that are clearly unacceptable. These would include issues such as return too low, risk too high, or direct violation of constraints. Excessive cash would reduce expected return and be a reason to eliminate. More subtle issues, such as starting with a 60/40 equity/FI allocation for an average risk investor, might indicate more or less appropriate asset allocations. If more than one portfolio remains, higher return to risk rankings would be selected.

6. **C** Loss aversion means investors prefer uncertain losses to smaller certain losses. Rather than give up and take a small loss, investors would rather take their chances with a larger loss, as long as there is still the possibility of a gain. These investors will tend to hold losing investments too long.

7. **C** Advisers benefit from an IPS because it serves as the document formally stating
          an understanding and agreement with clients. If questions arise regarding specific
          investment decisions, the IPS can be consulted for clarification as to the appropriateness
          of such decisions. Because most IPSs contain a stated review process, the document
          should indicate, or at least provide, direction for dispute resolution. The document
          should identify issues that could eventually become problems.

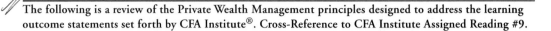

The following is a review of the Private Wealth Management principles designed to address the learning outcome statements set forth by CFA Institute®. Cross-Reference to CFA Institute Assigned Reading #9.

TAXES AND PRIVATE WEALTH MANAGEMENT IN A GLOBAL CONTEXT[1]

Study Session 4

EXAM FOCUS

Any of the calculations in this topic assignment are reasonable for the exam. Understanding the terminology is also required. For example, what are accrual equivalent after-tax returns, accrual equivalent taxes, TEA, and TDA? In addition, recognize when a given tax regime favors a particular investment strategy. In other words, what maximizes after-tax value under various tax rules? In addition to making calculations, there may be questions where the facts are sufficient to indicate what the best strategy will be even though insufficient details are provided to perform a calculation.

GLOBAL TAXATION REGIMES

LOS 9.a: Compare basic global taxation regimes as they relate to the taxation of dividend income, interest income, realized capital gains, and unrealized capital gains.

CFA® Program Curriculum, Volume 2, page 226

There are three primary categories of taxes:

1. *Taxes on income:*
   - Paid by individuals, corporations, and other legal entities on various types of income including wages, interest, dividends, and capital gains.

2. *Wealth-based taxes:*
   - Paid on the value of assets held and on wealth transfers.

3. *Taxes on consumption:*
   - Sales taxes: Paid by the consumer.
   - Value-added taxes: Paid at each intermediate production step according to the amount of value added at the step; ultimately borne by the consumer (added into the purchase price).

Governments use taxes as a source of funding for operations and to encourage or discourage certain actions. For example, to encourage savings many governments provide favorable tax treatment on retirement accounts. Tax regimes are generally classified as flat or progressive. In a flat system the same tax rate is paid, regardless of the amount of income. In a progressive tax system the tax rate increases as the level of income increases.

---

1. The terminology used throughout this topic review is industry convention as presented in Reading 9 of the 2018 Level III CFA exam curriculum.

In 2009 in the United States, for example, single individuals pay 10% of income up to $8,350. On income above $8,350 up to $33,950, they pay at a rate of 15%.

The tax rate paid on the very last (highest) dollar of income is referred to as the *marginal tax rate*. A single (unmarried) taxpayer in the United States with a total taxable income of $20,000, for example, would have a marginal tax rate of 15% because that is the highest rate at which taxes are assessed. Using those rates, the individual's tax bill on $20,000 of taxable income is $(0.10)(\$8,350) + (0.15)(\$20,000 - \$8,350) = \$2,582.50$. The individual's *average tax rate* is $\$2,582.50 / \$20,000 = 0.1291 \cong 12.9\%$. In other words, had the individual paid taxes at a rate of 12.91% on all income earned, he would have paid $2,582.50.

Example: Total taxes, marginal tax rate, and average tax rate

Assume ordinary income of $173,000. Tax rates in Table 1 apply:

Table 1: 2009 Tax Rates for a U.S. Individual Filing as a Single

Taxable Income		Bracket Amount (Col 2 – Col 1)	Tax Rate %	Plus
(1) Over	(2) Up to			
0	$8,350	$8,350	10	
$8,350	33,950	25,600	15	$835
33,950	82,250	48,300	25	4,675
82,250	171,550	89,300	28	16,750
171,550	372,950	201,400	33	41,754
372,950			35	108,216

Before we perform any calculations, let's discuss the "Plus" column in the table. That column saves you the trouble of calculating accumulated taxes at rates lower than the marginal rate. For example, according to the first tax bracket the individual pays 10% on income up to $8,350. If an individual has taxable income of exactly $8,350, she will pay $(0.10)(\$8,350) = \$835$. If the individual has income of $9,000, however, she will pay taxes at 10% on the first $8,350 and 15% on income between $8,350 and $9,000. The tax bill will be $(0.10)(\$8,350) + (0.15)(\$650) = \$932.50$. Notice that instead of calculating the taxes on the first $8,350, we could simply have calculated the taxes on the amount over $8,350 and added $835. Likewise, an individual with income falling in the highest tax bracket would pay $108,216 plus 35% on all income over $372,950.

Now let's return to the example.

A. **Calculate** the individual's *total tax bill*.

   The individual's taxable income (all taxed as ordinary income) is $173,000, so she falls in the second highest tax bracket. She will pay $41,754 (shaded in the table) plus 33% of all income above $171,550 and her tax bill will be:

$$\$41,754 + (0.33)(\$173,000 - \$171,550) = \$42,232.50$$

Let's calculate the tax bill the *long way* (without using the "Plus" column) by multiplying each successive amount of income by its respective tax rate:

$$\text{taxes due} = (0.10)(\$8{,}350) + (0.15)(\$25{,}600) + (0.25)(\$48{,}300)$$
$$+ (0.28)(\$89{,}300) + (0.33)(\$173{,}000 - \$171{,}550)$$
$$= \$835 + \$3{,}840 + \$12{,}075 + \$25{,}004 + \$478.50 = \underline{\$42{,}232.50}$$

Notice that we arrive at exactly the same number.* That's because the Plus column at each bracket sums up the total taxes due on all lower brackets. Because our individual fell in the second highest (fifth) tax bracket, the Plus column contained the taxes due on all income in the first four brackets (up to $171,550).

B. **Determine** the individual's *marginal tax rate.*

The individual's marginal tax rate is simply the highest tax rate applied. In this case, that is 33%.

C. **Calculate** the individual's *average tax rate.*

The individual's average tax rate is calculated as total taxes paid divided by total taxable income and indicates the average rate paid on each dollar of taxable income.

$$\text{average tax rate} = \frac{\text{total taxes paid}}{\text{total taxable income}} = \frac{\$42{,}232.50}{\$173{,}000} = 0.244118 \cong 24.4\%$$

Check: $0.244118(\$173{,}000) = \underline{\$42{,}232.50}$

* The typical tax table does not include column 3, which shows the total taxable income in each bracket. You would have had to calculate those numbers to determine taxes the "long way."

For the Exam: Consider these necessary warm-up calculations needed for later material. Be able to perform them.

In addition to imposing progressive tax rates on *ordinary income*,[2] many countries tax investment returns differently depending on whether they are in the form of interest, dividends, or capital gains. For example, interest and dividends might be taxed at a reduced rate or taxed at ordinary rates after they exceed some amount. Long-term capital gains are often taxed at a lower rate than short-term capital gains, with long-term definitions varying from one to five years or so. In most countries, capital gains taxes are paid only when capital gains are realized (i.e., when the investment is sold).

---

2. The $173,000 taxable income in our example was assumed to be ordinary income, which consists of salary, wages, commissions, et cetera, and is subject to taxation at standard rates. If a tax regime does not provide special treatment for income from investments, then dividends, interest, and capital gains would be added to income from salary, et cetera and taxed as ordinary income.

Table 2 shows seven global tax regimes delineated by whether the ordinary income tax rate is progressive or flat and by the treatment of investment income (i.e., interest, dividends, and capital gains).

Table 2: Seven Global Tax Regimes

Tax Regime	Ordinary Income Tax Structure	Favorable Treatment for Interest Income?	Favorable Treatment for Dividend Income?	Favorable Treatment for Capital Gains?
Common Progressive	Progressive	Yes*	Yes	Yes
Heavy Dividend Tax	Progressive	Yes*	No	Yes
Heavy Capital Gain Tax	Progressive	Yes*	Yes	No
Heavy Interest Tax	Progressive	No	Yes	Yes
Light Capital Gain Tax	Progressive	No	No	Yes
Flat and Light	Flat	Yes*	Yes	Yes
Flat and Heavy	Flat	Yes*	No	No

* Some countries may provide favorable tax treatment or exemption for some types of interest (e.g., tax-free bonds in the United States).

The first regime, **Common Progressive**, is the most frequent regime observed globally. There is, however, considerable variation in the special treatment of investment income, with some countries providing exemption for only part of investment income and other countries providing exemption for all investment income. The United States, United Kingdom, China, France, Italy, Japan, and many other countries fall under this category. The **Light Capital Gain Tax** regime is the second most common regime, while only one country, Colombia, fell under the **Heavy Capital Gain Tax** regime.

TAX REGIMES

LOS 9.b: Determine the effects of different types of taxes and tax regimes on future wealth accumulation.

LOS 9.c: Explain how investment return and investment horizon affect the tax impact associated with an investment.

CFA® Program Curriculum, Volume 2, pages 229 and 232

The effect of taxes on investment returns is substantial. The effect will vary depending on the tax rate, the return on the investment, the frequency, and the form (regime) of taxation. Given the variety of tax methods, some form of consistent notation is necessary. In general, the following will apply in this reading:

- r: pretax return.
- n: number of time periods (years).
- t_i: tax rate on income or interest.

- t_{cg} and t_w: tax rates on capital gains and wealth, respectively.
- B: the basis, the ratio of cost basis to current market value where cost basis is not subject to capital gains tax at sale.
- p_i, p_d, p_{cg}: The portion (%) of return subject to interest, dividend, and capital gains tax in a time period.
- FVIF: Future value of an investment factor (e.g., the FV of an initial dollar invested at the end of time period n).
- AT and PT: After-tax and pretax, respectively.

Professor's Note: Whether "i" refers to income in general or interest income in particular will depend on the context of the question. No one will try and trick you on that and there will be enough information to tell. You may see capital letters used occasionally instead of small cap (e.g., T_{CG} for t_{cg}); the meaning is the same, tax rate on capital gains.

Simple Accrual Taxation

Accrual taxes are a periodic (usually annual) tax at a single tax rate on income or return. Most countries apply accrual taxation to dividends and interest. The future value of an investment after-tax under accrual taxation is:

$$FVIF_{AT} = [1 + r(1 - t_i)]^n$$

For accrual taxation $r(1 - t_i)$ is the after-tax rate of return so the computation is simply the after-tax value of a single initial currency unit invested. However, the ultimate effect of taxes on future value is complicated. One way to measure the effect is **tax drag**. Tax drag can be computed as both an amount and as a percentage. For example, for a U.S. investor:

tax drag$_\$$ = gain lost to taxes
= gain with no taxes – gain after taxes
= $FV_{PT} - FV_{AT}$

tax drag$_\%$ = % of gain lost to taxes
= tax drag$_\$$ / gain with no taxes

Example: Account subject to annual accrual taxes

$1,000 is invested for 20 years at a pretax return of 10%. Return is subject to an annual tax rate of 30%. Compute the ending after-tax account value and the tax drag.

Answer:

$$FV_{AT} = \$1,000[1 + 0.10(1 - 0.30)]^{20} = \$3,869.68$$

This is a gain after tax of $3,869.68 − 1,000 = $2,869.68

With no tax, the FV is $1,000(1 + 0.10)^{20} = \$6,727.50$ and the gain would have been:

gain no tax: $6,727.50 − 1,000 = $5,727.50

gain lost to taxes: $5,727.50 − $2,869.68 = $2,857.82 = tax drag$_\$$
$2,857.82 / $5,727.50 = 49.9% = tax drag$_\%$

For accrual taxes, it can be generalized that:

1. Over a time horizon of more than one period (n > 1), the tax drag percentage exceeds the tax rate because the periodic payment of taxes reduces the benefits of tax-free compounding over time. In the following illustration, the 37.5% tax drag exceeds the tax rate of 30%:

			FV	Gain	Tax Drag	
n =	10					
t =	**30%**	with tax:	$172.44	$72.44	$43.45	**37.5%**
r =	8%	no tax:	$215.89	$115.89		
PV =	100					

2. The adverse effects increase as the time horizon increases. Both the tax drag amount and percentage increase because the effects of lost pretax compounding increase. This is illustrated by increasing the time horizon from 10 to 20 years. Tax drag increases from $43.45 and 37.5% to $168.74 and 46.1%:

			FV	Gain	Tax Drag	
n =	**20**					
t =	30%	with tax:	$297.36	$197.36	$168.74	46.1%
r =	8%	no tax:	$466.10	$366.10		
PV =	100					

3. The adverse effects increase at higher rates of return as the dollar amount consumed by taxes is higher each year. Again this leads to a loss of pretax compounding. Both the tax drag amount and percentage increase. This is illustrated by increasing the return from 8% to 12% over a 10-year horizon. Tax drag increases from $43.45 and 37.5% to $86.56 and 41.1%:

n =	10		FV	Gain	Tax Drag
t =	30%	with tax:	$224.02	$124.02	**$86.56 41.1%**
r =	12%	no tax:	$310.58	$210.58	
PV =	100				

4. The time horizon and level of return effects compounding, meaning tax drag is further increased when both time horizon and rates of return are longer and higher. This is illustrated by computing the drag over 20 years at a 12% return. This further increases the tax drag to $462.77 and 53.5%:

n =	**20**		FV	Gain	Tax Drag
t =	30%	with tax:	$501.86	$401.86	**$462.77 53.5%**
r =	12%	no tax:	$964.63	$864.63	
PV =	100				

Deferred Capital Gains Taxation

Capital gains taxes are applied only to the gain in value on an asset. Generally, the timing of the tax can be controlled as it is only imposed when the asset is sold. By deferring the tax, the benefits of pretax compounding of return can be realized to lower the tax drag. If the initial starting value for the analysis period is the tax cost basis of the investment (i.e., the basis, B, equals 1.00), the future value of an investment after-tax under capital gains taxation is:

$$FVIF_{AT} = (1 + r)^n (1 - t_{cg}) + t_{cg}$$

The advantage of the formula is it can be adjusted for the tax implications of a basis other than 1.00 and the resulting additional tax issues. It becomes:

$$FVIF_{AT} = (1 + r)^n (1 - t_{cg}) + t_{cg}B$$

B   = cost basis / asset value at start of period n

Professor's Note: This formula may appear unfamiliar. The intuition is simple. Before the "+" sign, the after-tax value is computed as if both the gain and initial investment are taxed at the end of the analysis period. Because the initial cost basis is not taxed under capital gains taxation, the tax on that amount is added back (that is the final "+ $t_{cg}B$" term). You are probably used to computing the gain, the capital gains tax owed, and then the after-tax ending value, or some variation of that process. If your method matches the above formula, it is correct.

However, the formula approach simplifies the analysis of the basis. If the investment is purchased at the start of the analysis period, for example at $100, then the cost basis and the start of analysis value are both $100 and the basis is 100 / 100 = 1.00. However, suppose the investment had been made prior to the start of the analysis period for $90, then the basis is 90 / 100 = 0.90 and there is an unrealized gain that will be taxed at the end of the analysis. Or suppose the investment had been made prior to the start of the analysis period for $115. Then the basis is 115 / 100 = 1.15 and the gain from $115 will be taxed, not from $100. There are also some types of assets, such as real estate, where the basis may be adjusted over time.

Example: Account subject to deferred capital gains taxation

Part 1: $1,000 is invested for 20 years at a pretax return of 10%. Return is subject to a deferred capital gains tax of 30%. **Compute** the ending after-tax account value and the tax drag. The cost basis is also $1,000 for B = 1.00.

Answer:

$$FV_{AT} = \$1,000[(1 + 0.10)^{20}(1 - 0.30) + 0.30(1.00)] = \$5,009.25$$

This is a gain after tax of $5,009.25 – 1,000 = $4,009.25

With no tax, the FV is $1,000(1 + 0.10)^{20} = $6,727.50 and the gain would have been:

gain no tax: $6,727.50 – 1,000 = $5,727.50

gain lost to taxes: $5,727.50 – $4,009.25 = $1,718.25 = tax drag$_\$$

$1,718.25 / $5,727.50 = 30.0% = tax drag$_\%$

Part 2: **Compute** the ending after-tax account value and the tax drag if all other facts are the same except the cost basis is $800 or $1,200.

Answer:

If cost basis is $800, B = 800 / 1,000 = 0.80

$$FV_{AT} = \$1,000[(1 + 0.10)^{20}(1 - 0.30) + 0.30(0.80)] = \$4,949.25$$

This is a gain after tax of $4,949.25 − 1,000 = $3,949.25

With no tax, the FV and gain are still $6,727.50 and $5,727.50.

gain lost to taxes: $5,727.50 − $3,949.25 = $1,778.25 = tax drag$_\$$
$1,778.25 / $5,727.50 = 31.0% = tax drag$_\%$

Answer:

If cost basis is $1,200, B = 1,200 / 1,000 = 1.20

$$FV_{AT} = \$1,000[(1 + 0.10)^{20}(1 - 0.30) + 0.30(1.20)] = \$5,069.25$$

This is a gain after tax of $5,069.25 − 1,000 = $4,069.25

With no tax, the FV and gain are still $6,727.50 and $5,727.50.

gain lost to taxes: $5,727.50 − $4,069.25 = $1,658.25 = tax drag$_\$$
$1,658.25 / $5,727.50 = 29.0% = tax drag$_\%$

For capital gains taxes, it can be generalized that:

- Unlike accrual taxation, there is no lost compounding of return due to paying taxes periodically. All tax is paid at the end of the time horizon.
- The tax drag amount will increase as the time horizon and/or rate of return increase because the tax will be on a larger pretax ending value.
- The relationship of the tax drag percentage and stated tax rate will depend on the basis (B):
  - If there is no initial unrealized gain or loss and B equals 1.00, the tax drag percentage is equal to the tax rate.
  - If there is an initial unrealized gain and B is less than 1.00, the tax drag percentage is greater than the tax rate because there is an additional initial gain subject to tax.
  - If there is an initial unrealized loss and B is greater than 1.00, the tax drag percentage is less than the tax rate because the portion of the return earned during the period back to the cost basis is untaxed.

Annual Wealth Based Taxation

A **wealth tax** is imposed on total value, not just on return. For example, if a portfolio of GBP100 declines to GBP90 or increases to GBP 110, the tax would be imposed on GBP90 and GBP 110, respectively. Some countries impose annual wealth taxes on the value of real estate, often called a property tax. (Estate and gift taxes are another form of wealth tax but they are only imposed at death or time of the gift, not periodically).

The future value of an investment after-tax under wealth taxation is:

$$FVIF_{AT} = [(1 + r)(1 - t_w)]^n$$

Compared to the accrual tax formula ($FVIF_{AT} = [1 + r(1 - t_i)]^n$), the tax applies to end of period value $(1 + r)$ and not just to return (r) each period. For the same tax rate, the effect of a wealth tax is much larger than for the other forms of taxation because the wealth tax applies to both start of period value and return earned. As a result, wealth tax rates tend to be lower than accrual or capital gains tax rates. For example, suppose the wealth tax is 4% and the return is 3%. Over one period, the tax is $1,000(1.03)(0.04) = 41.20$ and exceeds the return earned of 30.00. But if the return increases to 5%, the tax only increases to $1,000(1.05)(0.04) = 42.00$ and is now less than the return of 50.00.

Example: Account subject to annual wealth taxation

$1,000 is invested for 20 years at a pretax return of 10%. The investment is subject to an annual wealth tax of 3%. Compute the ending after-tax account value and the tax drag.

Answer:

$$FV_{AT} = \$1,000[(1 + 0.10)(1 - 0.03)]^{20} = \$3,658.38$$

This is a gain after tax of $\$3,658.38 - 1,000 = \$2,658.38$

With no tax, the FV and gain are still $6,727.50 and $5,727.50.

$$\text{gain lost to taxes: } \$5,727.50 - \$2,658.38 = \$3,069.12 = \text{tax drag}_\$$$
$$\$3,069.12 / \$5,727.50 = 53.6\% = \text{tax drag}_\%$$

For an annual wealth tax, it can be generalized that:

1. Wealth taxes are more onerous than other taxes because they apply to total value, not just return. To illustrate using the previous examples for 20 years, 10% return, and B = 1.00:
    *   The 30% accrual tax drags were $2,857.82 and 49.9%.
    *   The 30% capital gains tax drags were $1,718.25 and 30%.
    *   But for only a 3% annual wealth tax, they were $3,069.12 and 53.6%.

2. The adverse effects increase as the time horizon increases. Both the tax drag amount and percentage increase due to the loss of pretax compounding. This is illustrated by increasing the time horizon from 10 to 20 years:

n =	10		FV	Gain	Tax Drag
t =	3%	with tax:	$191.27	$91.27	**$68.11 42.7%**
r =	10%	no tax:	$259.37	$159.37	
PV =	100				

n =	20		FV	Gain	Tax Drag
t =	3%	with tax:	$365.84	$265.84	**$306.91 53.6%**
r =	10%	no tax:	$672.75	$572.75	
PV =	100				

3. But at higher rates of return the tax drag percentage declines even as the dollar amount increases. A large part of the tax is on the beginning value and is essentially "fixed" (i.e., not based on the return for the period). But tax drag percentage is related to gain and therefore tax drag percentage declines as the return increases. This is illustrated by increasing the return from 8% to 12% over a 10-year horizon.

n =	10		FV	Gain	Tax Drag
t =	3%	with tax:	$159.20	$59.20	**$56.69 48.9%**
r =	8%	no tax:	$215.89	$115.89	
PV =	100				

n =	10		FV	Gain	Tax Drag
t =	3%	with tax:	$229.03	$129.03	**$81.55 38.7%**
r =	12%	no tax:	$310.58	$210.58	
PV =	100				

4. The net result is that:
   - Tax drag amount increases with both longer time horizon and higher rate of return.
   - Tax drag percentage increases with longer time horizon but decreases with higher rate of return.

- Tax drag percentage is minimized at moderate time horizon and return and is higher at either (1) a shorter time horizon and lower return or (2) a longer time horizon and higher return. This is illustrated by comparing the three following scenarios.

				FV	Gain	Tax Drag	
n =	5						
t =	3%	with tax:		$109.60	$9.60	$18.03	65.3%
r =	5%	no tax:		$127.63	$27.63		
PV =	100						

				FV	Gain	Tax Drag	
n =	10						
t =	3%	with tax:		$191.27	$91.27	$68.11	42.7%
r =	10%	no tax:		$259.37	$159.37		
PV =	100						

				FV	Gain	Tax Drag	
n =	20						
t =	3%	with tax:		$890.00	$790.00	$746.65	48.6%
r =	15%	no tax:		$1,636.65	$1,536.65		
PV =	100						

Blended Taxation

Most portfolios are subject to multiple taxation methods and earn a portion (p) of the return from interest (i), dividends (d), and realized capital gains (rcg). In many cases, each portion is subject to a different tax rate. If all capital gains are realized and taxed each year, the three portions will sum to 100% and the annual tax rate is a weighted average of the component tax rates. But in many cases, the three will not sum to 100% as a portion of return is unrealized capital gain or loss (urcg) and the tax on that portion is deferred until sale. When there is a deferred tax portion, the annual tax rate computation will involve additional steps (but starting with the simple weighted average based on the realized tax portions).

Example 1: Blended tax

An account was worth $100,000 at the beginning of the year and $110,000 at year-end. The client did not add or remove any funds (meaning all interest and dividends received remain in the account). The portfolio return includes $300 of interest taxed at 30%, $4,000 in dividends taxed at 20%, and $2,200 of realized gains taxed at 20%.

Calculate the total portfolio pretax return in amount and percentage. **Label** and **calculate** the four percentage portions of return that sum up to the total return. **Calculate** the weighted average realized tax rate for the year and the percentage return after realized taxes for the year. **Explain** how the last calculation overstates true return for the year.

Answers:

Pretax return is:

$$EV - BV = \$110,000 - 100,000 = \$10,000$$

Percentage return is: $(EV / BV) - 1 = (EV - BV) / BV = 10,000 / 100,000 = 10\%$

- Interest portion is: $\$300 / 10,000 = 3\% = p_i$
- Dividend portion is: $\$4,000 / 10,000 = 40\% = p_d$
- Realized capital gain portion is: $\$2,200 / 10,000 = 22\% = p_{cg}$
- Unrealized capital gain portion must be:
  $\$10,000 - 300 - 4,000 - 2,200 = \$3,500$
  $\$3,500 / 10,000 = 35\% = p_{urcg} = 1 - 0.03 - 0.40 - 0.22$

The weighted average realized tax rate (wartr) for the year is:

$$wartr = p_i t_i + p_d t_d + p_{cg} t_{cg}$$

$$= (0.03)(30\%) + (0.40)(20\%) + (0.22)(20\%) = 13.3\%$$

The return after realized taxes for the year is:

$$r^* = r[1 - (p_i t_i + p_d t_d + p_{cg} t_{cg})] = r(1 - wartr)$$

$$= 10\%\{1 - [(0.03)(30\%) + (0.40)(20\%) + (0.22)(20\%)]\} = 8.67\%$$

$$= 10\%(1 - 0.133) = 8.67\%$$

The 8.67% overstates true after-tax return because there is an unrealized gain of $3,500 and a potential future tax liability to be paid on this gain.

The effect of the deferred capital gains on ultimate after-tax return is complex. The greater the portion of annual return that is taxed annually, the less the deferred taxes will matter as there is only a smaller portion of return to be subject to deferred taxes. But time horizon will also matter as the longer the holding period before the gain is realized, the greater the benefit of deferred tax compounding.

The net result can be projected in steps. (1) Begin with the after realized tax return (r^*) based on the realized tax rate (wartr). (2) Then calculate an effective capital gains tax rate (T^*) that reflects the capital gains rate that would apply to the deferred return. This T^* reflects the effect of all taxes already paid on interest, dividends, and realized capital gains and that the stated CG tax rate only applies to a portion of the return. (3) Treat this effective capital gains tax rate (T^*) as if it applied to 100% of the after realized tax return (which considers the taxes already paid). Lastly, and like the CG tax computation, this must be adjusted for any initial unrealized gain or loss [i.e., the basis (B)].

The process and its application are summarized using our previous blue box example. The additional required assumptions are a time horizon for deferral of eight years and an initial cost basis of $75,000 for the starting market value of $100,000, making B equal 0.75.

1. Based on the initial 10% pretax return and realized tax rate (wartr) of 13.3%, the after realized tax return (r^*) was computed to be 8.67%.

2. In the example, 65% of return was taxed annually and 35% was subject to deferred capital gains tax. The effective capital gains tax rate T^* is:

$$T^* = t_{cg} \left[\frac{1 - \left(p_i + p_d + p_{cg} \right)}{1 - \left(p_i t_i + p_d t_d + p_{cg} t_{cg} \right)} \right]$$

This formula is the capital gains tax rate times the ratio of the portion of return subject to deferred taxes over one minus the realized tax rate:

$$T^* = t_{cg} [p_{deferred\ cg} / (1 - wartr)]$$

$$= 20\% [0.35 / (1 - 0.133)] = 0.0807$$

3. Then apply these to a modified version of the standard deferred capital gains FV formula:

Standard formula: $FVIF_{AT} = (1 + r)^n (1 - t_{cg}) + t_{cg} B$

Modified formula:

$$FVIF_{AT} = (1 + r^*)^n (1 - T^*) + T^* - (1 - B) t_{cg}$$

$$= \$100,000 [(1 + 0.0867)^8 (1 - 0.0807) + 0.0807 - (1 - 0.75)(0.20)]$$

$$= \$100,000 [(1.9448)(0.9193) + 0.0807 - 0.05] = \$181,855$$

Study Session 4
Cross-Reference to CFA Institute Assigned Reading #9 – Taxes and Private Wealth Management in a Global Context

Study Session 4

Professor's Note: Some candidates complain this process is complicated and not intuitive. That is a realistic assessment. One way to think of it is this: 1.9448 is the FV of an initial investment unit after the annual realized taxes are considered but before any deferred taxes. 0.9193 then treats this as if it is 100% taxed at the effective capital gains tax rate (T*). The +0.0807 is an addback to reflect that some of the return was already taxed annually. –0.05 is a reduction in final result to reflect the effect of the initial unrealized gain and its tax liability.

TAX LOCATION

LOS 9.d: Discuss the tax profiles of different types of investment accounts and explain their effects on after-tax returns and future accumulations.

CFA® Program Curriculum, Volume 2, page 245

Many countries offer accounts that allow funds to be deposited and invested in a tax-advantaged manner. There are generally specified limits on how much can be invested in these accounts and they are typically restricted to specified purposes such as retirement or health care. These accounts provide a tax advantage. No taxes are imposed on return while funds are in the account, allowing pretax compounding of returns. These accounts can generally be classified as:

- Tax-deferred accounts (TDA): Pretax funds are deposited. The investor can take a tax deduction for the amount contributed, reducing taxable income and taxes due. All tax is deferred until withdrawal, allowing tax deferred compounding. Because no tax was paid on the funds deposited, tax is due on the full amount of withdrawals. The tax rate will be the rate at the end of time n (t_n) and the after-tax future value will be:

$$\text{FVIF}_{AT} = (1 + r)^n (1 - t_n)$$

- Tax-exempt accounts (TEA): Because after-tax funds are deposited, no tax is due on the returns earned or on withdrawals. Therefore, the after-tax future value does not explicitly depend on tax rate and is:

$$\text{FVIF}_{AT} = (1 + r)^n$$

In the absence of tax-preferenced accounts or when the limits on contributions are reached, after-taxed savings are invested in taxable accounts where returns are subject to annual taxes. Taxable accounts provide no initial tax advantage or tax deferred compounding.

Example: Accounts subject to different tax treatments

Assume that $100,000 is invested in each of four accounts:

1. An account taxed annually (accrual taxes; $FVIF_{AT}$).

2. A tax-deferred account ($FVIF_{TDA}$).

3. An account with deferred capital gains and an initial cost basis of $100,000 ($FVIF_{CGBT}$).

4. A tax-exempt account ($FVIF_{TEA}$).

Calculate the after-tax value of each account in 30 years, if each account earns 9% annually and all investment income and returns are taxed at 35%.

Answer:

1. $FVIF_{AT} = [1 + r(1 - t_i)]^n$ $\Rightarrow \$100,000[1 + 0.09(1 - 0.35)]^{30}$
$$= \$550,460$$

2. $FVIF_{TDA} = (1 + r)^n (1 - t_n)$ $\Rightarrow \$100,000[(1 + 0.09)^{30}(1 - 0.35)]$
$$= \$862,399$$

3. $FVIF_{CGBT} = (1 + r)^n(1 - t_{cg}) + t_{cg}B$ $\Rightarrow \$100,000[(1 + 0.09)^{30}(1 - 0.35) + 0.35(1.0)]$
$$= \$897,399$$

4. $FVIF_{TEA} = (1 + r)^n$ $\Rightarrow \$100,000(1 + 0.09)^{30}$
$$= \$1,326,768$$

It is not surprising the tax exempt account provides the highest wealth accumulation and fully taxable accrual taxation, the lowest. Both capital gains taxation and the tax-deferred account provide tax benefits and so rank in the middle of results. This implies that investors should locate assets in the type of account that provides greatest wealth accumulation and subject to the limits of how much can be located where.

Tax-Advantaged Accounts and Asset Allocations

It is common to examine an investor's asset allocation on a pretax basis. For example, consider an investor with €1,000,000 in assets, with €600,000 invested in equity in a TDA, and €400,000 invested in bonds in a TEA. Assume the investor's tax rate is 30%.

Traditional (pretax) analysis indicates 60% equity and 40% bonds—a 60/40 asset allocation. However, after-tax analysis may lead to a different conclusion.

The bond assets are in a TEA and purchased with after-tax funds. They are not subject to any future tax liability. The equity assets are in a TDA, were purchased with pretax funds, and are subject to a tax liability at 30% on withdrawal of €600,000 × (0.30) = €180,000. Their after-tax value is only €420,000 and the total portfolio after-tax value is only 420,000 + 400,000 = 820,000 for a 51.2/48.8 allocation. Further complicating the analysis, the allocation depends on the time horizon assumptions as the deferred tax due on the equity compounds over time.

Choosing Account Tax Type

Superficially, it appears the TEA is superior to the TDA because there is no tax due on withdrawals. However, this ignores that TEA contributions are made with after-tax funds and TDA with pretax funds. Suppose an investor has $100 pretax available for savings and is in a 30% tax bracket. The full $100 can be contributed to a TDA and invested. If that contribution is not made, the investor will owe $30 in taxes now and have available only $70 for contribution to the TEA. The valid future value comparison is:

$$\text{TDA: } FV_{AT} = \$100(1 + r)^n(1 - t_n)$$

$$\text{TEA: } FV_{AT} = \$100(1 - t_0)(1 + r)^n$$

The relevant difference and key consideration is whether the tax rate is lower now (t_0) or expected to be lower in the future (t_n).

- If t_0 is lower, pay the taxes now and use the TEA.
- If t_n is lower, pay the taxes in the future and use the TDA.
- If t_0 and t_n are the same, the accounts produce the same ending value.

Example: Tax-deferred vs. tax-exempt accounts

An investor pays current and future taxes at 25% and is willing to give up $3,000 in consumption. The investor can contribute $3,000 in after-tax dollars to a tax-exempt account or $4,000 to a tax-deferred account.

 Professor's Note: At a tax rate of 25%, the investor will have to earn $4,000 and pay taxes of $1,000 to contribute $3,000 to a tax-exempt account. Alternatively, the investor can deposit the entire $4,000 into a tax-deferred account.

Assuming pretax income of $4,000 is available to be saved and earns an investment return of 8% for 20 years and the tax rate is 25%, **calculate** the future values of the following three account structures:

1. A TDA (e.g., retirement account).

2. A TEA (e.g., tax-exempt bonds).

3. An account taxed annually (e.g., savings account).

Answer:

The corresponding formulas and future value calculations, considering after-tax contributions:

$$1. \ FV_{TDA} = (1+r)^n (1-t_n) \Rightarrow \$4,000\left[(1+0.08)^{20}(1-0.25)\right] = \$13,983$$

$$2. \ FV_{TEA} = (1+r)^n \qquad\qquad \Rightarrow \$3,000(1+0.08)^{20} \qquad\quad = \$13,983$$

$$3. \ FV_{AT} = \left[1+r(1-t_i)\right]^n \Rightarrow \$3,000\left[1+0.08(1-0.25)\right]^{20} = \$9,621$$

Example: Unequal current and future tax rates

Assume the investor in the previous example pays current taxes at 25% and expects a future tax rate of 20%. **Determine** whether the TDA or TEA will have the greater future value.

Answer:

In this case, the investor faces a lower future tax rate. The investor's current situation is unchanged. She will still have to earn $4,000 to invest $3,000 in the tax-exempt account or be able to invest the entire $4,000 in the tax-deferred account:

$$FV_{TDA} = (1+r)^n (1-t_n) \Rightarrow \$4,000\left[(1+0.08)^{20}(1-0.20)\right] = \$14,915$$

$$FV_{TEA} = (1+r)^n \quad\quad\quad \Rightarrow \$3,000(1+0.08)^{20} \quad\quad = \$13,983$$

The future after-tax accumulation of the tax-exempt account is still $13,983. Because the future rate is expected to be 20%, the TDA now produces a greater future value.

Equal Limits on Contributions (A Special Case)

Contribution amounts are normally stated as a nominal amount and may be the same for both TDAs and TEAs. If the investor has additional disposable (not needed for other purposes) funds that can be contributed, the TEA can (in this situation) be superior for maximizing future wealth even if the current and future tax rates are equal.

Returning to the previous example, where current and future tax rates were 25% and the pretax rate of return was 8% (giving an after-tax rate of return of 6%), a $4,000 pretax deposit into a TDA and a $3,000 after-tax deposit into a TEA had the same value at the end of the 20-year period of $13,983.

Now suppose regulations limit the contribution to either account to $3,000 (this will be in pretax terms for a TDA and in after-tax terms for a TEA) and assume, once again, that the investor has $4,000 (pretax) that she is prepared to divert away from current consumption.

If she chooses the TEA, then all of the $4,000 will be taxed; this means $1,000 will be paid in tax, leaving $3,000 for the TEA (exactly equalling the limit on contributions). As we saw previously, this will grow to $13,983 over 20 years.

If, instead, she chooses the TDA, then only $3,000 of the $4,000 can be invested, due to the contribution limit, and this will grow over the 20 years to $3,000 × 1.08^{20} × (1 – 0.25) = $10,487. The $1,000 that is not put into the TDA will be subject to tax, leaving $750, which we can assume will be invested in a taxable account earning 6% net after-tax per year, compounding over the 20 years to $750 × 1.06^{20} = $2,405. In total, the TDA and the taxable residue will have a value of $10,487 + $2,405 = $12,892 at the end of the 20 years.

The TEA is the superior choice, even though current and future tax rates are the same, because the limit on contributions is, in effect, more generous for the TEA (where the limit applies to the after-tax value) than for the TDA (where the limit applies to the pretax value).

TAXES AND INVESTMENT RISK

LOS 9.e: Explain how taxes affect investment risk.

CFA® Program Curriculum, Volume 2, page 250

Taxes reduce return, which means they also reduce the variability of return and the after-tax risk of the investment. Suppose pretax return on an investment can be either +10% or –10% and the investor's tax rate is 40%. Then the after-tax returns can be either +6% or –6%. The +6% is obviously 10%(1 – 0.40) and –6% is –10%(1 – 0.40). The reasoning for –6% is that the pretax loss can be used to reduce otherwise taxable income from other sources (i.e., the government shares in the upside and downside of the investment). The after-tax standard deviation of the + to – 6% returns must be lower than the pretax standard deviation of the + to – 10%. After-tax return and risk are calculated as:

$$r_{AT} = r(1 - t)$$

$$\sigma_{AT} = \sigma(1 - t)$$

Example: Risk reduction

Suppose an investor has half her portfolio in stocks and half in bonds. No tax deferred accounts are available. The returns on the stock investment are taxed at an annual rate of 20% and the bond returns are taxed at a rate of 30%. The pretax standard deviation of stock returns is 16% and the pretax standard deviation of bond returns is 6%.

Calculate the pretax and after-tax standard deviations of portfolio returns, assuming the correlation between stocks and bonds is 1.

Answer:

If the correlation between stocks and bonds is 1, the **pretax standard deviation** of portfolio returns is a simple weighted average of the individual standard deviations:

$$\sigma_{P,\text{before-tax}} = 0.5(16\%) + 0.5(6\%) = 11.0\%$$

After-tax standard deviation is:

$$\sigma_{P,\text{after-tax}} = 0.5(16\%)(1 - 0.2) + 0.5(6\%)(1 - 0.3) = 8.5\%$$

Example: Risk reduction with accrual and deferred taxes

Now assume the bonds are held in a tax-exempt account. **Calculate** the after-tax standard deviation of portfolio returns.

Answer:

$$\sigma_{P,\text{after-tax}} = 0.5(16\%)(1-0.2) + 0.5(6\%) = 9.4\%$$

In this case, the standard deviation of portfolio returns increases from 8.5% when the returns are fully taxable, to 9.4%. The increase in variability is because the government does not absorb part of the variability of the bond returns. Because the stock returns are taxed annually, however, there is still an amount of risk reduction.

GENERATING TAX ALPHA

The account type where assets are held (i.e., the asset location) is important for tax management. From strictly a tax-management standpoint, an investor should locate assets that would be heavily taxed in tax-advantaged accounts and hold more lightly taxed assets in taxable accounts. More lightly taxed can refer to either lower tax rates and/or tax deferral. The value created by this effective tax management of investments is referred to as **tax alpha**.

Assuming there are limits on how much can be placed in the tax-deferred locations, this generally favors holding bonds in tax-deferred accounts because the bonds produce most of their return from income. In contrast, equities can be held in the taxable accounts. The equity return is typically made up mostly of capital gains rather than dividend income and capital gains can be deferred. By extending the holding period, the T_{AE} can be reduced even in the fully taxable location to improve the equity after-tax return and generate tax alpha.

In more complicated situations, both tax location and asset allocation can be optimized by using leverage. Suppose an investor has $75,000 in tax-deferred accounts (either TDA or TEA) all invested in bonds and $25,000 in equities in fully taxable accounts to maximize tax alpha. However, the 25/75 equity/bond allocation is not optimal and 60/40 is the desired allocation. There are two possibilities:

1. Shift $35,000 of the tax-deferred account holdings from bond to equity to produce the 60/40 allocation. However, this will reduce tax alpha even though it increases expected return with a shift to higher return equity.

2. Or borrow and invest in the taxable account the desired amount of increased equity holdings ($35,000). Borrowing is the equivalent of shorting bonds, [i.e., you pay interest on the borrowings (a short position) while you receive interest on bonds owned (a long position)]. This optimizes tax alpha and produces the desired allocation.

Location	Asset Class	Before Leverage		After Leverage	
		Market Value	% Allocation	Market Value	% Allocation
TDA or TEA	Bond	$75,000	75%	$75,000	75%*
Taxable	Equity	$25,000	25%	$60,000	60%
	Short Bond			–$35,000	–35%*
Total		$100,000	100%	$100,000	100%

* The net bond allocation is now 75 – 35 = 40%.

LOS 9.f: Discuss the relation between after-tax returns and different types of investor trading behavior.

CFA® Program Curriculum, Volume 2, page 254

Generally, the more frequent the trading, the less the ability to defer taxes, increasing tax drag and decreasing after-tax return. Trading behavior can be differentiated as:

1. **Traders**—due to frequent trading, all gains are realized frequently and taxed at a generally higher rate with no deferred tax compounding. Tax alpha is lost.

2. **Active investors**—trade less frequently than traders so that many of their gains are longer term and taxed at lower rates.

3. **Passive investors**—buy and hold equity so that gains are deferred to benefit from pretax compounding and are taxed at lower long-term rates.

4. **Exempt investors**—avoid taxation altogether.

Example: The effects of trading behavior on taxes

Consider the case of four equity traders who invest $1,000 for 30 years and earn 9% annually. They pay a tax of 30% on gains realized in less than a year and a tax of 20% on gains held a year or longer. What are the future accumulations for each trader?

Answer:

Trader—realizes all gains as short term and pays 30% tax annually:

$$FVIF_{AT} = \left[1 + r(1 - t_i)\right]^n : \$1,000[1 + 0.09(1 - 0.30)]^{30} = \$6,252$$

Active investor—simplify by assuming realizes all gains as long term and pays 20% tax annually:

$$FVIF_{AT} = \left[1 + r\left(1 - t_i\right)\right]^n : \$1,000[1 + 0.09(1 - 0.20)]^{30} = \$8,051$$

Passive investor—defers all gains until the end of the investment horizon and pays a 20% tax at that time:

$$FVIF_{cgt} = \left(1 + r\right)^n \left(1 - t_{cg}\right) + t_{cg} : \$1,000[(1 + 0.09)^{30}(1 - 0.20) + 0.20] = \$10,814$$

Exempt investor—does not pay taxes:

$$FVIF_{TEA} = \left(1 + r\right)^n : 1,000(1 + 0.09)^{30} = \$13,268$$

Professor's Note: You should conclude that:

Asset allocation is more important than asset location.
Borrowing to optimize both tax alpha and asset allocation is an unusual strategy.

- *More frequent trading, even if it increases pretax return, may reduce after-tax return when the additional tax burden is considered (i.e., + pretax alpha may not generate + after-tax alpha).*
- *Once an appropriate asset allocation is achieved, then it is appropriate to utilize legal methods to maximize after-tax value.*

ADDITIONAL STRATEGIES FOR GENERATING TAX ALPHA

LOS 9.g: Explain tax loss harvesting and highest-in/first-out (HIFO) tax lot accounting.

CFA® Program Curriculum, Volume 2, page 255

Tax Loss Harvesting

Tax loss harvesting refers to realizing losses to offset realized gains or other taxable income. It reduces the taxes due now but generally does not reduce eventual total taxes. If the benefit is taken now to lower taxes now, it cannot be used in the future and taxes in the future will be higher. Even so, tax loss harvesting is beneficial. Think of it as saving $100 in taxes now versus paying $100 at a future date.

Example: Tax loss harvesting

An investor has a realized capital gain of $100,000 and pays a capital gains tax rate of 20%. The investor is considering selling Stock A to reduce his tax bill. Stock A has a cost basis of $120,000 and has fallen to a current market value of $80,000.

Calculate the investor's tax payment if Stock A is not sold, if it is sold, and the difference in tax payments this year.

Answer:

If Stock A is not sold, the investor will have to pay capital gains taxes on the full $100,000 capital gain: $0.20 \times \$100,000 = \$20,000$.

If Stock A is sold, there is a capital loss: $\$80,000 - \$120,000 = -\$40,000$. This $40,000 loss can be applied against the $100,000 gain such that the net taxable gain is only $60,000. The tax bill is $0.20 \times \$60,000 = \$12,000$, so the tax savings is $\$20,000 - \$12,000 = \$8,000$.

The tax loss harvesting saves $8,000 in tax payments this year.

For the Exam: In a simple case like this, the immediate tax savings from the loss harvest can be calculated directly as the capital loss multiplied by the tax rate: $\$40,000 \times 0.20 = \$8,000$. This is the most likely question.

In practice, taxing authorities have many different ways of treating tax loss harvesting. In many cases, there are restrictions on loss harvesting. On the exam, always read the question and apply the case facts as given.

When a tax loss is harvested, the proceeds are typically reinvested, and the reinvested sale proceeds become a new lower cost basis. When the new asset is eventually sold, there is a higher realized gain (or lower loss) for higher tax due (or less tax sheltering) in the future. Taking the loss now means that loss amount is unavailable in the future.

Example: Loss harvest with purchase of a nearly identical stock

Continuing the previous example with an investor who holds Stock A with a market value, cost basis, and unrealized loss of $80,000, $120,000, and $40,000 respectively. The investor also has $100,000 of already realized gains.

Assume the investor can sell Stock A this year and reinvest in a stock with similar return expectations, Stock B. Assume both stocks then double in price and are liquidated next year. **Calculate** and **show** your calculations of the total tax bills this year and next for the investor if:

1. Stock A is sold next year.

2. Stock A is sold this year and the sale proceeds are reinvested in Stock B.

3. Stock A is sold this year and the sale proceeds plus year 1 tax savings are reinvested in Stock B.

Answer:

Option 1:
Taxes year 1: $100,000 already realized gain @ 20% = $20,000
Taxes year 2: Projected sale price of A is $80,000 × 2 = $160,000
    Less cost basis of $120,000 for gain of $40,000
    Tax on sale is $40,000 @ 20% = $8,000

Cumulative tax bill of $28,000.

Option 2:
Taxes year 1: $40,000 tax loss harvest from selling A reduces gain to $60,000 @ 20% = $12,000
Taxes year 2: Sale of Stock A in year 1 generates $80,000 invested in Stock B; Stock B then doubles in value to $160,000 for a taxable gain when Stock B is sold of $80,000 @ 20% = $16,000

Cumulative tax bill of $28,000; $8,000 less in year 1 but $8,000 more in year 2 than Option 1.

Option 3:
Taxes year 1: $40,000 tax loss harvest from selling Stock A reduces gain to $60,000 @ 20% = $12,000
Taxes year 2: sale of Stock A in year 1 generates $80,000 and $8,000 tax savings for $88,000 invested in Stock B; Stock B then doubles in value to $176,000 for a taxable gain when Stock B is sold of $88,000 @ 20% = $17,600

Cumulative tax bill of $29,600; a higher tax bill than Option 2 because more funds were invested in the appreciating Stock B.

Despite paying more in taxes, the investor maximizes ending wealth with Option 3 because the tax savings were reinvested (in an asset with a positive return).

Highest-In/First-Out (HIFO) Tax Lot Accounting

Most tax authorities allow a form of specific inventory accounting. When an investor makes a partial sale and has acquired the stock on different dates, each at different cost basis, the investor can select which tax lots are applied to the sale. In that case, the tax lots that produce the lowest tax bill should be designated as sold. Consider an investor who bought 100 shares of stock on three different dates for $10,000, $12,000, and $15,000. The investor just sold 100 shares.

Highest-in/first-out (HIFO) is generally optimal and the 100 shares with a cost basis of $15,000 should be designated as sold. If the sale price is higher than $15,000, this will minimize the gain and capital gains tax due now. If the sale price is less than $15,000, this will maximize the realized loss and immediate tax benefits.

In a special case where future tax rates are expected to be higher than current tax rates, **lowest-in/first-out (LIFO)** may be better and the 100 shares with a cost basis of $10,000 should be designated as sold. It will create a higher immediate tax bill. But it defers the higher tax lots for sale in the future. That will lower the realized gain or increase the realized loss at a future date and higher tax rates. In other words, it will reduce the realized gain or maximize the loss until a period of higher rates and greater tax benefit.

HOLDING PERIOD MANAGEMENT

Many tax authorities impose a higher capital gains tax rate on shorter-term versus longer-term holdings. While it is generally desirable to extend the holding period to defer the tax, it is particularly desirable to extend the holding period when it also lowers the tax rate.

> **Example: Expected returns, tax classifications, and after-tax returns**
>
> Investor 1 is an extremely active trader whose returns are always taxed at the ordinary tax rate of 40%. Investor 2 follows a minimum trading strategy, only recognizing long-term capital gains taxes of 20% each year. Both recognize gains and pay taxes annually. Both investors earn a pretax return of 12%. **Determine** the after-tax value of a $1.00 over a 1-year and 10-year holding period for both investors and the value ratio of the two investors.

Answer:

Over 1-year holding period:
Investor 1: after-tax annual return = {1 + [0.12(1 − 0.40)]} × $1.00 = $1.072
Investor 2: after-tax annual return = {1 + [0.12(1 − 0.20)]} × $1.00 = $1.096
A ratio favoring the patient trader (Investor 2) of 1.096 / 1.072 = 1.022

Over 10-year holding period:
Investor 1: after-tax annual return = {1 + [0.12(1 − 0.40)]}^{10} × $1.00 = $2.004
Investor 2: after-tax annual return = {1 + [0.12(1 − 0.20)]}^{10} × $1.00 = $2.501
A ratio favoring the patient trader (Investor 2) of 2.501 / 2.004 = 1.247

The advantage is growing with longer time periods.

The implications of a higher short-term versus lower long-term gains taxation rate are:

- The ratios of ending after-tax value of the patient and rapid trader (1.022 and 1.247 over 1- and 10-year investment horizons) increase in favor of the patient trader:
  - At higher rates of return (e.g., 2% versus 4%).
  - Over longer investment horizons (e.g., five years versus ten years).
- Rapid trading would require a much higher pretax return to break even on an after-tax basis. In the example, the active trader would have to earn 16% per year pretax to stay even with the more patient investor earning 12% pretax. The 16% is a 33% higher pretax return. Calculations to support this conclusion are shown below:

    Rapid trader, t = 40%; 16% (1 − 0.40) = 9.6% after-tax
    Patient trader, t = 20%; 12% (1 − 0.20) = 9.6% after-tax

Another dimension of holding period management is the timing of sales in relation to tax year end. If a sale is being considered near the tax year end, make the sale:

- Before year end if it is a loss in order to place the loss in the current tax year and offset gains this year. This will lower taxes this year but raise taxes next year.
- After year end if it is a gain. This will defer the gain and tax until next year's tax return.

If tax rates are going to change, the analysis could become more complicated. If, for example, tax rates will rise next year, it may become more advantageous to incur the gain now, at the lower rate, than wait.

TAXES AND MEAN-VARIANCE OPTIMIZATION

LOS 9.h: Demonstrate how taxes and asset location relate to mean–variance optimization.

CFA® Program Curriculum, Volume 2, page 260

In the previous sections, we discussed how taxes affect the after-tax returns and risk of investments. Ideally then, the efficient frontier of portfolios should be viewed on an after-tax basis. Furthermore, because the tax status of an investment depends on the type of account it is in (i.e., its asset location), the same asset could appear on the efficient frontier in both taxable and non-taxable forms.

For example, an investor holds stocks and bonds in taxable, tax-deferred, and tax-exempt accounts. In this case, there are effectively six different assets to consider. Of course, the optimization process would have to be constrained to account for limits on the amount of funds that can be placed in tax-advantaged accounts and the type of assets that can be allocated to them.

The mean-variance optimization should optimally allocate assets and determine the optimal asset location for each asset. Accrual equivalent after-tax returns would be substituted for before-tax returns, and risk on an after-tax basis would be substituted for before-tax risk.

KEY CONCEPTS

LOS 9.a

Tax Regime	Ordinary Income Tax Structure	Favorable Treatment for Interest Income?	Favorable Treatment for Dividend Income?	Favorable Treatment for Capital Gains?
Common Progressive	Progressive	Yes*	Yes	Yes
Heavy Dividend Tax	Progressive	Yes*	No	Yes
Heavy Capital Gain Tax	Progressive	Yes*	Yes	No
Heavy Interest Tax	Progressive	No	Yes	Yes
Light Capital Gain Tax	Progressive	No	No	Yes
Flat and Light	Flat	Yes*	Yes	Yes
Flat and Heavy	Flat	Yes*	No	No

* Some countries may provide favorable tax treatment or exemption for some types of interest (e.g., tax-free bonds in the United States).

LOS 9.b

- annual accrual taxation: $FVIF_{AT} = [1 + r(1 - t_i)]^n$

  deferred capital gains taxation: $FVIF_{AT} = (1 + r)^n(1 - t_{cg}) + t_{cg}B$

  $$B = \text{cost basis / asset value at start of period n}$$

  annual wealth taxation: $FVIF_{AT} = [(1 + r)(1 - t_w)]^n$

blended taxation:

  weighted annual realized tax rate: $wartr = p_i t_i + p_d t_d + p_{cg} t_{cg}$

  return after realized taxes: $r^* = r[1 - (p_i t_i + p_d t_d + p_{cg} t_{cg})] = r(1 - wartr)$

  effective capital gains tax rate: $T^* = t_{cg}[p_{deferred\ cg} / (1 - wartr)]$

  future value of the investment: $FVIF_{AT} = (1 + r^*)^n(1 - T^*) + T^* - (1 - B)t_{cg}$

LOS 9.c
For accrual taxes:
- If $n > 1$, tax drag percentage > t.
- As *n* and/or *r* increase, tax drag percentage and amount increase.

For deferred capital gains taxes:
- As n and/or r increase, tax drag amount increases.
  - If B = 1.0, tax drag percentage = t.
  - If B < 1.0, tax drag percentage > t.
  - If B > 1.0, tax drag percentage < t.

For annual wealth taxes:
- Tax effects are more onerous as the tax rate applies to total value, not just return.
- As n increases, tax drag percentage and amount increase.
- But as r increases, tax drag percentage decreases even as amount increases.
- Tax drag percentage is lower at moderate time horizon and return.

LOS 9.d
Both TDA and TEA provide tax deferred compounding of return.

Tax-deferred account (TDA) contributions provide a front-end tax advantage; contributions are pretax, but all withdrawals are taxed.

$$FVIF_{AT} = (1 + r)^n (1 - t_n)$$

Tax-exempt account (TEA) contributions provide a back-end tax advantage; contributions are after-tax, and withdrawals are not taxed.
- If the current and the expected future tax rate are equal, TDA and TEA provide equal future value.
- If the future tax rate is expected to be lower, use the TDA.
- If the future tax rate is expected to be higher, use the TEA.

LOS 9.e
After-tax return is less variable than pretax return as taxes take a portion of the upside and reduce the downside.

$$r_{AT} = r(1 - t)$$

$$\sigma_{AT} = \sigma(1 - t)$$

LOS 9.f
High turnover lowers tax alpha as the benefits of tax-deferred compounding are lost. In addition, more gains are taxed at higher short-term rather than lower long-term rates.

In order from lowest tax alpha (highest turnover) to highest tax alpha (lowest turnover) are: traders, active investors, and passive investors. Exempt investors do not pay taxes.

LOS 9.g
Tax loss harvesting uses investment losses to offset investment gains or income, resulting in a tax savings. This initial tax savings is overstated because the tax savings is taken now and the low cost basis is not available in the future. Harvesting is a deferral of taxes.

Investors often accumulate a security position through a series of trades, each occurring at different points in time and at different prices. If a partial sale of the position is being made, it is generally best to designate the highest cost basis lot as being sold first (HIFO) to minimize the tax gain or maximize the tax loss. If future tax rates are expected to be higher than current rates, designating the lowest cost basis as being sold (LIFO) may be better as it accelerates tax payments to the present and lowers them in the future.

LOS 9.h

Ideally, the efficient frontier of portfolios should be viewed on an after-tax basis. For example, an investor holds both stocks and bonds in both taxable and tax-exempt accounts. In this case, there are four different assets that could appear on the efficient frontier. Of course, the optimization process would have to be constrained to account for limits on the amount of funds that can be placed in tax-advantaged accounts and the type of assets that can be allocated to them.

The mean-variance optimization should optimally allocate assets and determine the optimal asset location for each asset.

CONCEPT CHECKERS

1. Of the seven primary global tax regimes, **determine** which of the following does *not* provide potentially favorable tax treatment of interest income.
   A. The Flat and Heavy regime.
   B. The Common Progressive regime.
   C. The Light Capital Gain Tax regime.

2. An individual pays taxes as a single tax payer. During 2009 her taxable income totaled $412,950. Applying the following rates, her tax bill and average tax rate for 2009 are *closest* to:

Taxable Income		Bracket Amount (Col 2 – Col 1)	Tax Rate %	Plus
(1) Over	(2) Up to			
0	$8,350	$8,350	10	
$8,350	33,950	25,600	15	$835
33,950	82,250	48,300	25	4,675
82,250	171,550	89,300	28	16,750
171,550	372,950	201,400	33	41,754
372,950			35	108,216

   A. $122,216; 30%.
   B. $136,274; 33%.
   C. $144,533; 35%.

3. An investor is evaluating various assets and strategies for her portfolio. Based solely on tax effects, **determine** which of the following investments would *most likely* be favored in a Heavy Interest Tax Regime.
   A. Growth stocks with high turnover.
   B. Bonds with periodic payment of interest.
   C. Value stocks held for a long period of time.

4. An investment of $1,000 earns annual interest of 5% (no capital gains). Assuming accrual taxes of 30%, the expected after-tax value of the investment in ten years is *closest* to:
   A. $1,035.
   B. $1,140.
   C. $1,411.

5. In Question 4, the tax drag in percentage terms is *closest* to:
   A. 1.6%.
   B. 34.7%.
   C. 53.2%.

6. Consider the following statements about an account subject to accrual taxes and **select** the best answer:

   Statement 1: As the investment horizon *increases*, the tax drag *increases*.
   Statement 2: As the investment return *increases*, the tax drag *decreases*.

   A. Both of the statements are correct.
   B. Statement 1 is incorrect; the tax drag decreases as the investment horizon increases.
   C. Statement 2 is incorrect; the tax drag increases as the investment return increases.

7. An initial starting investment of $1,000 earns an annual return of 9%, all of which is deferred capital gains. At a capital gains tax rate of 20%, **determine** which of the following is *closest* to the after-tax value of the investment in ten years.
   A. $1,894.
   B. $2,094.
   C. $2,367.

8. For Question 7, the tax drag in percentage terms is *closest* to:
   A. 20.0%.
   B. 25.0%.
   C. 34.6%.

9. Consider the following two statements about an account with a basis (B) of 1.0 that produces only fully tax-deferred capital gains:

   Statement 1: As the investment horizon increases ⇒ the tax drag percent is constant.
   Statement 2: As the investment return increases ⇒ the tax drag percent increases.

   A. Both of the statements are correct.
   B. Only Statement 1 is correct.
   C. Only Statement 2 is correct.

10. An investment of $1,000 is expected to earn an annual return of 12% in fully deferred capital gains. If the capital gains tax rate is 20% and the cost basis is $800, **determine** which of the following is *closest* to the expected value of the investment in ten years.
    A. $2,485.
    B. $2,645.
    C. $3,106.

11. An initial investment of $1,000 will earn an annual return of 14%. If the wealth-based tax is 3% and no other taxes are paid on the account, **determine** which of the following is *closest* to the value of the investment in 15 years.
    A. $4,520.
    B. $6,924.
    C. $7,138.

12. For Question 11, **determine** the approximate tax drag in percentage terms.
    A. 3.5%.
    B. 42.6%.
    C. 74.4%.

13. Consider the following two statements assuming only wealth taxes apply:

    Statement 1: As the investment horizon increases ⇒ the tax drag $ increases.
    Statement 2: As the investment return increases ⇒ the tax drag % decreases.

    A. Both statements are correct.
    B. Only Statement 1 is correct.
    C. Only Statement 2 is correct.

14. A portfolio generates a total return of 15%. The tax rates on interest, dividends, and capital gains are 35%, 20%, and 20%, respectively. The proportions of the portfolio return from interest, dividends, and realized capital gains are 10%, 25%, and 35%, respectively. Using the data, the net return after all taxes is *closest* to:
    A. 11.25%.
    B. 11.50%.
    C. 12.68%.

15. In Question 14, the effective capital gains tax rate is *closest* to:
    A. 5.07%.
    B. 7.10%.
    C. 35.50%.

16. In Question 14, assume the return proportions continue for seven years and the account's cost basis is €100,000. The expected balance in the account in seven years after payment of all taxes is *closest* to:
    A. €184,260.
    B. €221,361.
    C. €224,013.

17. In Question 14, assume the account's basis is €80,000 instead of €100,000 and the investment's current value is €100,000. The expected balance in the account in seven years after payment of all taxes is *closest* to:
    A. €180,361.
    B. €217,361.
    C. €220,014.

18. Assume €100,000 is invested in a tax-deferred account. The expected after-tax balance that can be withdrawn after 20 years, assuming a tax rate of 30% and a pretax return of 10%, is *closest* to:
    A. €386,968.
    B. €470,925.
    C. €672,750.

19.   Assume €100,000 is invested in a tax-exempt account. The expected balance in
        the account after 20 years, assuming a tax rate of 30% and pretax return of 10%,
        is *closest* to:
        A. €386,968.
        B. €500,925.
        C. €672,750.

20.   An investor has €800,000 equity in a tax-deferred account and €600,000 in
        bonds in a tax-exempt account. Assuming a tax rate of 40%, the after-tax asset
        allocation is *closest* to:
        A. 44.4% stocks; 55.6% bonds.
        B. 57.1% stocks; 42.9% bonds.
        C. 31.0% stocks; 69.0% bonds.

21.   An investor pays 20% current taxes but will pay future taxes at 30%. The
        investor is willing to give up $2,000 in current consumption and expects to earn
        12% in a tax-advantaged account for 30 years. Assuming no contribution limits,
        determine which account will have the highest future after-tax accumulation.
        A. A tax-deferred account.
        B. A tax-exempt account.
        C. The accounts provide the same future accumulations.

22.   Of the following assets, **determine** which one would be the *most* appropriate
        asset to locate in a tax-deferred account rather than a taxable account in a <u>Flat
        and Heavy Tax regime</u>.
        A. Tax-exempt bonds.
        B. High-growth stocks.
        C. Corporate bonds.

23.   All else equal, which of the following will usually have the lowest risk?
        A. A tax-deferred account.
        B. A taxable account.
        C. A tax-exempt account.

24.   All else equal, which of the following investors would have the lowest future
        accumulation?
        A. A trader.
        B. An active investor.
        C. A passive investor.

25.   An investor has a realized capital gain of £80,000 and pays a capital gains tax
        rate of 30%. The investor can sell another stock with a cost basis of £140,000
        and a current market value of £90,000. The tax savings (tax alpha) from
        harvesting the loss is *closest* to:
        A. £9,000.
        B. £10,000.
        C. £15,000.

26. In the previous question, assume the investor can either:

    Strategy 1: Sell the stock now and recognize the loss in the current year.
    Strategy 2: Hold the stock and sell it at the end of the second year.

    In either case, the old or new stock is sold at the end of the second year after earning a 10% return for that year. Any current tax savings (tax alpha) is immediately reinvested in very similar stock. **Determine** which of the strategies provides the highest future accumulation.
    A. Strategy 1.
    B. Strategy 2.
    C. The strategies provide the same future after-tax accumulation.

27. To perform mean-variance optimization from the perspective of a specific taxable investor, use:
    A. accrual equivalent after-tax returns and after-tax standard deviations.
    B. accrual equivalent after-tax returns and before-tax standard deviations.
    C. annual pretax returns and after-tax standard deviations.

ANSWERS – CONCEPT CHECKERS

1. **C** The Light Capital Gain Tax regime provides potentially favorable treatment for capital gains but not for interest and dividend income. The Flat and Heavy regime provides potentially favorable treatment for interest income but not capital gains and dividend income. The Common Progressive regime provides potentially favorable treatment for interest income, dividend income, and capital gains.

2. **A** With total taxable income of $412,950, the individual falls in the highest tax bracket (*marginal tax rate* = 35%). As such, she pays $108,216 plus 35% of any amount above $372,950. Her total tax bill is:

   $108,216 + ($412,950 − $372,950)(0.35) = $122,216

   Her average tax rate is the average rate paid on her entire taxable income, which is determined by dividing taxes paid by taxable income:

   $$\frac{\$122,216}{\$412,950} = 29.6\%$$

3. **C** Bonds with periodic payment of interest would not be favored due to the high tax on interest in this environment. Low-turnover strategies are favored over high-turnover strategies because long-term capital gains are usually taxed less than short-term gains. Furthermore, in most countries, capital gains are paid only when realized (i.e., when the investment is sold).

4. **C** Expected future value after paying annual (accrual) taxes:

   $$\begin{aligned} FV_{IT} &= V_P\left[1+r\left(1-t_i\right)\right]^n \\ &= \$1,000\left[1+0.05\left(1-0.30\right)\right]^{10} \\ &= \$1,410.60 \end{aligned}$$

5. **B** If the tax rate were zero in the previous question, the expected value of the investment would have been:

   $$\begin{aligned} FV_{IT} &= V_P\left[1+r\left(1-t_i\right)\right]^n \\ &= \$1,000\left[1+0.05\left(1-0\right)\right]^{10} \\ &= \$1,628.89 \end{aligned}$$

   The effect of taxes is a reduction of investment value of $218.29 (= $1,628.89 − $1,410.60). On a percentage basis, the tax drag is 34.7% [= $218.29 / ($1,628.89 − $1,000)].

6. **C** Statement 1 is correct. Statement 2 is incorrect.

   A higher investment return results in a higher tax drag when considering tax on investment income. In the example above, if the return is changed from 5% to 10%, the tax drag increases from 34.7% to 39.3% (= $626.59 / $1,593.74).

Study Session 4
Cross-Reference to CFA Institute Assigned Reading #9 – Taxes and Private Wealth Management in a Global Context

Study Session 4

7. **B** Expected future value after paying deferred capital gains taxes only:

$$FV_{CGT} = V_P\left[(1+r)^n\left(1-t_{cg}\right)+t_{cg}\right]$$
$$= \$1,000\left[(1+0.09)^{10}(1-0.20)+0.20\right]$$
$$= \$2,093.89$$

Note that because the question indicates the $1,000 investment is made at the start of the analysis period, there can be no initial unrealized gain or loss and the basis, B, must be 1.0.

8. **A** When only deferred capital gains taxes are paid, tax drag % is the same as the tax rate, in this case 20%.

9. **B** Only Statement 1 is correct. Tax drag % is constant when capital gains taxes are fully deferred, regardless of the investment horizon or investment return.

10. **B** Expected future value when both deferred capital gains taxes and cost basis are considered:

$$FV_{CGBT} = V_P[(1+r)^n(1-t_{cg})+t_{cg}B]$$
$$= \$1,000[(1+0.12)^{10}(1-0.20)+0.20(0.80)]$$
$$= \$2,644.68$$

11. **A** Expected future value with wealth taxes only:

$$FV_{WT} = V_P[(1+r)(1-t_w)]^n$$
$$= \$1,000[(1+0.14)(1-0.03)]^{15}$$
$$= \$4,520.11$$

12. **B** If the wealth tax rate in the previous question were zero, the expected future value of the investment would have been:

$$FV = \$1,000[(1+0.14)(1-0)]^{15}$$
$$= \$7,137.94$$

The effect of taxes is a reduction of investment value of $2,617.83 ($7,137.94 − $4,520.11). On a percentage basis, the tax drag is 42.65% [$2,617.83 / ($7,137.94 − $1,000)].

13. **A** Both statements are correct. The tax drag as a proportion of the future investment value increases with the investment horizon. However, as the investment return increases, the tax drag % on the future investment value decreases.

14. **C** The return after taxes on interest income, dividends, and realized capital gains factors in the proportions of the return sources and the respective taxes on each:

$$r^* = r[1-(p_it_i+p_dt_d+p_{cg}t_{cg})] = r(1-wartr)$$
$$= 0.15\left[1-0.10(0.35)-0.25(0.20)-0.35(0.20)\right]$$
$$= 0.15(0.845) = 0.12675 \cong 12.68\%$$

15. **B** The effective capital gains tax rate that adjusts for the annual taxes already paid is:

$$T^* = t_{cg}[p_{deferred\ cg} / (1 - wartr)]$$

$$wartr = p_i t_i + p_d t_d + p_{cg} t_{cg}$$

$$= 0.20 \left[\frac{1 - 0.10 - 0.25 - 0.35}{1 - 0.10(0.35) - 0.25(0.20) - 0.35(0.20)} \right]$$

$$= 0.20 \left(\frac{0.30}{0.845} \right) = 0.0710 = 7.10\%$$

16. **B** Expected future value after all taxes ($FVIF_T$) using the effective capital gains tax rate (i.e., some capital gains realized annually and some deferred):

$$FV_T = V_p[(1 + r^*)^n(1 - T^*) + T^* - (1 - B)t_{cg}]$$
$$= €100,000[(1 + 0.1268)^7(1 - 0.0710) + 0.0710 - (1 - 1)0.20] = €221,361.22$$

17. **B** The expected balance in the account in seven years after payment of all taxes:

$$FV = €100,000[(1 + 0.1268)^7(1 - 0.0710) + 0.0710 - (1 - 0.80)0.20] = €217,361.22$$

18. **B** The expected after-tax balance in the account in 20 years:

$$FV_{TDA} = V_p(1 + r)^n(1 - t_n)$$
$$= €100,000[(1.10)^{20}(1 - 0.30)]$$
$$= €470,925$$

19. **C** The expected balance in the account in 20 years (no taxes are paid):

$$FV_{TEA} = V_p(1 + r)^n$$
$$= €100,000(1.10)^{20}$$
$$= €672,750$$

€386,968 is the expected future value of an account taxed annually (accrual taxes). €500,925 is the expected future value of an account with deferred capital gains taxes and a basis of €100,000.

20. **A** The investor has €480,000 [(€800,000 × (1 – 0.40)] after-tax invested in equity. The bonds in the tax-exempt account are not subject to taxation and thus are not adjusted. On an after-tax basis, the investor has 44.4% in equity [€480,000 / (€480,000 + €600,000)] and the other 55.6% in bonds [€600,000 / (€480,000 + €600,000)].

21. **B** Because the current tax rate is less than the future tax rate, the tax-exempt account will have a higher expected future accumulation, even though contributions are made from after-tax dollars. The following calculations are unnecessary to answer the question but illustrate its proof.

If the investor pays current taxes at 20% and is willing to give up $2,000 in consumption, she can contribute $2,500 to a tax-deferred account. Because contributions to TDAs are treated as tax deductions against income, the $2,500 contribution will save her $2,500 × 0.20 = $500 in taxes. Therefore, her net consumption would be reduced by only $2,000.

Alternatively, she could invest $2,000 in after-tax dollars in a tax-exempt account. Future value calculations:

FVIF Formula	Future Value
$FVIF_{TDA} = (1+r)^n (1-t_n)$	$\$2,500\left[(1+0.12)^{30}(1-0.30)\right] = \$52,430$
$FVIF_{TEA} = (1+r)^n$	$\$2,000(1+0.12)^{30} = \$59,920$

22. **C** Some countries exempt the interest income for some types of bonds from taxation. Because most of the return from bonds is income, there is no benefit to placing such tax-exempt bonds in a tax-deferred account because no tax is owed. The after-tax return from standard (taxable) corporate bonds would benefit from locating them in the TDA because their income return is generally taxed. High-growth stocks pay small dividends and provide most of their return from capital gains. By extending the holding period, tax deferral will be possible even in a taxable account. So the greatest benefit is from locating the corporate bonds in the TDA.

23. **B** The taxable account will have the lowest risk because the government (taxing authority) effectively shares the risk of the investment with the investor. Assuming before-tax standard deviation of σ, the after-tax standard deviation of the investment is $\sigma(1 - T_I)$.

24. **A** The trader will have the lowest future accumulation because her capital gains will be short term, taxed at a high rate, and taxed every year. The active investor will have the next lowest future accumulation because, although gains are taxed at a lower rate, the gains are taxed every year. The passive investor will pay a low tax rate on a deferred basis and have the highest accumulations of the three investors.

25. **C** If the stock is sold, there is a capital loss of £90,000 – £140,000 = –£50,000, making net taxable gain £30,000. The tax is 0.30 × £30,000 = £9,000.

   If the stock is not sold, the taxes on the full gain are £80,000 × 0.30 = £24,000. The recognition of the capital loss would result in a tax savings of £24,000 – £9,000 = £15,000. In this case, the tax alpha from harvesting the loss can also be calculated as the capital loss multiplied by the tax rate: £50,000 × 0.30 = £15,000.

26. **A** While this may look like a calculation question, it is really a concept question. The appreciation rate is the same in both cases and assuming future tax rates do not change (which is the only acceptable assumption when nothing is said), there is a benefit to the tax deferral inherent in tax loss harvesting. Tax loss harvesting changes the pattern of tax payments [i.e., the payment(s) is (are) pushed further into the future]. However, if the stock is sold in the current year, the tax savings of $15,000 can be immediately reinvested and earn the 10% return. Thus, Strategy 1 will provide the higher future accumulation.

27. **A** Both the risk and return of the asset classes would be adjusted to reflect the tax rates and situation of that specific investor.

ESTATE PLANNING IN A GLOBAL CONTEXT

Study Session 4

EXAM FOCUS

As with the previous reading, the purpose here is not to teach law and regulation of a specific country but concepts and calculations relevant to wealth management. Be prepared to make calculations and understand the implications discussed in this section.

ESTATE PLANNING

LOS 10.a: Discuss the purpose of estate planning and explain the basic concepts of domestic estate planning, including estates, wills, and probate.

CFA® Program Curriculum, Volume 2, page 273

Your **estate** is everything you own: financial assets; real estate (a.k.a. *immovable property*); collections such as art, stamps, or coins; businesses; and non-tangible assets, such as trademarks, copyrights, and patents. **Estate planning** is the planning process associated with transferring your estate to others during your lifetime or at death so that the assets go to the individuals or entities you intend and in the most efficient way.

The most common tool used to transfer assets is a **will** (a.k.a. a *testament*). A will is the legal document that states the rights others will have to your assets at your death. The person transferring assets through a will is known as the *testator*.

Probate is a legal process that takes place at death, during which a court determines the validity of the decedent's will, inventories the decedent's property, resolves any claims against the decedent, and distributes remaining property according to the will. Probate involves considerable paperwork and court appearances, and all costs associated with the probate process, which can be significant, are borne by the decedent's estate. If the decedent leaves no will or if the will is deemed invalid, the decedent is said to have died *intestate* and the distribution of assets is determined by the court.

Assets *solely owned* by the decedent must be transferred by a will through the probate process. Due to the cost, the time it takes, and the public nature of the probate process, however, individuals often take steps to avoid it. This can be accomplished through joint ownership with rights of survivorship, living trusts, retirement plans, life insurance, and other means which transfer assets outside the probate process (i.e., without the need for a will).

WEALTH TRANSFER TAXES

LOS 10.b: Explain the two principal forms of wealth transfer taxes and discuss effects of important non-tax issues, such as legal system, forced heirship, and marital property regime.

CFA® Program Curriculum, Volume 2, page 276

The two primary means of transferring assets are through **gifts** and **bequests**. Gifts are referred to as *lifetime gratuitous* (without the intent of receiving value in return) *transfers* or *inter vivos* (between living individuals) transfers and may be subject to **gift taxes**. Whether the gift is taxed and who pays the tax is determined by the taxing authorities involved. Assets transferred through bequests are referred to as *testamentary* (after death) *gratuitous transfers* and can be subject to **estate taxes**, paid by the grantor (i.e., transferor), or **inheritance taxes**, paid by the recipient.

Professor's Note: The tax treatment of testamentary transfers varies across tax systems and even in the same system according to the relationship between the transferor and recipient. In many cases, for example, transfers between spouses are not subject to taxes. Even when not between spouses, most transfers are subject to exclusions (statutory allowances), which state a maximum that may be transferred tax free.

Many jurisdictions that impose gift taxes also provide exclusions. As of 2009 in the United States, for example, the first $13,000 given to a single recipient is exempt from taxation, subject to limitations depending upon the location and type of the asset and the tax status of the recipient. For example, the asset might be cash or securities or even real estate located in another country, and the entity could be a relative, friend, or charity in the same or another country. Thus, the first $13,000 is exempt from U.S. gift taxes, but the recipient could have to pay gift taxes under another tax regime.

Tax laws across the globe can vary dramatically. Many of the differences are due to the foundations upon which the tax systems are based. For example, a **civil law** system is based on old Roman law. In this system, laws are handed down (i.e., a top down system) by a legislative body.

Common law systems, based primarily on old English law, are more "bottom up." Judges play very important roles in common law systems by refining any existing laws to meet particular situations. Once made by a judge, the decisions become *precedent* to be applied in future cases.

Ownership Rights

Although on the surface it might seem rather clear cut, the precise legal meaning of *ownership* can be shaped by the legal regime. Some regimes provide statutory ownership that effectively gives one person the right to the assets of another. If the system has **forced heirship** rules, for example, children have a right to a portion of a parent's estate, regardless of the location of the child vis-à-vis the parent, the relationship that exists between the parent and child, or even the relationship between the parents.

Knowing the situation could arise, wealthy individuals might try to avoid forced heirship rules by gifting assets or moving them "offshore" into a trust where they fall under a different taxing authority with no forced heirship rule. Recognizing this, many regimes apply **clawback** provisions that add the values back to the decedent's estate before calculating the child's share. If the estate isn't sufficient to meet the child's entitlement, the child may in some cases legally seek the difference from those who received the gifts.

In addition to marital rights provided under forced heirship rules, spouses can also have marital property rights according to the type of marriage they are in. Under a **community property rights** regime, each spouse is entitled to one-half of the estate *earned during* the marriage. Gifts and inheritances received before or during the marriage may be held separate from marital assets. Assets not distributed under community property rights are distributed according to the will.

 Professor's Note: Assets that are not considered part of marital assets under a community property rights regime are considered part of the total estate for purposes of forced heirship rules. Also, a marital right to the estate is a form of forced heirship.

Under a **separate property rights** regime, which is common in civil law countries, each spouse owns and controls his or her property, separate from the other. Each spouse may, barring the presence of other forced heirship rules, bequeath assets as they wish.

Example: Property rights and forced heirship

Hope and Larry have been married for 40 years. They have two married children, Emma, age 32, and Toby, age 34. The community property regime under which the family lives provides that at the death of a spouse, the surviving spouse has the right to one-half the marital estate (community property). In addition, a forced heirship rule entitles a surviving spouse to 30% of the estate, and children are entitled to split 30% of the estate. During the marriage, Larry inherited $500,000 from his parents. His inheritance is not considered part of marital assets, which total $1,300,000.

If Larry should die:

A. **Determine** the amount Hope would inherit under both of the forced heirship rules.

B. **Determine** the amount each child would inherit under the forced heirship rule.

Answer:

A. Under the community property provision, the surviving spouse is entitled to one-half the *marital estate*. The marital estate includes assets totaling $1.3 million. Larry's $500,000 inheritance is considered part of the *total estate*, but not part of community property (marital estate).

When the country has both community property rights and forced heirship rules, as in this case, the surviving spouse is entitled to the *greater* of the two amounts:

- Under community property, Hope is entitled to half the marital property or $1,300,000 / 2 = $650,000.
- Under the forced heirship rule, Hope is entitled to 30% of the *total estate* or (0.30)($1,800,000) = $540,000.
- Hope is entitled to the greater of the two amounts, so she would receive $650,000 under community property rights. She could inherit more based on the stipulations of Larry's will.

B. Under the forced heirship rules, the two children are entitled to *split* 30% of the total estate for (0.30)($1,800,000) = $540,000 in total for $270,000 to each child.

In total, only $650,000 + $540,000 = $1,190,000 of the total $1.8 million is distributed according to forced heirship rules. (The marital community property rights provision is a type of forced heirship rule.) The remaining $610,000 would be distributed through a probate process according to Larry's will.

Example: Clawback provision

Assume a country with forced heirship rules entitling children to split 33% of the estate of a deceased parent, subject to clawback provisions. The estate of the (unmarried) decedent is worth $500,000 after gifting $2,750,000 to two of his children in anticipation of death. An estranged child has now come forth to claim his legal right under the community property described in the question data. *Based solely on this information*, **determine** the amount the estranged child is entitled to under the forced heirship rule.

Answer:

The three children of the deceased are entitled to *split* 33% of the parent's estate or 0.33($3,250,000) = $1,072,500.

 Professor's Note: According to the clawback provision, we use the total value of the estate ($500,000 + $2,750,000 = $3,250,000) before the gifts.

Because there are apparently three children (the two who received gifts and the estranged child), each is entitled to $1,072,500 / 3 = $357,500 under the forced heirship rule.

Because the estate is worth $500,000 after the gifts, the estranged child is able to receive $357,500 without resorting to lawsuits to reclaim part of the gifts from the other two children.

CORE CAPITAL

LOS 10.c: Determine a family's core capital and excess capital, based on mortality probabilities and Monte Carlo analysis.

CFA® Program Curriculum, Volume 2, page 278

To understand the concepts of core and excess capital, consider a balance sheet; assets are on the left side and liabilities and equity are on the right; of course, equity equals asset minus liabilities.

On an individual's balance sheet, assets consist of the financial and other assets currently held by the individual plus the *present value* of net employment income expected to be generated over the lifetime, referred to as **human capital** or **net employment capital**. (Human capital is discussed at length in Topic Review 12.) In other words, the individual's *total assets* equal the value of assets currently held plus the individual's ability to accumulate more assets in the future through employment (i.e., generate more future income than is required to meet all future expenses).

The individual's liabilities on the balance sheet are the present values of all current and future costs necessary to sustain a given lifestyle. These consist of any explicit liabilities, such as mortgage or other loan payments plus costs of living and any planned gifts and bequests. Just as with a financial balance sheet, then, the individual's **excess capital** (i.e., equity capital) is the difference between total assets and total liabilities.

The amount of assets necessary to meet all the individual's liabilities plus a reserve for unexpected needs is considered the individual's (or family's) **core capital**. It's the amount that must be maintained to meet all present and future liabilities as described previously. Any amount above core capital is considered excess capital and can be used for other purposes. Hint: In the following examples, no reserve for unexpected needs is given so one is not included. On the exam you should only include such an amount if given clear direction.

Mortality Probabilities

A major problem associated with estimating the individual's human capital and total liabilities, of course, is determining the values of future net employment income and required future outlays. Compounding the problem is determining the individual's lifetime. To estimate an individual's remaining expected life, statisticians developed *mortality tables*. Mortality tables show an individual's expected remaining years based upon attaining a given age. For example, one of these tables might show that a male who has reached the age of 80 has approximately an 87% probability of living one more year and a 16% probability of living to age 93.

For the Exam: The probabilities of survival change every year. They are based on the individual's current age and show the probability for the *average individual* who has attained that age. In our previous discussion, once the 80-year-old male reaches 85, the probability of him living to 93 increases somewhat because at 80, living to 93 means surviving another 13 years, while at 85, it means surviving only another eight years. Of course, the probability of surviving a set *number* of years decreases as the individual ages. If you are required to perform related calculations on the exam, the question will have to include a mortality table.

Consider the following mortality table, which is adapted from the 2017 CFA Level III curriculum.[1] The husband and wife are currently 79 and 68, respectively. From the table we see that the husband has a 93.55% probability (Prob.) of living one more year, to the age of 80, and a 46.74% probability of living eight more years, to the age of 87. The wife has a 98.31% probability of living one more year (age 69) and 82.52% probability of living eight more years (age 76). Additional explanation follows the table.

Figure 1: Individual and Joint Mortality Probabilities and Core Capital

Yrs	Husband		Wife		Combined Prob.	Real Annual Spending	Expected Real Spending	Present Value	Total
	Age	Prob.	Age	Prob.					
1	80	0.9355	69	0.9831	0.9989	200,000	199,780	195,863	195,863
2	81	0.8702	70	0.9649	0.9954	204,000	203,062	195,177	391,040
3	82	0.8038	71	0.9457	0.9893	208,080	205,854	193,981	585,021
4	83	0.7339	72	0.9249	0.9800	212,242	207,997	192,157	777,178
5	84	0.6686	73	0.9025	0.9677	216,486	209,494	189,745	966,923
6	85	0.6001	74	0.8785	0.9514	220,816	210,084	186,549	1,153,472
7	86	0.5327	75	0.8526	0.9311	225,232	209,714	182,569	1,336,041
8	87	0.4674	76	0.8252	0.9069	229,737	208,348	177,823	1,513,864
9	88	0.4048	77	0.7958	0.8785	234,332	205,861	172,255	1,686,119
10	89	0.3459	78	0.7646	0.8460	239,019	202,210	165,883	1,852,002
11	90	0.2912	79	0.7311	0.8094	243,799	197,331	158,706	2,010,708

- **Combined Prob.** is the (joint) probability that one or both will live to the given age. For example, there is a 98% probability that *at least* one of them will live four years.
- **Real Annual Spending** (i.e., living expenses) for the coming year is expected to be $200,000 and is expected to increase at a rate of 2% per year.
- **Expected Real Spending** is *Real Annual Spending* multiplied by *Combined Prob.* It shows the expected amount required for the year based on the probability of either or both remaining alive.
- **Present Value** is *Expected Real Spending* discounted to year zero at the real, risk-free rate of 2%.
- **Total** is a running total. It's the amount of core *capital required* to meet living expenses through the given year. For example, assuming no further contributions, it will take a portfolio of $1,153,472 (today) to meet estimated expenses for six years.

---

1. 2018 CFA Level III curriculum, Exhibit 2, Vol. 2, p. 281.

Professor's Note: The full table includes enough rows for both to reach 100 years of age. At 100 years old, individuals are assumed to have 0% probability of living another year.

Example: Calculating core capital using a mortality table

A. Using the mortality table, **determine** the probability that either the husband, the wife, or both will be alive in ten years.

B. Based on expenditures in the table, **calculate** the core capital required for the next ten years.

C. If the family has a portfolio of $2,500,000, **determine** (based solely on the information provided) the maximum amount they could give to charity.

Answer:

A. From the mortality table, we see the probability of surviving ten years for the husband and wife is 34.59% and 76.46%, respectively. The probability that one or both will survive ten years (Combined Prob.) is calculated as follows:

$$\text{prob(joint survival)} = \text{prob(husband survives)} + \text{prob(wife survives)}$$
$$- \text{prob(husband survives)} \times \text{prob(wife survives)}$$
$$= 0.3459 + 0.7646 - (0.3459)(0.7646) = \mathbf{84.60\%}$$

B. The amount of core capital required for ten years is:

$$\text{core capital}_{10\,\text{years}} = \sum_{t=1}^{10} \frac{P(\text{surv}_t)(\text{spending}_t)}{(1+r)^t}; \quad r = \text{real risk-free rate}$$
$$= \frac{P(\text{surv}_1)(\text{spending}_1)}{(1.02)^1} + ... + \frac{P(\text{surv}_{10})(\text{spending}_{10})}{(1.02)^{10}}$$
$$= \$1,852,002$$

$1,852,002 is calculated by multiplying the real annual spending requirement for each year by the joint probability associated with that year, finding the present value of the result at the risk-free rate, and then summing the present values for all ten years. For example, the core capital requirement (portfolio value required today) for the next *three* years is:

$$\text{core capital}_{3\,\text{years}} = \frac{P(\text{surv}_1)(\text{spending}_1)}{(1+r)^1} + \frac{P(\text{surv}_2)(\text{spending}_2)}{(1+r)^2} + \frac{P(\text{surv}_3)(\text{spending}_3)}{(1+r)^3}$$

$$= \frac{0.9989(\$200,000)}{(1.02)} + \frac{0.9954(\$204,000)}{(1.02)^2} + \frac{0.9893(\$208,080)}{(1.02)^3} = \$585,021$$

> *Professor's Note: The data provided in this question gave projected real spending needs; therefore, the real risk-free rate was used to discount the needs. If the data had given projected nominal spending needs, the nominal risk-free rate would have been used to discount the needs. Either method will produce the same result. Using real data excludes future inflation from both the numerator and denominator of the underlying time value of money calculations, while using nominal data includes future inflation in both the numerator and denominator.*
>
> *It is important that all data be either all real or all nominal. The choice of approach is based purely on expediency—whichever approach seems easiest in the situation. But the analysis always uses some form of a risk-free (not a risky) rate to reflect the importance of meeting the needs. As long as the portfolio assets earn at least the (low) discount rate used, the future distribution needs can be met. Using a risk-free rate is the conservative approach.*

C. Excess capital is any amount above the core capital requirement. Based solely on the information provided and using a 10-year planning horizon, they have excess capital of $2,500,000 – $1,852,002 = $647,998, which they could give to charity.

Safety Reserve

Mortality tables are based on average life expectancy. If the amount in excess of the core capital calculated with a mortality table were gifted away, there is an approximate 50% chance the gift giver will outlive the remaining capital. Thus, core capital should be increased by a safety reserve.

In addition, the core-capital model implicitly assumes an average risk-free rate of return on assets, ignoring the possibility of poor market returns. Finally, the spending needs could have been underestimated or could be front loaded (i.e., more spending is needed now even if spending diminishes later). Either lower initial portfolio returns or more initial spending could create a path dependency risk of drawing down the portfolio and diminished chances of recovery later.

Monte Carlo Simulation

Monte Carlo analysis is commonly used in retirement planning. Depending on the sophistication of the model, the user can input the starting portfolio value and assumptions for:

- Distribution amounts, both recurring and irregular one-time distributions.
- Inflation rates.
- Asset class returns and correlations.
- Return distributions, either normal or non-normal.
- Tax rates.
- And any other relevant factors.

Hundreds or thousands of simulation runs can be generated and ranked with output displayed in various forms.

One common display would chart the value of the portfolio over time at some specified probability. For example, plot the portfolio value at the 5% probability, allowing the client and manager to see how long the portfolio is expected to last. If the results are unacceptable, then adjustments can be made. Common changes would be to adjust the asset mix and expected return or the distribution amount and/or start date of the distributions.

A particular benefit of the analysis is to capture the interaction of distribution and the sequence of returns, a form of path dependency. Without distributions, the sequence of returns is not important. A portfolio that increases and then decreases 20% in value has the same ending value as one that decreases and then increases 20%. But with distributions the sequence will matter. If the portfolio first declines, the distribution will consume a larger portion of the portfolio and the portfolio value will be diminished when return rebounds. This increases the chances the client will run out of funds.

Another display format is to show the **probability of ruin** (reaching a zero portfolio value) based on differing start dates for retirement (start of withdrawals) and distribution percentage. Delaying retirement or lowering the distribution percentage make it less likely the portfolio can be exhausted.

Consider the following ruin probability table based on the example from the CFA text. The table is built on an assumed 5% average arithmetic return with a 12% standard deviation. It shows that if the initial distribution starts at 3% of portfolio value, the distribution amount increases with inflation, and retirement begins at age 55, there is a 6.3% chance of exhausting the portfolio by the median age of death at 83. If retirement is delayed until age 60, the ruin probability declines to 5.2% by the median age of death at 83.4.

Figure 2: Ruin Probabilities and Spending Rates

Retirement Age	Median Age at Death	Hazard Rate		Real Spending Rate		
				2%	3%	4%
55	83.0	2.48	Probability of Ruin	1.8	6.3	14.0
60	83.4	2.96		1.5	5.2	11.6

RELATIVE AFTER-TAX VALUES OF GIFTS

LOS 10.d: Evaluate the relative after-tax value of lifetime gifts and testamentary bequests.

LOS 10.e: Explain the estate planning benefit of making lifetime gifts when gift taxes are paid by the donor, rather than the recipient.

CFA® Program Curriculum, Volume 2, pages 288 and 293

A client with excess capital can gift the capital now or bequest it at death. There are practical issues to consider: Gifting now likely gives up control and cannot be revoked if circumstances change. There are also tax issues to consider that can affect the ultimate value of the gift/bequest to the receiver.

One approach is to calculate a ratio of a gift now versus bequest at death. A ratio above/below 1 indicates that from a tax perspective it is favorable/unfavorable to gift now. The calculations are based on the FV after-tax to the receiver. Any FV after-tax calculations require assumptions and the conclusions are only as good as the assumptions.

The basic form of the ratio is:

$$\frac{\text{FV after tax to the receiver if gifted now}}{\text{FV after tax to the receiver if bequested at death}}$$

There are three tax scenarios to consider:

- The gift now is tax free to both the receiver and the donor.
- The gift now is taxable with the tax paid by the receiver.
- The gift now is taxable with the tax paid by the giver, also called the donor.

The relevant tax factors to consider are:

- r_g and t_{ig} are the pretax return earned and the applicable tax rate on those earnings for assets held by the gift receiver.
- r_e and t_{ie} are the pretax return earned and the applicable tax rate on those earnings for assets held by the gift giver.
- T_e is the estate tax rate and would be paid from the estate.
- T_g is the gift tax rate, paid by the giver (or by the receiver if specified by the facts in the question).

The three potential RV ratios are:

RV of a tax-free gift, $T_g = 0$

$$RV_{\text{tax-free gift}} = \frac{\left[1 + r_g\left(1 - t_{ig}\right)\right]^n}{\left[1 + r_e\left(1 - t_{ie}\right)\right]^n \left(1 - T_e\right)}$$

RV of a taxable gift, T_g paid by receiver

$$RV_{\text{taxable gift}} = \frac{FV_{\text{taxable gift}}}{FV_{\text{bequest}}} = \frac{\left[\left(1-T_g\right)\right]\left[1+r_g\left(1-t_{ig}\right)\right]^n}{\left[1+r_e\left(1-t_{ie}\right)\right]^n\left(1-T_e\right)}$$

RV of a taxable gift, T_g paid by giver

$$RV_{\text{taxable gift}} = \frac{\left(1-T_g+T_gT_e\right)\left[1+r_g\left(1-t_{ig}\right)\right]^n}{\left[1+r_e\left(1-t_{ie}\right)\right]^n\left(1-T_e\right)}$$

Notice that each formula is a cumulative variation on the previous formula.

RV of a tax-free gift, T_g = 0: The numerator projects FV after-tax of the investment if held by the receiver. The denominator projects the FV after-tax if held by the giver and then subject to estate taxes.

RV of a taxable gift, T_g paid by receiver: This is a variation on the tax-free gift formula with a subtraction in the numerator of $-T_g$ to reflect the receiver of the gift must pay a tax and has less to invest. All else the same, it makes gifting now less attractive.

RV of a taxable gift, T_g paid by giver: This is a variation on the taxable gift if paid by receiver formula with the addition of $+T_gT_e$ in the numerator. All else the same, it makes gifting now more attractive. The addition reflects that by gifting now and paying a gift tax, the giver's estate is reduced and therefore the future estate tax will be lower. One interpretation is gifting now creates a partial gift tax credit against the estate tax bill.

Mary Jane is considering making a gift now or at bequest. The assumptions are:

- Life expectancy is 20 years.
- Jane's pretax return and investment tax rate are 8% and 35%.
- Receiver's pretax return and investment tax rate are also 8% and 35%.
- T_g and T_e are 25% and 40%.

Scenario 1: Assuming the gift is not subject to gift taxes, **compute** the relative attractiveness of a gift or bequest and **recommend** the best approach:

$$[1 + (0.08(1 - 0.35))]^{20} / [(1 + (0.08(1 - 0.35)))^{20} (1 - 0.40)]$$
$$= 2.756 / ((2.756)(0.60)) = 2.756 / 1.654 = 1.67$$

Gifting now is more attractive. Also notice because the giver and receiver's after-tax investment return is assumed to be the same, the ratio is just $1 / (1 - T_e)$, a special case of the formula.

Scenario 2: Assuming the gift is subject to gift taxes and the tax is paid by the receiver, **compute** the relative attractiveness of a gift or bequest and **recommend** the best approach:

$$[(1 - 0.25)(1 + (0.08(1 - 0.35)))^{20}] / [(1 + (0.08(1 - 0.35)))^{20} (1 - 0.40)] =$$
$$((0.75)(2.756)) / ((2.756)(0.60)) = 2.067 / 1.654 = 1.25$$

Gifting now is not as favorable but still best. Also notice because the giver and receiver's after-tax investment return is assumed to be the same, the ratio is just $(1 - T_g) / (1 - T_e)$, a special case of the formula.

Scenario 3: Assuming the gift is subject to gift taxes and the tax is paid by the giver, **compute** the relative attractiveness of a gift or bequest and **recommend** the best approach:

$$[(1 - 0.25 + (0.25)(0.40))(1 + (0.08(1 - 0.35)))^{20}] / [(1 + (0.08(1 - 0.35)))^{20} (1 - 0.40)] = ((0.75 + 0.10)(2.756)) / ((2.756)(0.60)) = 2.343 / 1.654 = 1.42$$

Gifting now is still best and more attractive than if the receiver pays the tax. Also notice because the giver and receiver's after-tax investment return is assumed to be the same, the ratio is just $(1 - T_g + T_e T_g) / (1 - T_e)$, a special case of the formula.

ESTATE PLANNING STRATEGIES

LOS 10.f: Evaluate the after-tax benefits of basic estate planning strategies, including generation skipping, spousal exemptions, valuation discounts, and charitable gifts.

CFA® Program Curriculum, Volume 2, page 296

Generation Skipping

In the absence of generation-skipping transfer taxes, as in the United States, transferring assets directly to a third generation avoids possible double taxation. When the first (i.e., oldest) generation transfers assets to the second generation, the transfer is typically subject to taxes. Then when the second generation transfers the assets to the third generation, the assets are taxed again.

Example: Generation skipping

Assume an expected after-tax return of 5% on assets that will ultimately be transferred to the third generation from the second generation. We'll assume the first generation will transfer the assets to the second generation in 15 years, and the second generation will transfer the assets 30 years after that to the third generation. We'll also assume equal gift and inheritance tax rates of 40%.

Answer:

The value of the assets to the third generation in 45 years, without generation skipping and with generation skipping, is:

$$
\begin{aligned}
\text{FV}_{\text{no skipping}} &= \text{PV}\left[(1+0.05)^{15}(1-0.40)\right]\left[(1+0.05)^{30}(1-0.40)\right] \\
&= \text{PV}(2.0789)(0.60) \times (4.3219)(0.60) = \text{PV}(3.2344)
\end{aligned}
$$

$$
\text{FV}_{\text{skipping}} = \text{PV}(1+0.05)^{45}(1-0.40) = \text{PV}(5.3910)
$$

With the ability to skip generations, the value to the third generation is increased by a factor of $1 / (1 - t)$, where t is the gift/inheritance tax rate:

$$
\frac{1}{1-t} = \frac{1}{1-0.40} = \frac{5.3910}{3.2344} = 1.6667 = \textbf{relative value} \text{ of generation skipping}
$$

The amount to be transferred, PV, is the excess above the core capital requirements for both the first and second generations. The first generation must first determine its core capital to determine the total excess that can be transferred to future generations. After calculating and then deducting the core capital for the second generation, any remaining excess (PV) can be transferred directly to the third generation.

Spousal Exemptions

Many countries allow tax-free transfers of estates between spouses. Whether or not this is optimal from a tax perspective depends upon other possible gift and inheritance exclusions. For example, assume tax laws permit tax-free transfers of estates less than $500,000. If the decedent leaves a large estate, and assuming the spouse's core capital is satisfied, $500,000 of the estate could be transferred immediately to his children.

In this fashion, $500,000 of the estate is transferred immediately to the children tax free, while if the surviving spouse waited until later to transfer the assets, they could be subject to gift and/or inheritance taxes.

Valuation Discounts

Assets such as marketable securities have readily determined fair market values, but valuing ownership claims in partnerships and other privately held interests can be difficult. Because valuation discounts can reduce the value of wealth transfers and the associated transfer taxes, high net worth individuals will utilize them whenever possible by, for example, transferring interest in a family business.

The value of a nonpublicly traded family business is determined using financial models with discount rates and other assumptions from otherwise comparable publicly traded firms. The resulting value, of course, implicitly assumes the family business is also publicly traded, so the valuator must reduce it to reflect the family business's **lack of liquidity**. In addition, the *proportion* of the family business transferred may not give the recipient control of the firm's operations, so the value could also be subject to a **minority interest discount**.

An important consideration is that discounts are not typically additive. For example, a 20% liquidity discount plus a 20% minority discount do not necessarily imply a total discount of 40%. The total discount is subject to court approval and both tend to be inversely related to firm size; as the size of the firm increases, the percentage discount falls.

Charitable Gifts (Charitable Gratuitous Transfers)

Returning to the topic of gifting excess capital now or bequesting at death, what if the receiver is a tax-exempt charity? This is another variation of the RV formulas. The denominator is the same as in the previous discussion; the giver invests, an estate tax is paid at death, and then the bequest is made. The numerator, which is the FV to the receiver if gifted now, is different and almost always higher because:

- The charity can invest and the asset return earned is not taxed. This is the $(1 + r_g)^n$ term.
- The giver can take an immediate tax deduction for the gift and this will reduce the giver's current tax bill by T_{oi} for each dollar gifted. T_{oi} is the giver's tax rate on ordinary income. Therefore a $1.00 gift would produce a tax savings of $1.00(T_{oi})$. The formula compounds this tax savings to a FV subject to estate taxes and then bequested at death, as an addition to the gift made now. This is the remainder of the formula in the numerator.

RV of a gift to a charity:

$$RV_{\text{charitable donation}} = \frac{\left(1+r_g\right)^n + T_{oi}\left[1+r_e\left(1-t_{ie}\right)\right]^n\left(1-T_e\right)}{\left[1+r_e\left(1-t_{ie}\right)\right]^n\left(1-T_e\right)}$$

r_g = expected return on the assets in the charity's portfolio

T_{oi} = tax rate on ordinary income

r_e = expected return on the assets in the donor's portfolio

t_{ie} = donor's tax rate on investment income

T_e = estate tax rate

Now assume:

$r_g = r_e = 8\%$

$T_{oi} = 40\%$

$t_{ie} = 30\%$

$T_e = 50\%$

n = 20 years

$$= \frac{(1.08)^{20} + 0.40\left[1+0.08(0.70)\right]^{20}(0.50)}{\left[1+0.08(0.70)\right]^{20}(0.50)}$$

$$= \frac{4.6610 + 0.40(2.9736)0.50}{(2.9736)0.50} = 3.5349$$

The assets FV to the receiver are 3.5349 times greater if given now than if given as a bequest at death.

TRUSTS

LOS 10.g: Explain the basic structure of a trust and discuss the differences between revocable and irrevocable trusts.

CFA® Program Curriculum, Volume 2, page 299

Trusts are a means by which a **grantor** (or **settlor**) can transfer assets to beneficiaries outside of the probate process. The trustee (i.e., manager of the trust) holds the assets and manages them in the best interests of the beneficiaries according to the constraints of the trust documents.

Professor's Note: Asset ownership can be a fuzzy concept with trusts. It might help to think of the assets as being placed into limbo somewhere between the settlor and the beneficiary. A trustee actually has possession of and manages the assets for the benefit of the settlor and/or beneficiaries and may be considered the owner of the assets for tax purposes only. Legal ownership of the assets may be held by the settlor or transferred to the trustee or beneficiaries, while ownership for tax purposes may reside with the settlor or the trustee. Thus, the legal owner and the owner for tax purposes may be two different entities, depending on the structure of the trust.

In a **revocable trust**, the settlor can rescind (i.e., revoke) the trust and resume ownership of the assets. The settlor is considered the legal owner of the assets for tax and reporting purposes, and creditors, divorcing spouses, et cetera can make claims against the trust assets.

In an **irrevocable trust**, the settlor relinquishes ownership and control. The trustee is considered the owner of the assets for tax purposes and is responsible for reporting and paying taxes on income generated by the trust. The irrevocable trust protects the trust assets from claims against the settlor.

Professor's Note: A trust will not protect assets if it is deemed to have been created in anticipation of a claim.

The trustee may be responsible for distributing assets to the beneficiaries. In a **fixed trust**, the pattern of distributions to the beneficiaries is predetermined by the settlor and incorporated into the trust documents. When setting up a trust for a minor, for example, the settlor may wish the trustee to distribute a fixed portion of the assets when the minor reaches 21 years of age and then distribute a given percentage each year until they are depleted.

With a **discretionary trust**, the trustee determines how the assets are to be distributed. The primary concern is that the assets are distributed to produce the greatest benefit to the beneficiary or beneficiaries. The settlor can convey her general wishes through the trust documentation or separately through a *letter of wishes*. Beneficiaries have no legal right to either the income or the assets of the discretionary trust. Thus, the trust assets are protected from claims *against the beneficiaries*.

A **spendthrift trust** is used to transfer assets to a beneficiary who is too young or is otherwise unable to manage the assets. It provides a means for the settlor to transfer assets outside the probate process while maintaining some control over the distribution of the assets.

In some countries, trusts are recognized as legally transferring the ownership of assets but not for tax purposes. If that is the case, the settlor remains responsible for taxes on income generated by the trust.

Trusts are recognized by, and are thus most prevalent in, common law countries but can be found in (i.e., are recognized by) some civil law countries. Foundations, on the other hand, are most prevalent in civil law countries but can also be found in common law countries.

LIFE INSURANCE

LOS 10.h: Explain how life insurance can be a tax-efficient means of wealth transfer.

CFA® Program Curriculum, Volume 2, page 302

As the only assets transferred by the grantor (policy owner) are the premiums paid,[2] life insurance policies represent a very efficient means for transferring assets or even helping beneficiaries pay inheritance taxes. In most jurisdictions, life insurance proceeds pass to beneficiaries without tax consequences, and, depending on jurisdiction, the policy might provide tax-free accumulation of wealth and/or loans to the policy holder on beneficial terms.

Life insurance can be used in combination with a trust. By establishing a trust on behalf of the beneficiaries and making that trust the direct beneficiary of the life policy, the policy holder can transfer assets to young, disabled, et cetera, beneficiaries outside the probate process.

TAX JURISDICTION

LOS 10.i: Discuss the two principal systems (source jurisdiction and residence jurisdiction) for establishing a country's tax jurisdiction.

LOS 10.j: Discuss the possible income and estate tax consequences of foreign situated assets and foreign-sourced income.

CFA® Program Curriculum, Volume 2, pages 305 and 307

Income Taxes

- Under **source jurisdiction** (a.k.a. **territorial tax system**) a country levies taxes on all income generated within its borders, whether by citizens or foreigners.
- Under **residence jurisdiction**, the most prevalent type of jurisdiction, a country taxes the income of its residents, whether generated inside or outside the country. Citizens of residence jurisdiction countries pay taxes on their worldwide income, regardless of their current place of residence (i.e., whether currently living in the country or not).

Countries use many different tests to determine residency. They may utilize subjective standards such as personal ties (e.g., family, house) or economic ties (e.g., own a local business) to the country. They may also use objective measures such as the number of days residing within the country's borders.

---

2. The premiums are not usually considered part of the grantor's estate for tax purposes, but in some jurisdictions the premiums are considered gifts to the beneficiary and may be subject to taxation.

Wealth Transfer Taxes

- Under **source jurisdiction**, transfer taxes are levied on assets located within (e.g., real estate) or transferred within a country, whether by citizens or foreigners.
- Under **residence jurisdiction**, citizens and residents pay transfer taxes, regardless of the worldwide location of the assets.

Exit Taxes

In an effort to avoid residence taxation, individuals may renounce their citizenship and move to a less strict jurisdiction. In response, some residence jurisdictions impose an **exit tax**. The amount is usually based on the gains on assets leaving, as if the individual sold the assets and realized the gains. (This is referred to as a **deemed disposition**.) The exit tax could include a tax on income earned for a period (called a **shadow period**) following the expatriation.

RELIEF FROM DOUBLE TAXATION

LOS 10.k: Evaluate a client's tax liability under each of three basic methods (credit, exemption, and deduction) that a country may use to provide relief from double taxation.

CFA® Program Curriculum, Volume 2, page 307

Due to overlapping tax systems, two countries may lay claim to the same income and/or assets for tax purposes. In a **residence-residence conflict**, for example, two countries claim residence for the same individual and hence claim taxing authority over the individual's world-wide assets and income. Alternatively, two countries could claim authority over the same income in a **source-source conflict** (think of a multinational company with operations that generate income in several countries).

In another possible double taxation scenario, an individual might be subject to residence jurisdiction and receive income on assets in a foreign country with source jurisdiction. This is a **residence-source conflict**, because the individual's world-wide assets and income are taxed by the residence jurisdiction, and income generated by the foreign assets is taxed again under the source jurisdiction. In response, some countries have adopted policies that help relieve the double taxation.

The **exemption method** provides complete relief from double taxation. Suppose an individual is subject to 50% residence tax and has $100 of income from and subject to a source country taxing at 40%. Forty dollars will be owed to the source country and the $100 is not then subject to tax in the residence country.

The **credit method** also provides complete relief though not always the lowest total tax bill. Forty dollars would be owed to the source country and $50 to the residence country. A $40 credit for taxes paid can be taken against the $50 and only $10 will be owed to the residence country, making the total tax owed between both countries $50. Had the rates been reversed, $50 is owed to the source country and a $40 credit can be taken against the $40 owed to the residence country making the residence country tax bill $0. The total tax bill is $50. In the same situation and under the exemption method, the total tax bill is also $50 as the source country collects $50 and the income is exempt in the residence country.

The **deduction method** provides only partial resolution of the residence-source conflict. Under the deduction method, the individual pays the full tax to the source country and is only allowed to *deduct* the amount of taxes paid to the source country in calculating total world-wide income.

Example: Residence-source conflict

An individual living in a country that bases income tax on residency has total worldwide income of 1,500,000. 600,000 of that amount is generated in a source jurisdiction country. The domestic country charges 40% income taxes on worldwide income, and the source country charges 35% taxes on income generated within its borders.

Determine the income taxes paid on the foreign source income and the country or countries to which it is owed under the:

A. Credit method.

B. Exemption method.

C. Deduction method.

Answer:

A. Credit method:

- Source country tax is: 600,000(0.35) = $210,000.
- Residence country tax would have been: 600,000(0.40) = $240,000. Taking a 210,000 credit leaves $30,000 owed to residence country.
- Total taxes are $240,000.

B. Exemption method:

- Source country tax is: 600,000(0.35) = $210,000.
- Residence country: The income is exempt.
- Total taxes are $210,000.

C. Deduction method:

- Source country tax is: 600,000(0.35) = $210,000.
- Residence country taxable income is: 600,000 – 210,000 = 390,000. Tax is: 390,000(0.40) = 156,000 to residence country.
- Total taxes are $366,000.

INTERNATIONAL TRANSPARENCY

LOS 10.l: Discuss how increasing international transparency and information exchange among tax authorities affect international estate planning.

CFA® Program Curriculum, Volume 2, page 310

In the estate planning process, financial advisers should attempt to structure estates to hold and transfer assets in the most tax-efficient ways. This could include holding foreign assets and even holding funds in a foreign country to more efficiently provide living and/or business expenses.

Tax avoidance is legal. Any tax-paying entity or individual would be expected to minimize the amount of taxes paid through various legal tax-reduction strategies. **Tax evasion**, on the other hand, is hiding, misrepresenting, or otherwise not recognizing income so as to *illegally* avoid taxation. To avoid complications related to tax evasion strategies that are ultimately uncovered through global tax treaties, it is important to structure estates as efficiently and legally as possible.

Most countries attempt to maximize the amount of taxes to which they are legally entitled and to do so enter into global treaties which provide for the sharing of information. In an effort to maximize world-wide taxation on its residents and citizens, for example, the United States demands that global banks disclose the names of U.S. securities owners, whether U.S. citizens or not. In response, many global banks became Qualified Intermediaries (QIs). To avoid disclosing the names of all their customers, the QIs collect all the required information but provide the information on their U.S. customers only. A similar agreement exists in the European Union, by which EU member banks exchange customer information with each other.

KEY CONCEPTS

LOS 10.a
A **will** (also known as a *testament*) is used to transfer estate assets at death. **Probate** is a legal process to validate and implement the will after death. Probate can be costly and make details of the will public. Joint ownership with rights of survivorship, living trusts, retirement plans, life insurance, and other means can sometimes be used to transfer assets outside the probate process.

LOS 10.b
Gifts are *lifetime gratuitous transfers* or *inter vivos transfers* and may be subject to **gift taxes**. Bequests are *testamentary gratuitous transfers* and can be subject to **estate taxes**, paid by the grantor, or **inheritance taxes**, paid by the recipient.

Forced heirship rules provide statutory ownership. Many regimes apply **clawback** provisions. Under a **community property rights** regime, each spouse is entitled to one-half of the estate earned *during* the marriage. Under a **separate property rights** regime, each spouse owns and controls his or her property, separate from the other.

LOS 10.c
Core capital is the amount necessary to meet all of an individual's liabilities plus a reserve for unexpected needs. It is the sum of the products of expected spending for each year and the probability of living that long. An individual has 50% probability of outliving mortality table expected life, so incorporate a **safety reserve** into core capital.

Monte Carlo simulation gives the expected portfolio value and distribution of possible values at retirement. The probability of running out of money is known as the *probability of ruin*. Level of spending and probability of ruin are usually positively correlated.

LOS 10.d
Relative value ratios (RV) project the future value to the recipient of making the gift now during the giver's life versus leaving a bequest (gift) at death. An RV > 1 indicates the value of the gift now is higher.

$$RV_{\text{tax-free gift}} = \frac{FV_{\text{tax-free gift}}}{FV_{\text{bequest}}} = \frac{\left[1 + r_g\left(1 - t_{ig}\right)\right]^n}{\left[1 + r_e\left(1 - t_{ie}\right)\right]^n \left(1 - T_e\right)}$$

$$RV_{\text{taxable gift}} = \frac{FV_{\text{taxable gift}}}{FV_{\text{bequest}}} = \frac{\left[\left(1 - T_g\right)\right]\left[1 + r_g\left(1 - t_{ig}\right)\right]^n}{\left[1 + r_e\left(1 - t_{ie}\right)\right]^n \left(1 - T_e\right)} \quad \text{If the receiver pays the gift tax}$$

r_g = pretax return on the stock if gifted and held by the recipient
t_{ig} = tax rate on investment returns if gifted
r_e = pretax return on the stock if held in the estate
$t_{i,e}$ = tax rate on investment returns in testator's portfolio
T_e = estate tax rate

LOS 10.e

When the *donor pays the gift taxes*, the future value of the gift to the recipient is increased by an amount equal to the product of the estate and gift tax rates (t_g and t_e) and the value of the gift:

$$RV_{\text{taxable gift}} = \frac{\left(1 - T_g + T_g T_e\right)\left[1 + r_g\left(1 - t_{ig}\right)\right]^n}{\left[1 + r_e\left(1 - t_{ie}\right)\right]^n \left(1 - T_e\right)} \quad \text{If the giver pays the gift tax}$$

LOS 10.f

Skipping a generation can avoid the double taxation of assets. It increases the FV of the gift by a factor of $1 / (1 - t)$ if all others factors are the same:

$$FV_{\text{no skipping}} = PV[(1 + r)^{n1} (1 - t)][(1 + r)^{n2} (1 - t)]$$

$$FV_{\text{skipping}} = PV[(1 + r)^N (1 - T_e)] \qquad\qquad [N = n1 + n2]$$

Many countries allow: (1) **spousal exemptions**. (2) **Valuation discounts** can be employed to reduce the taxable value of gifts or the estate. (3) The donor to take a **tax deduction** in the amount of the **charitable gift**. Value of a gift to charity relative to leaving it in a bequest is:

$$RV_{\text{charitable donation}} = \frac{FV_{\text{charitable gift}}}{FV_{\text{bequest}}} = \frac{\left(1 + r_g\right)^n + T_{oi}\left[1 + r_e\left(1 - t_{ie}\right)\right]^n \left(1 - T_e\right)}{\left[1 + r_e\left(1 - t_{ie}\right)\right]^n \left(1 - T_e\right)}$$

LOS 10.g

In a **revocable trust**, the settlor can rescind the trust and is considered the legal owner of the assets for tax purposes. In an **irrevocable trust**, the settlor relinquishes ownership. The trustee is considered the owner of the assets for tax purposes. An irrevocable trust protects the trust assets from claims against the settlor.

In a **fixed trust**, the pattern of distributions to the beneficiaries is predetermined by the settlor and incorporated into the trust documents. In a **discretionary trust**, the trustee determines how the assets are distributed. A **spendthrift trust** is used to transfer assets to a beneficiary who is too young or is otherwise unable to manage the assets.

LOS 10.h

Premiums paid on life insurance are not usually considered part of the grantor's estate for tax purposes. In most jurisdictions, life insurance proceeds pass to beneficiaries without tax consequences, and, depending on jurisdiction, the policy might provide tax-free accumulation of wealth and/or loans to the policy holder on beneficial terms. By establishing a trust on behalf of the beneficiaries and making that trust the direct beneficiary of a life policy, the policy holder transfers assets to young, disabled, et cetera, beneficiaries outside the probate process.

LOS 10.i

Under **source jurisdiction** (a.k.a. **territorial tax system**) a country levies taxes on all income generated within its borders. Under **residence jurisdiction**, a country taxes the global income of its residents.

LOS 10.j

In response to citizens who renounce their citizenship to avoid taxes, some residence jurisdictions impose an exit tax, usually based on the gains on assets leaving, as if they were sold (deemed disposition). This could include a tax on income earned for a shadow period.

LOS 10.k

In a **residence-residence conflict**, two countries claim residence for the same individual. In a **source-source conflict**, two countries claim authority over the same income. In a **residence-source conflict**, an individual is subject to residence jurisdiction and receives income on assets in a foreign country with source jurisdiction.

Tax treaties may partially or fully resolve the double taxation of residence-source conflicts. The income is taxed by the source country and then:

- Exemption method: Not taxed by the residence country.
- Credit method: The tax owed to the residence country is computed, and a credit for taxes paid to the source country is applied:
  - If more is owed the residence country, the difference is paid.
  - If less is owed the residence country, the bill is zero.
- Deduction method: Taxes owed the source country reduce the taxable income in (and thereby partial reduce the tax owed to) the residence country.

LOS 10.l

In the estate planning process, financial advisers should attempt to structure estates to hold and transfer assets in the most tax-efficient ways. This could include holding foreign assets and even holding funds in a foreign country to more efficiently provide living and/or business expenses. **Tax avoidance** is legal. **Tax evasion** is hiding, misrepresenting, or otherwise not recognizing income so as to illegally avoid taxation.

Many countries enter into global treaties which provide for the sharing of information. QIs collect all the information required by the United States but provide the information on their U.S. customers only. A similar agreement exists in the European Union, by which EU member banks exchange customer information with each other.

CONCEPT CHECKERS

1. Which of the following are the main objectives of estate planning and the results of the techniques used to facilitate those objectives? The main objectives of estate planning are to minimize taxes and:
    A. achieve effective diversification. The results of the techniques used can include tax efficiency, access to assets to be transferred, and control over those assets.
    B. transfer assets to heirs or recipients of charitable bequests in an efficient manner. The results of the techniques used can include asset protection from creditors, creating liquidity, and transferring assets for a specific purpose.
    C. transfer assets to heirs or recipients of charitable bequests in an efficient manner. The results of the techniques used can include tax efficiency, access to assets to be transferred, control over the management of those assets, and the ability to maximize excess returns.

2. Individuals must generally be concerned with tax planning on:
    A. two levels.
    B. three levels.
    C. four levels.

3. What are the main targets for taxation, the fundamental methodologies for improving after-tax returns, and a key feature in the tax code to assist married couples in pursuing one or both of these methodologies? The main targets for taxation are:
    A. income, assets held, assets transferred, and expenditures. The two main methodologies for improving after-tax returns are to realize income and capital gains in the most advantageous way so that taxes are minimized and to defer the realization of gains for as long as possible. The provision in the tax code that permits the tax-free transfer of assets between spouses upon the death of one can assist married couples in pursuing one or both of these tax-reducing methodologies.
    B. income and assets transferred. The two main methodologies for improving after-tax returns are to realize income and capital gains in the most advantageous way so that taxes are minimized and to defer the realization of gains for as long as possible. The provision in the tax code that permits the tax-free transfer of assets between spouses upon the death of one can assist married couples in pursuing one or both of these tax-reducing methodologies.
    C. income, assets held, assets transferred, and expenditures. The two main methodologies for improving after-tax returns are to realize income and capital gains in the most advantageous way so that taxes are minimized and to defer the realization of gains for as long as possible. The provision in the tax code that resets the cost basis of assets after transfer of assets to the surviving spouse and payment of related estate taxes can assist married couples in pursuing one or both of these tax-reducing methodologies.

4. Which of the following is *most correct*? When investors make charitable gifts of appreciated securities, they are usually able to:
   A. avoid capital gains taxes but are not able to take a deduction for the gift.
   B. take a deduction in an amount designed to exactly offset the capital gains tax.
   C. avoid gift transfer taxes and can take an income tax deduction equal to the current fair market value of the gift.

5. Under a community property regime, which of the following is *most correct*? When one spouse dies, estate taxes on:
   A. all marriage assets (community property) are avoided.
   B. at least one-half of the marriage assets are avoided.
   C. at least one-half of the marriage assets are deferred.

6. For estate planning purposes, investments in privately held companies are usually tax:
   A. efficient because gains realized are usually taxed at long-term rates.
   B. inefficient because it is difficult to determine fair market value, thus the correct amount to be taxed cannot be determined.
   C. efficient because they can be transferred from an estate using a valuation discount, which reduces the basis on which the transfer tax is calculated.

7. What is usually the *most important* concern with determining the level of feasible retirement income, and what is the *best* method used to address this concern? The main concern with determining the level of feasible retirement income is:
   A. outliving one's assets and income, and this can be addressed by estimating core capital with Monte Carlo analysis and incorporating a safety reserve.
   B. outliving one's assets and income, and this can be addressed by multiplying expected future cash flows by the probability that each cash flow will be needed, which is called a survival probability.
   C. maintaining purchasing power, and this can be addressed by calculating the present value of anticipated spending over one's remaining life expectancy and incorporating a safety reserve.

8.   Joe Angelone, age 65, recently retired after a long career in the aerospace industry, first as a fighter pilot in the Vietnam war, then as a fighter test pilot, and finally as a project manager overseeing the testing and production of fighter planes. He and his wife Charlene, age 63, recently retired in Texas. Even though they are retired, they prefer to maintain their current lifestyle with spending needs of $80,000 per year in real terms. Inflation is expected to be 3% with the nominal risk-free rate equal to 5%. The Angelones' survival probabilities for the next three years are shown in the table below.

Year	Joe Age	Joe P(Survival)	Charlene Age	Charlene P(Survival)	
1	66	0.992	64	0.997	= 0.999976
2	67	0.982	65	0.987	= 0.999766
3	68	0.972	66	0.967	

A.   **Determine** the probability that either Joe or Charlene will survive for three years.

B.   **Calculate** the capitalized value of the Angelones' core spending needs over the next three years.

For more questions related to this topic review, log in to your Schweser online account and launch SchweserPro™ QBank; and for video instruction covering each LOS in this topic review, log in to your Schweser online account and launch the OnDemand video lectures, if you have purchased these products.

ANSWERS – CONCEPT CHECKERS

1. **B** The primary objectives of estate planning are to minimize taxes and to facilitate the tax-efficient transfer of assets to heirs or recipients of charitable bequests. Diversification and the ability to maximize excess returns are usually not the objectives of estate planning and are part of the grantor's/settlor's investment policy statement while accumulating assets throughout working years and throughout retirement.

   Estate planning tools include trusts that allow for the control of those assets, asset protection from creditors, and reduced taxes for either the settlor or beneficiary depending upon how the trust is structured. Foundations are used to transfer assets for specific purpose, such as helping to fund hospitals, libraries, or colleges. Life insurance is a liquidity planning technique that can be used to pay estate and gift taxes. Investing in partnerships or having a controlling interest in a foreign company may also be effective tax-reducing strategies.

2. **C** Individual taxation generally occurs on four levels—tax on income, tax on spending, tax on wealth, and tax on assets when they are transferred to others.

3. **A** The main targets for taxation are income, assets held, assets transferred, and expenditures. The two main methodologies for improving after-tax returns are to realize income and capital gains in the most advantageous way so that taxes are minimized and to defer the realization of gains for as long as possible. The provision in the tax code that permits the tax-free transfer of assets between spouses upon the death of one of them can assist married couples in pursuing one or both of these tax-reducing methodologies. In virtually all cases, this feature of the tax code allows couples to defer the payment of estate taxes, often for a considerable period of time, until the death of the surviving spouse. To the extent that future tax rates are lower than those present at the time the assets are transferred between spouses, there will also be some reduction in the effective tax rate.

4. **C** When an investor makes a charitable gift of appreciated securities, the investor is usually able to avoid gift transfer taxes and can take an income tax deduction equal to the current fair market value of the gift. The appreciated securities continue to avoid capital gains taxes once transferred to the tax-exempt organization.

5. **C** Under a community property regime, the surviving spouse is entitled to one half of marriage assets, which are considered community property. This means that estate taxes that would have been paid immediately on at least half of the marriage assets are deferred until the surviving spouse's death. The remaining property is divided according to the testator's will and other asset transfer mechanisms.

6. **C** Investments in privately held companies are usually tax-efficient from an estate planning perspective, because they can be transferred after taking a valuation discount. The discount relates to uncertainty of true value as well as lack of liquidity and sometimes control. It is true that they are also tax-efficient from the standpoint that any gains realized are usually taxed at favorable long-term rates, but this pertains to liquidating the assets that would normally not be done before transferring them in an estate.

7. **A** The main concern with determining the level of feasible retirement income is outliving one's assets and income. This potential problem can be addressed by all three methods mentioned. Calculating the present value of anticipated spending over one's remaining life expectancy has the weakness of being based on average life expectancies, thus half of all individuals will live longer than expected. A better method, but one that still uses a mortality table, is to multiply expected future cash flows by the probability that each cash flow will be needed, which is called a survival probability. These two methods do not consider market risk, however. The best method is by estimating core capital with Monte Carlo analysis, which uses thousands of simulations, meaning it considers market risk and is the most accurate (realistic) method. All three methods should incorporate a safety reserve to account for the risk of capital markets or a change in spending needs.

8. A. Joe and Charlene's joint probability of surviving for a given number of years is equal to the sum of their individual probabilities minus the product of their individual probabilities:

p(Joint) = p(Joe survives) + p(Charlene survives) – p(Joe survives)p(Charlene survives)

There is effectively 100% probability (0.99998) at least one of them will survive for one year:

Year 1 = 0.992 + 0.997 – (0.992)(0.997) = 1.0000

There is 99.98% probability at least one of them will survive for two years:

Year 2 = 0.982 + 0.987 – (0.982)(0.987) = 0.9998

There is 99.91% probability at least one of them will survive for three years:

Year 3 = 0.972 + 0.967 – (0.972)(0.967) = 0.9991

B. The capitalized value of the core spending needs is the sum of the product of the joint probability of survival and the real spending need discounted by the real risk-free rate.*

The real risk-free rate is calculated as:
(1 + nominal risk-free rate) / (1 + inflation rate) – 1 = (1.05 / 1.03) – 1 = 1.94%

Year	Spending	Joint p(Survival)	Expected Spending	Discount Factor	Discounted Value
1	80,000	1.0000	80,000	1.0194	$78,478
2	80,000	0.9998	79,984	$(1.0194)^2$	$76,969
3	80,000	0.9991	79,928	$(1.0194)^3$	$75,451

Total capitalized value of core spending needs = $230,898

* In this question, the spending needs were given in real terms so the real risk-free rate was used for discounting. If the spending needs had been given in nominal terms, the nominal risk-free rate would have been used for discounting.

CONCENTRATED SINGLE-ASSET POSITIONS

Study Session 5

EXAM FOCUS

This topic review presumes a basic understanding of taxation, particularly capital gains taxes, along with derivative payoff patterns and features. This background is covered in other sections of the Level III curriculum and is not more than what has already been utilized at Levels I and II. The material takes a global perspective, meaning that legal and tax specifics are not going to be covered. Do not implement these techniques without consulting a qualified, knowledgeable tax and legal advisor. This is a good introduction to a specialized area that would require years of additional experience and training in order to reach proficiency.

INTRODUCTION

Through work, inheritance, entrepreneurship, or for other reasons, individuals may come to hold concentrated positions in a single asset. Concentrated positions in a publicly traded single-stock position, a privately held business, or a real estate investment (not the primary residence) are covered in this discussion. A concentrated position can lead to inefficient asset allocation. An investment manager often works with the client to sell or otherwise monetize the asset. Such decisions often involve illiquidity, tax, legal, and emotional (behavioral finance) issues.

RISK ASSOCIATED WITH SINGLE-ASSET POSITIONS

LOS 11.a: Explain investment risks associated with a concentrated position in a single asset and discuss the appropriateness of reducing such risks.

CFA® Program Curriculum, Volume 2, page 324

Concentrated positions can have consequences for return and risk. The assets may not be efficiently priced and, therefore, not generate a fair risk-adjusted return. Illiquid assets can be difficult and costly to exit or non-income producing. The risk in such assets is both systematic and company- or property-specific.

- **Systematic risk** is the risk that cannot be diversified away through holding a portfolio of risky assets. In the single factor CAPM, this would be beta. In multifactor models there will be more than one systematic risk. Multifactor models might include unexpected changes in the business cycle or inflation as systematic risks.

- **Company-specific risk** is the nonsystematic risk of an investment that can be diversified away. It would derive from events that affect a specific investment but not the overall market. A corporate bankruptcy as a result of financial fraud would be an extreme example of company-specific risk. Nonsystematic risk increases the standard deviation of returns without additional expected return. This can be illustrated with a simulation, as shown in the following section.
- **Property-specific risk** for real estate is the direct counterpart to company-specific risk for a company. It is the additional, diversifiable risk associated with owning a specific property. It might arise, for example, from the discovery of environmental pollution on the site or the loss of a key tenant and rental income.

Simulation Assumptions[1]:

An investor holds an initial portfolio valued at $100 in a single stock with a zero cost basis. The investor can sell the asset and invest the after-tax proceeds in a diversified stock portfolio. In either case, at the end of 20 years, the portfolio is liquidated and any additional taxes are paid.

	Single Stock	*Diversified Portfolio*
Annual expected return:	10.0%	10.0%
Capital gains tax:	20.0%	20.0%
Dividend:	0.0%	1.2%
Standard deviation:	40.0%	17.0%

Simulation Results:

- Both portfolios have positive skew. Downside is limited to a 100% loss, while the probability of exceeding a 100% gain over a 20-year time horizon is significant.
- The single asset portfolio has more extreme positive skew for two reasons:
  - A higher average ending value reflecting the benefit of tax deferral. The full $100 can be compounded in the single asset portfolio, while selling the stock and reinvesting in the diversified portfolio incurs an initial $20 capital gains tax, allowing only $80 to compound over time.
  - A much higher probability of a 100% loss due to bankruptcy of a single asset.
- The median outcome is higher for the diversified portfolio, reflecting its lower probability of suffering a large or total loss.

The single asset portfolio appears superior when looking at only average ending value. However, when downside risk is considered, the diversified portfolio is superior for most investors.

Professor's Note: While the situation is somewhat different, this should sound like the conclusion reached in Monte Carlo simulations with path dependency factored in. A diversified portfolio that provides a return consistent with client objectives and constraints is preferable for most clients.

---

1. This analysis is derived from the information presented in Reading 11 *Concentrated Single-Asset Positions* by Thomas Boczar and Nischal R. Pai of the 2018 Level III CFA exam curriculum.

OBJECTIVES IN DEALING WITH A CONCENTRATED POSITION

LOS 11.b: Describe typical objectives in managing concentrated positions.

CFA® Program Curriculum, Volume 2, page 327

There are three common objectives when managing a concentrated position:

1. **Reduce the risk** caused by the wealth concentration.

2. **Generate liquidity** to meet diversification or spending needs.

3. **Optimize tax efficiency** to maximize after-tax ending value.

Reducing the concentrated position is not appropriate for all clients. There are other client specific objectives and constraints to consider:

- **Restrictions on sale**. Stock ownership in a public company may be received by a company executive as part of a compensation package, with company expectations or regulatory requirements that the executive will hold the stock for a certain length of time.
- **A desire for control**. Majority ownership brings control over the business.
- **To create wealth**. An entrepreneur may assume high specific risk in expectation of building the value of the business and his wealth. He may want to begin passing portions of the ownership to key employees as part of an incentive compensation plan or begin to transfer ownership to succeeding generations of the family.
- **The asset may have other uses**. Real estate owned personally could also be a key asset used in another business of the owner.

SPECIAL CONSIDERATIONS IN CONCENTRATED POSITIONS

LOS 11.c: Discuss tax consequences and illiquidity as considerations affecting the management of concentrated positions in publicly traded common shares, privately held businesses, and real estate.

CFA® Program Curriculum, Volume 2, page 328

Sale of a concentrated position may trigger a large capital gains **tax liability**. A large concentrated position is often accumulated and held for many years, resulting in a zero or low tax basis. A plan to defer, reduce, or eliminate the tax may be desirable.

Illiquidity and/or **high transaction** costs can be a factor even if there is no tax due. A public company trading with insufficient volume may require a price discount to sell. The expense of finding a buyer for a private business or real estate can be substantial. The intended use by the prospective buyer may affect the price.

LOS 11.d: Discuss capital market and institutional constraints on an investor's ability to reduce a concentrated position.

CFA® Program Curriculum, Volume 2, page 329

Institutional and capital market constraints such as tax law (covered previously) can significantly affect the costs of selling or monetizing a concentrated position. Legal issues can depend on the form of asset ownership: sole proprietorship, limited partnership, limited company, or public stock. Other specific issues that may exist include:

- **Margin lending rules** limit the percentage of the asset's value that can be borrowed. Derivative positions can be used to reduce the risk of the asset position and increase the percentage of value that can be borrowed. Rule-based systems tend to be rigid and define the exact percentage that can be borrowed, while risk-based systems consider the underlying economics of the transaction.

As an example of a rule-based system, the United States generally limits borrowing against a stock to 50% of value even if the stock is hedged with a protective put. However, U.S. regulations classify a prepaid variable forward (which also eliminates downside risk) differently and do not impose margin rules, leaving it up to the lender to decide what will be lent. This is economically inconsistent. A risk-based system would treat both transactions similarly and allow a 100% loan-to-value (LTV) ratio in both cases.

> *Professor's Note: A prepaid variable forward is discussed in more detail later. The point here is a rule-based system may ignore the similar results of the two hedging strategies. Remember, this material is not teaching specific laws but warning that such laws are not always logical or self-evident. Surely you know that from studying IFRS and GAAP.*

- **Securities law and regulations** may define the owner as an "insider" (who is presumed to have material, nonpublic information) and impose restrictions, regulations, and reporting requirements on the position.
- **Contractual restrictions and employer mandates** may impose restrictions (such as minimum holding periods or blackout periods when sales may not be made) beyond those of securities law and regulation.
- **Capital market limitations** in the form of market structure and regulation can have indirect consequences. Monetization strategies commonly require over-the-counter derivative trades with a dealer to hedge the security's risk and increase the LTV ratio. To offer such trades, dealers must be able to hedge the risks they assume. This may be impossible. For example, if the asset is an initial public offering (IPO) or trades infrequently, there will not be a price history on which the dealer can base a hedge. Borrowing and shorting the underlying asset is often required for the dealer to hedge their risk. This is prohibited in some markets. Without sufficient price history and liquidity in the underlying instruments, monetization techniques may be unavailable.

LOS 11.e: Discuss psychological considerations that may make an investor reluctant to reduce his or her exposure to a concentrated position.

CFA® Program Curriculum, Volume 2, page 331

Professor's Note: This section repeats material better covered in Behavioral Finance. It reiterates that cognitive biases are generally easier to overcome with education than are emotional biases. Managers may be able to help investors with emotional biases overcome them by asking questions such as: What would you do if the position were cash rather than a single asset? When grandmother left this stock to you, did the shares make more sense to hold? Reviewing past performance and current risk may help the investor gain perspective and think rationally.

Typical cognitive biases include *conservatism* in maintaining existing beliefs; *confirmation* in seeking support for what is already believed; *illusion of control* when the investor believes he can control what will happen to the investment; *anchoring and adjustment* in making decisions in reference to the current position held; and *availability in making decisions* based on ease of recalling information.

Typical emotional biases include *overconfidence*, *familiarity*, and *illusion of knowledge* leading the investor to overestimate the probability the investment will produce favorable returns; *status quo bias* and a failure to consider making changes; *naive extrapolation* of past results; *endowment* in expecting to be able to sell the asset for more than the investor would pay for it; and *loyalty bias* in retaining employer stock or feeling an obligation to retain an inherited position.

A Goal-Based Decision-Making Process

LOS 11.f: Describe advisers' use of goal-based planning in managing concentrated positions.

CFA® Program Curriculum, Volume 2, page 334

A **goal-based decision process** modifies traditional mean-variance analysis to accommodate the insights of behavioral finance theory. The portfolio is divided into tiers of a pyramid, or **risk buckets**, with each tier or bucket designed to meet progressive levels of client goals. The risk buckets and sequence of priority are:

1. Allocate funds to a **personal risk bucket** to protect the client from poverty or a drastic decline in lifestyle. Low-risk assets such as money market and bank CDs, as well as the personal residence, are held in this bucket. Safety is emphasized, but a below-market return is likely.

2. Next, allocate funds to a **market risk bucket** to maintain the client's existing standard of living. Portfolio assets in this bucket would be allocated to stocks and bonds earning an expected market return.

3. Remaining portfolio funds are allocated to an **aspirational risk bucket** holding positions such as a private business, concentrated stock holdings, real estate investments, and other riskier positions. Allocating these holdings to the aspirational risk bucket highlights their risky nature for the client. If successful, these high-risk investments could substantially improve the client's standard of living.

To implement a goal-based plan, the manager and client must determine the **primary capital** necessary to meet the goals of the first two risk buckets and the amount of any remaining **surplus capital** to meet *aspirational goals*. If a concentrated holding in the aspirational bucket leaves insufficient funds for the first two primary capital buckets, sale or monetization of the concentrated position must be discussed with the client. Some questions to address are:

*   What are the client's lifetime spending needs and desires?
*   What is the present value of those needs and desires?
*   What is the value of the concentrated position and do different approaches to sale or monetization produce different values?
*   What other assets does the client have and how liquid are they?
*   Would sale or monetization of the concentrated position be sufficient to fund any shortfall in the primary capital?

Example 1

Bill Cook is the founder, manager, and 100% owner of a private company. Through hard work he has built his company to an estimated value of GBP 30,000,000. While the country he resides in is not the U.K., it uses the GBP. His tax basis is near zero, and he has been planning for his daughter to take over the business when he retires in 3 years. He was shocked when she recently announced she is quitting the business to pursue a different life course. Both his grandchildren also work at the company and are advancing rapidly in their business skills. Cook has a home (mortgage free) and shorter-term government bonds valued at GBP 900,000. In addition, he has a stock and bond portfolio valued at GBP 1,700,000. He also owns the land and building where his business is located. The land and building are valued at GBP 2,000,000 and are mortgaged for GBP 2,000,000.

1. **Determine** the holdings and value of his three risk buckets.

Answer 1:

*   Personal risk bucket of GBP 900,000 composed of the home and short-term bonds.
*   Market risk bucket of GBP 1,700,000 composed of the stocks and other bonds.
*   Aspirational risk bucket of GBP 30,000,000 composed of the private company plus land and building less the mortgage on the land and building.

Working with an investment manager, Cook determines he requires GBP 20,000,000 today to fund the future value of his primary goals and objectives in retirement. Until retirement, his income from the business will fund his expenses.

---

2. Based on this information, **recommend** the next steps Cook should take in structuring a financial plan.

Answer 2:

Cook has only GBP 2.6 million in primary capital and GBP 30 million allocated to surplus capital. He has insufficient primary capital to fund the GBP 20 million to meet his primary needs. His allocation to higher-risk assets is too high. In addition, he will need a successor to manage the business in order to retire. He must develop a sale or monetization strategy which will (1) increase his allocation to primary capital and (2) find other management for the company.

Giving up control of the business is no longer an issue as he will not be leaving the business to his daughter, but he should structure a plan so that he can continue to work for the planned 3 years until retirement. As is common for an entrepreneur who builds a business over time, the tax basis of his holding is essentially zero. He currently has a GBP 30,000,000 unrealized gain and a substantial tax liability if he sells.

ASSET LOCATION AND TRANSFER

LOS 11.g: Explain uses of asset location and wealth transfers in managing concentrated positions.

CFA® Program Curriculum, Volume 2, page 337

Asset location determines the method of taxation that will apply. Location in a tax-deferred account would defer all taxes to a future date. In a taxable account, interest, dividends, and capital gains may be subject to different tax rates (or deferral possibilities in the case of when to realize capital gains). If the concentrated position owner has control over the asset, other tax strategies to maximize after-tax ending wealth will be discussed.

Wealth transfer involves estate planning and gifting to dispose of excess wealth. The specific strategies used depend on the tax laws of the country and the owner's situation. Key considerations include:

1. Advisors can have the greatest impact by working with clients before significant unrealized gains occur. If there are no unrealized gains, there are generally no financial limitations on disposing of the concentrated position.

2. Donating assets with unrealized gains to charity is generally tax-free even if there are gains.

3. An **estate tax freeze** is a strategy to transfer future appreciation and tax liability to a future generation. This strategy usually involves a partnership or corporate structure. A gift tax would be due on the value of the asset when the transfer is made; however, the asset (including any future appreciation in value) will be exempt from future estate and gift taxes in the giver's estate. Any tax owed is "frozen," meaning paid or fixed near an initial value.

Example 2

Cook has now decided to leave the company to his grandchildren. Cook's investment manager advises him to restructure the company into two classes of stock, a voting preferred class and a nonvoting common class of stock. The restructuring is done such that the voting preferred shares are worth GBP 30,000,000, and the common stock is worth GBP 0. Cook is advised to gift the common stock to a trust that will later disburse the stock to his grandchildren.

1. Assuming this transaction functions as an estate tax freeze, **explain** how it affects Cook's current and future tax situation as well as his other goals.

Answer 1:

The common stock has no current value, so there should be no tax on the initial gift. The preferred stock (with a fixed dividend) is not expected to increase in value as the company grows. The preferred stock will still be in Cook's estate and subject to taxes but at a value that is "frozen." Future growth of the business should increase the value of the common stock, which is not part of Cook's portfolio or estate. It will be taxed in the trust.

By retaining the voting preferred stock, Cook continues to have sole control of the business and can work there as long as he wishes. His cost basis is still zero, and he has a substantial unrealized gain in the preferred stock.

2. Cook is concerned that this strategy is overly complicated and is considering just giving ownership of the company to his grandchildren now. He will keep working for a few more years and, by then, they will be ready to take over. **Evaluate** whether this strategy is more appropriate than the estate tax freeze.

Answer 2:

This is less appropriate. While it is simple, a tax bill on the GBP 30,000,000 will be due immediately. In addition, Cook would no longer control the company. The grandchildren would have control, and there is no assurance they are currently ready to run the business. Cook will have no assurance he can continue to work there until retirement.

Minimizing transfer tax costs is more difficult when gains already exist. In the Cook example, the estate tax freeze shifts taxation of future appreciation but not of the existing gain.

Establishing a limited partnership and gifting may reduce taxes on existing appreciation. Cook could establish a limited partnership to hold the business and serve as general partner while gifting the limited partnership interests to his grandchildren. The partnership will own the business and, as general partner, Cook will make all business decisions. The tax value of the limited partnership interests can be reduced for gift taxes because they lack marketability and control. A total discount of 30% to 60% is plausible. Future appreciation in the value of the limited partnership positions would be taxed to the limited partners rather than Cook, moving the tax burden on future appreciation to the limited partners.

A five-step process can be used to make decisions for managing a concentrated position:

Step 1: Establish written objectives and constraints for the client. Nonfinancial issues such as retaining control of the asset and wealth transfer goals should be included in the document.

Step 2: Identify the techniques and strategies that best meet these objectives and constraints.

Step 3: Consider the tax advantages and disadvantages of each technique.

Step 4: Consider the other advantages and disadvantages of each technique.

Step 5: Document the decisions made.

TECHNIQUES TO MANAGE CONCENTRATED POSITION

Three broad techniques can be used to manage concentrated positions:

- **Sell the asset:** This will trigger a tax liability and loss of control.
- **Monetize the asset:** Borrow against its value and use the loan proceeds to accomplish client objectives.
- **Hedge the asset value:** Often done using derivatives to limit downside risk.

Hedging techniques often utilize over-the-counter (OTC) or exchange-traded derivatives. The choice of OTC instruments will (1) create counterparty credit risk, and (2) provide flexibility in setting the specific terms of the instrument. In contrast, exchange-traded instruments (1) facilitate closing the transaction early by entering an offsetting transaction, (2) provide price discovery because transaction prices are publicly reported, and (3) provide more transparent fees and transaction costs because it is easier for a dealer to embed transaction costs in complex OTC derivatives.

> *Professor's Note: We are going to follow the CFA curriculum and proceed through a variety of techniques that might be applicable for a given client. There is a chance a question will describe applicable tax or legal issues and then require comment on whether a specific strategy would be appropriate based on the information presented in the case.*

> *It bothers some candidates that tax and legal issues do not always make economic sense, may be inconsistent (the same economic result is treated differently) within a country or between countries, and that the CFA text does not cover the specifics of how a transaction will be taxed. The curriculum points out this should not be surprising. Generally market participants "invent" a strategy or technique to accomplish a goal such as maximizing after-tax value. Regulators in each country then attempt to determine which rules to apply or write new rules to apply to the transaction. The results can be inconsistent in hindsight. The curriculum cannot cover specifics that vary by country or regulator and over time.*

MANAGING CONCENTRATED STOCK POSITIONS

LOS 11.h: Describe strategies for managing concentrated positions in publicly traded common shares.

CFA® Program Curriculum, Volume 2, page 340

Monetization generally involves receiving cash for a position without triggering a tax event. It is a two-step process:

Step 1: Hedge a large part of the risk in the position. This is often complicated by tax regulations. If a perfect hedge removes all risk, it may be taxed as a sale. The hedge must be structured to eliminate as much risk as possible without the tax liability coming due.

Step 2: Borrow using the hedged position as collateral. The more effective the hedge, the higher the loan to value (LTV) ratio for the loan. For example, if a highly effective hedge can be established that limits the decline in value of a $10 million position to 5% (a $9.5 million ending value), it may now be possible to borrow $9.5 million (95% of initial LTV). The client can then use the $9.5 million to meet portfolio objectives.

To illustrate potential monetization tools, consider an investor with 100,000 shares of PBL, which is trading for $50 per share. Four tools can be considered for hedging the asset. They differ in how they hedge the asset, but all are designed to reduce the risk and increase the funds available to the investor.

1. **Short sale against the box**. The investor borrows 100,000 shares of PBL and sells them short. The investor is long and short the stock, a "riskless position" that is expected to earn the risk-free rate of return. The investor can use the short sale proceeds to meet portfolio objectives. Alternatively, regulations may require the investor to hold the short sale cash proceeds in an account to collateralize the short sale, but the investor could use that account as collateral to borrow close to 100% LTV of the hedged position.

2. **Equity forward sale contract**. The investor enters a forward contract to sell the 100,000 shares of PBL. The investor has a known sale price and does not share in any upside or downside price movement of PBL from that contract price.

3. **Forward conversion with options**. A pair of options is used to hedge the stock position, selling calls and buying puts with the same strike price. If a $50 strike price is used and the stock rises above $50, it will be called; if the stock falls below $50, it can be put. A hedged ending value of $50 is established.

4. **Total return equity swap**. The investor enters a swap to pay the total return on the $5,000,000 of PBL and receives LIBOR. The investor is fully hedged. If the return of PBL exceeds LIBOR, the investor pays the difference, which eliminates any gains on PBL. If the return of PBL is less than LIBOR, the investor receives the difference, so his return is LIBOR.

Selecting the tool will depend on tax treatment. The goal is to select the tool that will not trigger an existing tax liability. Critical questions will include what happens when a derivative is executed or closed, how the gains or losses are taxed, what expenses are involved, and the effects on the concentrated position.

It is also possible to use **modified hedging** to minimize downside risk while retaining upside in the underlying position. The following continues the discussion of the investor with 100,000 PBL shares.

Protective puts (sometimes called **portfolio insurance**): The investor would purchase puts on 100,000 shares of PBL. An at-the-money put with a strike price of $50 might cost $4.57 per share and protect against any decline if the price falls below $50. An out-of-the-money (OTM) put with a strike price of $48 might cost $2.98 per share. By using the OTM put, the investor is *self-insuring* the first $2 of stock price decline, but the OTM put will cost less initially. In all cases the options are a *wasting asset* that will be worthless if they expire out-of-the-money.

There are several ways to lower the cost of the protection:

- Purchase an out-of-the-money put as just described.
- Buy a put with a shorter time to expiration. The protection lasts for less time and will cost less.
- Use a pair of puts, buying a put with a higher strike price of X_H and selling a put with a lower strike price of X_L. Buying a put with a strike price of $48 protects against price declines below $48 but selling a put with a strike price of $40 removes any protection below that price. The investor is protected between X_H and X_L. The sale of puts reduces the initial cost.
- Add exotic features to the option (not found in standard options). For example, a **knock-out put** expires prior to its stated expiration if the stock price rises above a specified level. This may reduce the protection, and the option will cost less.
- **No-cost** or **zero-premium collars** are a common way to lower initial cost, in this case to zero, by giving up some stock upside. A put is purchased and a call is sold with different strike prices selected so the premiums are equal. For PBL, the investor could buy the 48 put for $2.98 and sell a 53 call for $2.98. The investor has a net expenditure of $0. The investor is protected if the stock price falls below 48, but the stock will be called at 53 if its price rises to that level. To increase the upside of the strategy, a call with a higher strike price can be sold. It will cost less, but to maintain the initial zero cost, a put with a lower strike price must be purchased. The upside potential is increased, but the downside protection is reduced.

> *Professor's Note: This CFA material assumes you remember the basics of options and forward contract payoffs. These same basics are also important in the derivatives and currency sections of the curriculum. We review the important basics in derivatives. Candidates may benefit by reviewing this section after the derivatives Study Session.*

> *The reason complex and multiple structures are presented is to leave enough risk and uncertainty so that the transaction is not treated as equivalent to a sale for tax purposes.*

Prepaid variable forwards (PVF) are economically similar to a collar and loan in one transaction. The owner of 100,000 PBL shares (currently priced at $50) could enter a PVF with a dealer. The dealer would pay the owner $45 per share now, equivalent to borrowing $45 per share. The loan will be repaid by delivering shares of PBL at a future date. The PVF could specify delivery of all 100,000 shares if PBL is below $50 per share on the repayment date but require delivery of a smaller number of shares if the price of PBL rises above $50.

Professor's Note: PVFs are considered "exotic" OTC instruments. The specifics of any contract vary. In this case the owner receives cash at initiation of the PVF, has a minimum sale price of $45 per share, and retains some price upside because fewer than 100,000 shares may be needed to close the PVF. The CFA text covers the concept of a PVF but not its details.

Example 3

An investor holds 50,000 shares valued at $100 per share. The investor simultaneously buys an OTC European style 6-month put with a strike price of 97 and sells a 1-year exchange-traded American style call with a strike price of 105. Both options cover the 50,000 shares, and the option premiums are equal. The relevant tax code specifies that option premiums received are taxed as ordinary income (t = 30%). Option premiums paid increase the tax basis of the underlying holding. In this case the underlying position is a long-term holding, and any gain will be taxed at 10% when realized.

1. **Comment** on whether this structure is more like a prepaid variable forward (PVF) or a zero cost collar (ZCC). Also, **comment** on how the risks in this transaction differ from a typical PVF or ZCC.

2. Are there any tax inefficiencies in the transaction?

Answer 1:

It is most like a zero cost collar because a put is purchased and a call sold on the 50,000 shares owned. The two premiums are equal, so there is a zero initial cost. It is unlike a PVF because no funds are received up front, and there is no variation in the number of shares to be delivered in the future.

It is not a standard ZCC because the options have different expiration dates and features. The put protection only lasts for 6 months. The OTC European style put option can only be exercised at expiration and will have limited liquidity until then. The American style call option can be exercised at any time up to expiration in 12 months and is marketable.

Answer 2:

The tax treatment is not optimal. The premiums received for selling the calls will be taxed now at 30%. The cost of the put increases the tax basis of the underlying stock. Any resulting tax savings are realized only when the shares are sold and reduce gains that would have been taxed at 10%.

TAX CONSIDERATIONS IN STRATEGY SELECTION

LOS 11.i: Discuss tax considerations in the choice of hedging strategy.

CFA® Program Curriculum, Volume 2, page 352

Example 3 described a **mismatch in character**, two items in a strategy that trigger different tax treatments. In that case it was the option premium received now and taxed at 30% versus a future reduction in long-term gain that would be taxed at 10%. A hedging strategy needs to consider any mismatch and select the tool or strategy that maximizes after-tax value for the investor.

Many tax codes treat employer stock options as an alternative to salary and tax any gains on the options as ordinary income. Hedging the options could produce a mismatch in character. As an example, a gain on stock options of $100,000 is taxed as ordinary income at 30%, while offsetting losses of $100,000 on the derivatives hedge are used to reduce long-term gains that are taxed at 10%. The tax of $30,000 is reduced by only $10,000 of capital gains tax not paid and only if the investor has $100,000 of capital gains to shelter. Whatever the strategy, it is essential to verify how it will be treated for tax purposes.

Yield enhancement with **covered calls** is another potential strategy. The owner of 100,000 shares of PBL priced at 50 could sell call options with a strike price of 53 for $2.98 a share. Because the stock will be called away if the price rises above $53, the owner is predetermining a liquidation value of $53. A manager could use a covered call program on a portion of the holding to psychologically prepare an investor to gradually reduce the concentrated position. The $2.98 of premium income received can be viewed as either enhancing the income yield of the stock or protecting against the first $2.98 of stock price decline.

Two **tax-optimization equity strategies** combine tax planning with investment strategy.

1. **Index tracking with active tax management.** Cash from a monetized concentrated stock position is invested to track a broad market index on a pretax basis and outperform the index on an after-tax basis. For example, if dividends are taxed at a higher rate than capital gains, the tracking portfolio could be structured with a lower dividend yield but higher expected price appreciation.

2. **A completeness portfolio** structures the other portfolio assets for greatest diversification benefit to complement (complete) the concentrated position. For example, if the concentrated position is an auto stock, the rest of the assets are selected to have low correlation with auto stocks such that the resulting total portfolio better tracks the return of the chosen benchmark.

Both of these tax-optimization strategies allow the investor to retain ownership of the concentrated position but may take time and sufficient other assets and funds to implement. (Tracking cannot be greatly improved if the investor has $9 million in the auto stock and $1 million of other assets.) Both strategies provide diversification while deferring the gain.

A perfect hedge is generally inappropriate if it will cause the underlying gain to be taxed or if the necessary derivatives do not exist. A **cross hedge** may be used instead. The investor who holds a large position in an auto stock but finds it cannot be shorted to create a hedge could consider three cross hedge possibilities:

1. Short shares of a different auto stock or another stock that is highly correlated with the concentrated position. The highly correlated short position will increase (decrease) in value to offset decreases (increases) in the auto stock.

2. Short an index that is highly correlated with the concentrated position. Shorting a different stock or an index will introduce company-specific risk. A negative event could affect the concentrated position but have no offsetting effect on the value of the short position.

3. Purchasing puts on the concentrated position is also considered a cross-hedge in that the put and stock are different types of assets.

Exchange funds are another possibility. Consider 10 investors, each of whom has a concentrated position in a single stock with a low cost basis. Each investor's position is in a different stock. The investors contribute their holdings into a newly formed exchange fund, and each now owns a pro rata share of the new fund. If investor H had a position worth EUR 5,000,000 with a cost basis of EUR 500,000 and the total value of the new fund is EUR 100,000,000, she now owns 5% of the new fund at a cost basis of EUR 500,000. The investor now participates in a diversified portfolio and defers any tax event until shares of the fund are sold.

MANAGING CONCENTRATED POSITIONS IN PRIVATELY HELD BUSINESSES

LOS 11.j: Describe strategies for managing concentrated positions in privately held businesses.

CFA® Program Curriculum, Volume 2, page 356

The previous strategy discussions will apply if the instruments necessary to implement a strategy exist. However, privately held businesses may be more concentrated (the owner could own 100% of the business and it may be close to 100% of her assets), the standalone and nonsystematic risk tends to be very high, and the asset is generally illiquid. Noninvestment psychological issues are often significant. The owner may derive a large part of his sense of self-worth as well as his income from the business. Business and personal life are often intermixed. If the concentrated position was received from a family member, there can be a strong sense of attachment to the holding.

Exit strategies for the business must be considered. Exit strategies include monetization, sale, a phased sale over time, or an adjustment to the business structure that will provide the owner with cash. Exit strategy analysis should consider:

- The value of the business.
- Tax rates that would apply to the potential exit strategies.
- Availability and terms of credit, as borrowing may be involved in financing any transaction.

- The buying power of potential purchasers.
- Currency values if the transaction involves foreign currencies.

The strategies to consider in managing a private business position include:

- **Strategic buyers** take a buy and hold perspective and generally offer the highest price to the seller. Strategic buyers seek to combine the business with an existing business of the buyer.
- A **financial buyer** or a **financial sponsor** is often a private equity fund planning to restructure the business, add value, and resell the business (typically in a 3 to 5 year period). They generally purchase more mature, established businesses and offer a lower price than a strategic buyer.
- **Recapitalization** is generally used for established but less mature (middle market) companies. In a **leveraged recapitalization** the owner may retain 20% to 40% of the equity capital and sell 60% to 80% of his shares back to the company. The owner continues to manage the business with a significant financial stake. A private equity firm could arrange the financing for the company to purchase the owner's stock. In exchange, the private equity firm receives equity in the company. This could be part of a *phased exit strategy* for the owner; sell and receive cash for a portion of his equity in the initial transaction, then participate in and sell his remaining shares when the private equity firm resells their position in a few years. Taxes are owed on the cash received in the initial recapitalization, but additional taxes are deferred until the owner's remaining stock is sold. If tax rates are expected to increase in the future, the transaction can be structured with more cash in the initial transaction.
- In a **sale to (other) management or key employees**, the owner sells his position to existing employees of the company. There are drawbacks:
  - Generally the buyers will only purchase at a discounted price.
  - The buyers may lack financial resources and expect the existing owner to finance a significant portion of the purchase with a loan or a promissory note, which is a promise that the buyers will pay in the future.
  - The promissory note is often contingent on future performance of the business with no assurance current employees or managers are capable of running the business and making the payments. This structure may be called a management buyout obligation (MBO) because existing managers buy the business in exchange for an obligation to pay for the business in the future.
  - Negotiation with employees to sell the business to them may fail and damage the continuing employer/employee relationship needed to continue operating the business.
- In a **divestiture, sale, or disposition of non-core business assets**, the owner sells nonessential business assets and then directs the company to use the proceeds to pay a large dividend to, or repurchase stock from, the owner. In either case, the owner receives cash while retaining the rest of the stock and control of the business.
- A **sale or gift to family members** could be structured with tax advantages such as the estate tax freeze or limited partnership valuation discounts discussed earlier. If the family members lack the financial resources to pay cash, the existing owner could do an MBO and accept a promissory note for the purchase price. Unfortunately, neither a gift nor MBO sale provides the existing owner much immediate cash flow.

- A **personal line of credit secured by company shares**. The owner can borrow from the company and pledge her company stock as collateral. If the company does not have the financial resources to make the loan, the company could borrow to obtain the cash for the loan to the owner. Interest paid by the company can be a tax-deductible business expense. Alternatively, the line of credit (loan to the owner) could be from a third-party lender. The company may offer the lender a put, allowing the lender to transfer the loan to the company for cash. This increases the lender's assurance of repayment in exchange for more favorable loan terms to the owner.

- With an **initial public offering (IPO)** the owner sells a portion of his shares to the public and transforms the remaining shares into liquid public shares. Generally, IPO purchasers will expect the owner to retain a significant ownership stake and continue to manage the business. The existing owner now faces the increased scrutiny of running a public company.

- With an **employee stock ownership plan (ESOP)**, the owner sells stock to the ESOP, which in turn sells the shares to company employees. In a leveraged ESOP, the company borrows the money to finance the stock purchase. In the United States (subject to additional restrictions), the owner's sale of shares may not trigger a capital gains tax.

EVALUATING THE STRATEGIES

Example 4

1. We previously considered the Bill Cook case. Cook has taken no actions regarding his ownership of a private company. His health has seriously deteriorated and is not expected to improve, but the company has thrived. Cook believes the company is worth "at least GBP 50 million." He wishes to retire next year and is now highly motivated to find the cash to fund a diversified portfolio of liquid stocks and bonds that will support his retirement and meet his medical expenses. He is no longer concerned with passing the company to family members.

He is considering several alternatives:

A. Sell 100% of the company to a strategic buyer for GBP 48 million.

B. Sell 100% to a financial buyer for GBP 46 million.

C. Sell 100% of the company to the existing employees in an MBO for GBP 50 million. Cook will receive GBP 4 million up front, accept a GBP 25 million promissory note from the employees payable in equal installments over 10 years at 0% interest, and the balance in a note at 4% interest that will pay if the company meets defined future performance targets. Default on payments returns the company to Cook.

D. Gift the business to his grandchildren.

Recommend the best alternative for Cook and support your decision with two reasons specific to Cook's objectives. **Give** one drawback to the recommended strategy. For each alternative not recommended, **give** one reason it is not appropriate.

Answer 1:

The strategic buyer (A.) is best. 1) Cook receives the most cash to fund a diversified portfolio. 2) He is completely out of the business and can concentrate on his health and retirement.

The primary disadvantage is that the sale will trigger a capital gains tax liability.

Alternatives not selected: (B) The financial buyer from Cook's perspective is identical to the strategic buyer but pays less. (C) The MBO price is higher but misleading. It provides minimal up-front cash, and the future payments are not certain. In addition, Cook could end up having to go back to running the company. (D) Gifting provides no money to Cook to meet his objectives.

2. The previous strategic and financial buyers withdraw their offers, and Cook negotiates to sell 85% of the company to a private equity fund for GBP 44 million. Cook will retire and no longer work for the company or have any further authority. He will receive 90% of the GBP 44 million in cash and 10% in a promissory note payable in five annual installments (0% interest) starting in 2 years. The private equity company's exit strategy is to sell the company to a strategic or financial buyer in 3 to 5 years. Cook's remaining shares will be included in that sale.

    Assuming Cook's tax basis is zero and tax is due when cash is received at a 12% long-term gains rate, **calculate** Cook's first-year tax bill. **Discuss** any tax deferral benefits of the transaction to Cook.

Answer 2:

Cook's cash received in the first year is 90% of GBP 44 million, which is GBP 39.6 million. With a zero cost basis, the full GBP 39.6 million is taxable at 12% for GBP 4.752 million in taxes due the first year.

There is some deferral benefit because taxes owed on the remaining 10% of GBP 44 million will be due as the promissory note payments are received. The tax on the remaining 15% of the company owned by Cook will be due when the private equity company makes a subsequent sale, anticipated in 3 to 5 years.

3. How does this transaction change Cook's allocation between primary and surplus capital? How does it change his exposure to nonsystematic and total risk?

Answer 3:

After tax, Cook has 44 – 4.752 or GBP 39.248 million more in primary capital that can be used to build a diversified portfolio to support his objectives. Cook lowers his nonsystematic risk as he shifts funds from a concentrated private company to a diversified portfolio of marketable securities. His total risk, measured as standard deviation of the portfolio, should decline.

MANAGING CONCENTRATED INVESTMENT REAL ESTATE POSITIONS

LOS 11.k: Describe strategies for managing concentrated positions in real estate.

CFA® Program Curriculum, Volume 2, page 366

A single investment in a real estate asset can be large and constitute a significant portion of an investor's assets, bringing a high level of concentrated, property-specific risk. Real estate is generally illiquid and, if held for a long time, may have a significant unrealized taxable gain. A seller considering sale or monetization of a property should consider its current value relative to historical and expected value in the future, taxes on any transaction, availability of credit, and interest rate levels. Strategies to consider include:

*   **Mortgage financing** can be an attractive strategy to raise funds without loss of control of the property. With a **nonrecourse loan** the lender's only recourse is to seize the property if the loan is not paid. The borrower effectively has a put option on the property. If the property value falls below the loan amount, the borrower can default on the loan, keep the loan proceeds, and "put" the property to the lender. A loan on income-producing property could have a zero cash flow effect on the borrower if the property's income covers the interest on the loan and other property expenses.

*   A **donor-advised fund** or **charitable trust** can allow the property owner to take a tax deduction, gift more money to the charity, and influence the use of the donation. For example, an investor owns property worth $5,000,000 and would like to make a $5,000,000 contribution to a local hospital in exchange for having a new children's clinic named after his mother. The property was originally purchased for $3,000,000 and the investor has deducted $1,300,000 in depreciation expense, making the current tax basis $1.7 million. If sold for $5,000,000, the owner would owe gains taxes of 15% on a $2,000,000 capital gain and recapture taxes of 12% on $1,300,000. Instead the owner can contribute the property to a donor advised fund for the hospital, take a $5,000,000 tax deduction, and the tax-exempt hospital can sell or retain the property with no tax due. The gains and depreciation recapture are never taxed.

- A **sale and leaseback** can provide immediate funds while retaining use of the property. For example, a small business owner also owns a warehouse that he uses in his business. The owner sells the warehouse to a financial buyer who leases the warehouse to the business for 10 years with an option for the business to renew the lease for another 10 years. The sale price is 100% of fair market value. The owner secures funds to meet portfolio objectives, and his business retains use of a key asset. The rental payments on the lease are a deductible business expense.

LOS 11.l: Evaluate and recommend techniques for tax efficiently managing the risks of concentrated positions in publicly traded common stock, privately held businesses, and real estate.

CFA® Program Curriculum, Volume 2, page 340

Many other strategies and combinations of strategies are possible to deal with concentrated asset positions in public or private equity and investment real estate. This final LOS refers to the entire topic and the examples and illustrations found throughout. Questions presume you understand the basic ideas, terminology, and tax calculations covered here. Any specific question has to provide necessary details, tax rules, rates, and specifics needed to solve the question. Don't forget to consider the psychological and nonfinancial issues often associated with these positions.

KEY CONCEPTS

LOS 11.a

Concentrated positions can have consequences for return and risk. The assets may not be efficiently priced and, therefore, not generate a fair risk-adjusted return. Illiquid assets can be difficult and costly to exit or non-income producing. The risk in such assets is both systematic and company- or property-specific.

- **Systematic risk** is the risk that cannot be diversified away through holding a portfolio of risky assets. In the single factor CAPM, this would be beta. In multifactor models there will be more than one systematic risk.
- **Company-specific risk** is the nonsystematic risk of an investment that can be diversified away. It would derive from events that affect a specific investment but not the overall market. A corporate bankruptcy as a result of financial fraud would be an extreme example of company-specific risk. Nonsystematic risk increases the standard deviation of returns without additional expected return.
- **Property-specific risk** for real estate is the direct counterpart to company-specific risk for a company. It is the additional, diversifiable risk associated with owning a specific property.

LOS 11.b

There are three common objectives when managing a concentrated position:

1. **Reduce the risk** caused by the wealth concentration.

2. **Generate liquidity** to meet diversification or spending needs.

3. **Optimize tax efficiency** to maximize after-tax ending value.

Reducing the concentrated position is not appropriate for all clients. There are other client specific objectives and constraints to consider:

- **Restrictions on sale.** Stock ownership in a public company may be received by a company executive as part of a compensation package, with company expectations or regulatory requirements that the executive will hold the stock for a certain length of time.
- **A desire for control.** Majority ownership brings control over the business.
- **To create wealth.** An entrepreneur may assume high specific risk in expectation of building the value of the business and his wealth.
- **The asset may have other uses.** Real estate owned personally could also be a key asset used in another business of the owner.

LOS 11.c

Sale of a concentrated position may trigger a large capital gains **tax liability**. A large concentrated position is often accumulated and held for many years, resulting in a zero or low tax basis. A plan to defer, reduce, or eliminate the tax may be desirable.

Illiquidity and/or **high transaction** costs can be a factor even if there is no tax due. A public company trading with insufficient volume may require a price discount to sell. The expense of finding a buyer for a private business or real estate can be substantial. The intended use by the prospective buyer may affect the price.

LOS 11.d

Institutional and capital market constraints such as tax law can significantly affect the costs of selling or monetizing a concentrated position. Legal issues can depend on the form of asset ownership: sole proprietorship, limited partnership, limited company, or public stock. Other specific issues that may exist include:

- **Margin lending rules** limit the percentage of the asset's value that can be borrowed. Derivative positions can be used to reduce the risk of the asset position and increase the percentage of value that can be borrowed. Rule-based systems tend to be rigid and define the exact percentage that can be borrowed, while risk-based systems consider the underlying economics of the transaction.
- **Securities law and regulations** may define the owner as an "insider" (who is presumed to have material, nonpublic information) and impose restrictions, regulations, and reporting requirements on the position.
- **Contractual restrictions and employer mandates** may impose restrictions (such as minimum holding periods or blackout periods when sales may not be made) beyond those of securities law and regulation.
- **Capital market limitations** in the form of market structure and regulation can have indirect consequences. Monetization strategies commonly require over-the-counter derivative trades with a dealer to hedge the security's risk and increase the LTV ratio. To offer such trades, dealers must be able to hedge the risks they assume. This may be impossible. For example, if the asset is an initial public offering (IPO) or trades infrequently, there will not be a price history on which the dealer can base a hedge. Borrowing and shorting the underlying asset is often required for the dealer to hedge their risk. This is prohibited in some markets.

LOS 11.e

Cognitive biases are generally easier to overcome with education than are emotional biases.

Typical cognitive biases include conservatism in maintaining existing beliefs; confirmation in seeking support for what is already believed; illusion of control when the investor believes he can control what will happen to the investment; anchoring and adjustment in making decisions in reference to the current position held; and availability in making decisions based on ease of recalling information.

Typical emotional biases include overconfidence, familiarity, and illusion of knowledge leading the investor to overestimate the probability the investment will produce favorable returns; status quo bias and a failure to consider making changes; naive extrapolation of past results; endowment in expecting to be able to sell the asset for more than the investor would pay for it; and loyalty bias in retaining employer stock or feeling an obligation to retain an inherited position.

LOS 11.f

A **goal-based decision process** modifies traditional mean-variance analysis to accommodate the insights of behavioral finance theory. The portfolio is divided into tiers of a pyramid, or **risk buckets**, with each tier or bucket designed to meet progressive levels of client goals.

1. Allocate funds to a **personal risk bucket** to protect the client from poverty or a drastic decline in lifestyle. Low-risk assets such as money market and bank CDs, as well as the personal residence, are held in this bucket. Safety is emphasized, but a below-market return is likely.

2. Next, allocate funds to a **market risk bucket** to maintain the client's existing standard of living. Portfolio assets in this bucket would be allocated to stocks and bonds earning an expected market return.

3. Remaining portfolio funds are allocated to an **aspirational risk bucket** holding positions such as a private business, concentrated stock holdings, real estate investments, and other riskier positions. If successful, these high-risk investments could substantially improve the client's standard of living.

To implement a goal-based plan, the manager and client must determine the **primary capital** necessary to meet the goals of the first two risk buckets and the amount of any remaining **surplus capital** to meet aspirational goals. If a concentrated holding in the aspirational bucket leaves insufficient funds for the first two primary capital buckets, sale or monetization of the concentrated position must be discussed with the client.

LOS 11.g

Asset location determines the method of taxation that will apply. Location in a tax-deferred account would defer all taxes to a future date. In a taxable account, interest, dividends, and capital gains may be subject to different tax rates (or deferral possibilities in the case of when to realize capital gains).

Wealth transfer involves estate planning and gifting to dispose of excess wealth. The specific strategies used depend on the tax laws of the country and the owner's situation. Key considerations include:

1. Advisors can have the greatest impact by working with clients before significant unrealized gains occur. If there are no unrealized gains, there are generally no financial limitations on disposing of the concentrated position.

2. Donating assets with unrealized gains to charity is generally tax-free even if there are gains.

3. An **estate tax freeze** is a strategy to transfer future appreciation and tax liability to a future generation. This strategy usually involves a partnership or corporate structure. A gift tax would be due on the value of the asset when the transfer is made; however, the asset (including any future appreciation in value) will be exempt from future estate and gift taxes in the giver's estate. Any tax owed is "frozen," meaning paid or fixed near an initial value.

A five-step process can be used to make decisions for managing a concentrated position:

Step 1: Establish written objectives and constraints for the client. Nonfinancial issues such as retaining control of the asset and wealth transfer goals should be included in the document.

Step 2: Identify the techniques and strategies that best meet these objectives and constraints.

Step 3: Consider the tax advantages and disadvantages of each technique.

Step 4: Consider the other advantages and disadvantages of each technique.

Step 5: Document the decisions made.

Three broad techniques can be used to manage concentrated positions:

- **Sell the asset:** This will trigger a tax liability and loss of control.
- **Monetize the asset:** Borrow against its value and use the loan proceeds to accomplish client objectives.
- **Hedge the asset value:** Often done using derivatives to limit downside risk.

Hedging techniques often utilize over-the-counter (OTC) or exchange-traded derivatives.

LOS 11.h

Monetization generally involves receiving cash for a position without triggering a tax event. It is a two-step process:

Step 1: Hedge a large part of the risk in the position. This is often complicated by tax regulations.

Step 2: Borrow using the hedged position as collateral. The more effective the hedge, the higher the loan to value (LTV) ratio for the loan.

To illustrate potential monetization tools, consider an investor with 100,000 shares of PBL, which is trading for $50 per share. Four tools can be considered for hedging the asset.

1. **Short sale against the box.** The investor borrows 100,000 shares of PBL and sells them short. The investor is long and short the stock, a "riskless position" that is expected to earn the risk-free rate of return. The investor can use the short sale proceeds to meet portfolio objectives.

2. **Equity forward sale contract.** The investor enters a forward contract to sell the 100,000 shares of PBL. The investor has a known sale price and does not share in any upside or downside price movement of PBL from that contract price.

3. **Forward conversion with options.** A pair of options is used to hedge the stock position, selling calls and buying puts with the same strike price. A hedged ending value of $50 is established.

4. **Total return equity swap.** The investor enters a swap to pay the total return on the $5,000,000 of PBL and receives LIBOR.

Selecting the tool will depend on tax treatment. The goal is to select the tool that will not trigger an existing tax liability.

It is also possible to use **modified hedging** to minimize downside risk while retaining upside in the underlying position.

Protective puts (sometimes called **portfolio insurance**): The investor would purchase puts on 100,000 shares of PBL.

There are several ways to lower the cost of the protection:

- Purchase an out-of-the-money put.
- Use a pair of puts, buying a put with a higher strike price of X_H and selling a put with a lower strike price of X_L.
- Add exotic features to the option (not found in standard options). For example, a **knock-out put** expires prior to its stated expiration if the stock price rises above a specified level. This may reduce the protection, and the option will cost less.
- **No-cost** or **zero-premium collars** are a common way to lower initial cost, in this case to zero, by giving up some stock upside. A put is purchased and a call is sold with different strike prices selected so the premiums are equal.

Prepaid variable forwards (PVF) are economically similar to a collar and loan in one transaction. The owner of 100,000 PBL shares (currently priced at $50) could enter a PVF with a dealer. The dealer would pay the owner $45 per share now, equivalent to borrowing $45 per share. The loan will be repaid by delivering shares of PBL at a future date. The PVF could specify delivery of all 100,000 shares if PBL is below $50 per share on the repayment date but require delivery of a smaller number of shares if the price of PBL rises above $50.

LOS 11.i

A **mismatch in character**, two items in a strategy that trigger different tax treatments. A hedging strategy needs to consider any mismatch and select the tool or strategy that maximizes after-tax value for the investor.

Many tax codes treat employer stock options as an alternative to salary and tax any gains on the options as ordinary income. Hedging the options could produce a mismatch in character. As an example, a gain on stock options of $100,000 is taxed as ordinary income at 30%, while offsetting losses of $100,000 on the derivatives hedge are used to reduce long-term gains that are taxed at 10%. The tax of $30,000 is reduced by only $10,000 of capital gains tax not paid and only if the investor has $100,000 of capital gains to shelter. Whatever the strategy, it is essential to verify how it will be treated for tax purposes.

Yield enhancement with **covered calls** is another potential strategy. The owner of shares could sell call options. The premium income received can be viewed as either enhancing the income yield of the stock or protecting against the stock price decline.

Two **tax-optimization equity strategies** combine tax planning with investment strategy.

1. **Index tracking with active tax management**. Cash from a monetized concentrated stock position is invested to track a broad market index on a pretax basis and outperform the index on an after-tax basis. For example, if dividends are taxed at a higher rate than capital gains, the tracking portfolio could be structured with a lower dividend yield but higher expected price appreciation.

2. **A completeness portfolio** structures the other portfolio assets for greatest diversification benefit to complement (complete) the concentrated position. For example, if the concentrated position is an auto stock, the rest of the assets are selected to have low correlation with auto stocks such that the resulting total portfolio better tracks the return of the chosen benchmark.

Both of these tax-optimization strategies allow the investor to retain ownership of the concentrated position but may take time and sufficient other assets and funds to implement. Both strategies provide diversification while deferring the gain.

A perfect hedge is generally inappropriate if it will cause the underlying gain to be taxed or if the necessary derivatives do not exist. A **cross hedge** may be used instead. The investor who holds a large position in an auto stock but finds it cannot be shorted to create a hedge could consider three cross hedge possibilities:

1. Short shares of a different auto stock or another stock that is highly correlated with the concentrated position. The highly correlated short position will increase (decrease) in value to offset decreases (increases) in the auto stock.

2. Short an index that is highly correlated with the concentrated position. Shorting a different stock or an index will introduce company-specific risk. A negative event could affect the concentrated position but have no offsetting effect on the value of the short position.

3. Purchasing puts on the concentrated position is also considered a cross-hedge in that the put and stock are different types of assets.

Exchange funds are another possibility. Consider 10 investors, each of whom has a concentrated position in a single stock with a low cost basis. Each investor's position is in a different stock. The investors contribute their holdings into a newly formed exchange fund, and each now owns a pro rata share of the new fund. The investor now participates in a diversified portfolio and defers any tax event until shares of the fund are sold.

LOS 11.j

Privately held businesses may be more concentrated (the owner could own 100% of the business and it may be close to 100% of her assets), the standalone and nonsystematic risk tends to be very high, and the asset is generally illiquid.

Exit strategies for the business must be considered. Exit strategy analysis should consider:

- The value of the business.
- Tax rates that would apply to the potential exit strategies.
- Availability and terms of credit, as borrowing may be involved in financing any transaction.
- The buying power of potential purchasers.
- Currency values if the transaction involves foreign currencies.

The strategies to consider in managing a private business position include:

- **Strategic buyers** take a buy and hold perspective and generally offer the highest price to the seller. Strategic buyers seek to combine the business with an existing business of the buyer.
- A **financial buyer** or a **financial sponsor** is often a private equity fund planning to restructure the business, add value, and resell the business (typically in a 3 to 5 year period).
- **Recapitalization** is generally used for established but less mature (middle market) companies. In a **leveraged recapitalization** the owner may retain 20% to 40% of the equity capital and sell 60% to 80% of his shares back to the company. The owner continues to manage the business with a significant financial stake. A private equity firm could arrange the financing for the company to purchase the owner's stock. In exchange, the private equity firm receives equity in the company. This could be part of a *phased exit strategy* for the owner; sell and receive cash for a portion of his equity in the initial transaction, then participate in and sell his remaining shares when the private equity firm resells their position in a few years.
- In a **sale to (other) management or key employees**, the owner sells his position to existing employees of the company. There are drawbacks:
  - Generally the buyers will only purchase at a discounted price.
  - The buyers may lack financial resources and expect the existing owner to finance a significant portion of the purchase with a loan or a promissory note.
  - The promissory note is often contingent on future performance of the business with no assurance current employees or managers are capable of running the business and making the payments. This structure may be called a management buyout obligation (MBO) because existing managers buy the business in exchange for an obligation to pay for the business in the future.
  - Negotiation with employees to sell the business to them may fail and damage the continuing employer/employee relationship needed to continue operating the business.
- In a **divestiture, sale, or disposition of non-core business assets**, the owner sells nonessential business assets and then directs the company to use the proceeds to pay a large dividend to, or repurchase stock from, the owner. In either case, the owner receives cash while retaining the rest of the stock and control of the business.
- A **sale or gift to family members** could be structured with tax advantages such as the estate tax freeze or limited partnership valuation discounts discussed earlier. The existing owner could do an MBO. Unfortunately, neither a gift nor MBO sale provides the existing owner much immediate cash flow.
- A **personal line of credit secured by company shares**. The owner can borrow from the company and pledge her company stock as collateral.
- With an **initial public offering (IPO)** the owner sells a portion of his shares to the public and transforms the remaining shares into liquid public shares.
- With an **employee stock ownership plan (ESOP)**, the owner sells stock to the ESOP, which in turn sells the shares to company employees. In a leveraged ESOP, the company borrows the money to finance the stock purchase.

LOS 11.k

A single investment in a real estate asset can be large and constitute a significant portion of an investor's assets, bringing a high level of concentrated, property-specific risk. Real estate is generally illiquid and, if held for a long time, may have a significant unrealized taxable gain. A seller considering sale or monetization of a property should consider its current value relative to historical and expected value in the future, taxes on any transaction, availability of credit, and interest rate levels. Strategies to consider include:

- **Mortgage financing** can be an attractive strategy to raise funds without loss of control of the property. With a **nonrecourse loan** the lender's only recourse is to seize the property if the loan is not paid. The borrower effectively has a put option on the property. If the property value falls below the loan amount, the borrower can default on the loan, keep the loan proceeds, and "put" the property to the lender.
- A **donor-advised fund** or **charitable trust** can allow the property owner to take a tax deduction, gift more money to the charity, and influence the use of the donation.
- A **sale and leaseback** can provide immediate funds while retaining use of the property.

LOS 11.l

This final LOS refers to the entire topic and the examples and illustrations found throughout. Questions presume you understand the basic ideas, terminology, and tax calculations covered here. Don't forget to consider the psychological and nonfinancial issues often associated with these positions.

CONCEPT CHECKERS

1. For which individual would reducing specific risk be *most* appropriate?
   A. An owner who holds 100% of a private business. The position is 40% of his assets.
   B. An executive owning shares of the company where she is employed. The position is 40% of her assets.
   C. The spouse who inherited an investment real estate position. Real estate makes up 10% of the spouse's assets.

2. Which of the following owners of a concentrated position would *most likely* wish to retain control of the position as part of a monetization strategy?
   A. The owner of a rental apartment property.
   B. The owner of a warehouse who leases the building to a private company he owns.
   C. Young children who inherit concentrated positions in public stock of the company where their mother worked and private stock in the company their father founded.

3. Illiquidity is *least likely* a factor in which concentrated position?
   A. Real estate held a couple of years.
   B. A private company acquired at the bottom of a past economic cycle.
   C. Publicly traded shares of stock recently awarded to a company executive.

4. Capital market limitations tend to make monetization strategies more difficult in:
   A. less regulated markets where dealers are able to take long and short positions in a variety of instruments.
   B. highly competitive markets with few barriers to entry or exit and a large number of unregulated dealers.
   C. regulated markets where each dealer is confined to trading specific instruments, allowing them to specialize and offer higher liquidity in a narrower range of products.

5. John Smith owns three apartment buildings. He employees himself as the business manager and pays himself a market wage for this function. Being recently divorced, this job has brought stability to his life. Financially, he does not need the "manager salary," but the job makes him feel better about himself. His advisor points out to Smith that the apartment buildings are exposing Smith to high property-specific risk. Smith agrees and embraces the idea of selling or monetizing the properties. Which of the following behavioral biases is Smith exhibiting and how has the manager addressed the bias? Smith is exhibiting:
   A. a cognitive bias, and the manager educated Smith.
   B. an emotional bias, and the manager educated Smith.
   C. an emotional bias, and the manager accommodated Smith.

6.   An investor owns a personal residence worth $1,000,000 and mortgaged for
      $700,000, a warehouse worth $3,000,000 and mortgaged for $2,000,000, a
      private business worth $6,000,000, a savings account of $150,000, and a stock
      and bond portfolio of $6,000,000. The present value of the investor's primary
      and secondary objectives are $6 and $4 million, respectively. Based on this
      information, the investor's advisor should:
      A. suggest monetizing the home.
      B. suggest selling the personal business.
      C. not recommend monetizing the home or selling the personal business.

7.   The primary purpose of an estate tax freeze is to:
      A. minimize total taxes paid.
      B. minimize taxes currently due.
      C. shift the tax burden from the current owner of an asset.

8.   A prepaid variable forward is economically most similar to a:
      A. collar.
      B. protective put.
      C. covered call writing program.

9.   An investor seeking to hedge a stock position executes appropriate at-the-
      money call and put options. Premiums paid are SFR 100,000 and received are
      SFR 70,000. The investor's country taxes option premiums received as income
      at 40%, while option premiums paid increase the cost basis of the underlying.
      Realized capital gains are taxed at 10%. What is the effect on the investor's
      current-period tax return based only on the information provided and assuming
      the asset is not sold in this period?
      A. SFR 12,000.
      B. SFR 28,000.
      C. SFR 40,000.

10.   The primary issue for a manager advising the holder of a concentrated position
      in a private business versus in a public company is determining:
      A. the investment's value.
      B. the relevant tax rates to apply.
      C. evaluating the impact of currency values.

11.   The owner of a factory building who executes a sale and lease back has *most
      likely*:
      A. lost control of the property.
      B. effectively bought a protective put on the property.
      C. triggered a tax liability based on the present value of the transaction.

12.   The following question has three parts for a total of 18 minutes

Patricia and Steve Peters meet with their advisor to discuss financial goals in retirement. The Peters are both age 54. Steve is the president and sole owner of a private company he founded 15 years ago. They have prepared a list of goals to discuss:

- Steve plans to retire in one year. He wants to make a clean break from the business with no more responsibility. Instead, he will focus on charity work and travel with his wife.
- Within the next several years the Peters want to gift 10% of their wealth to a charity for disadvantaged children.
- Steve estimates his company is worth at least $45 million and has no doubt it will grow in the future, just as it has in the past. His cost basis is $4 million, and capital gains tax rates are 20%. The company pays no dividend.
- Their only other asset is a $5 million diversified stock portfolio.
- Their primary goal is to maintain their standard of living, and their advisor estimates this will require $25 million in assets today.

A. **Discuss** three potential problems in meeting their goals and related to the business Steve owns.

(6 minutes)

B. The Peters's ask their advisor to consider several potential ways to monetize the business. In specific, they are interested in (1) an employee buyout, 70% funded by Steve, with the firm's middle management team, (2) a leveraged recapitalization with a private equity firm to purchase 60% of Steve's equity, or (3) a sale to a financial buyer. Which strategy is most plausible given their objectives? **Assume** each transaction has the same value for the entire firm. **Explain** why.

(4 minutes)

C. Patricia asks the advisor to explain a short sale against the box and an exchange fund. **Explain** each briefly and **determine** which might be most suitable for the Peters.

(8 minutes)

For more questions related to this topic review, log in to your Schweser online account and launch SchweserPro™ QBank; and for video instruction covering each LOS in this topic review, log in to your Schweser online account and launch the OnDemand video lectures, if you have purchased these products.

ANSWERS – CONCEPT CHECKERS

1. **B**   A 10% position is not that concentrated, and the contribution to portfolio specific risk not that great. Of the two 40% positions, the owner has less reason to diversify and reduce specific risk because the owner has much more control and is more likely to want the risk as a way to build wealth. The executive has less control with the most need to diversify and reduce specific risk.

2. **B**   Using the building in a business he also owns gives the building owner a reason to retain control.

3. **C**   Public shares of stock have an ongoing, traded market. Real estate and a private company require going out and seeking a buyer. While the publicly traded stock may represent a concentrated position in the holdings of the executive, there is no reason to assume it is so large a portion of trading volume that there will be a liquidity problem for the stock.

4. **C**   Monetization frequently requires a dealer market with a variety of OTC instruments. Dealers will only offer such OTC instruments if the dealers can take offsetting positions in other instruments. This requires that dealers be able to move freely among instruments and take needed positions. Regulation that segments markets and impedes dealers makes it difficult for them to offer the necessary tools to implement monetization.

5. **A**   Smith exhibits both rational cognitive behavior (paying himself a market wage) and emotional feelings from employing himself to manage the property he owns. It is common that behavior exhibits both cognitive and emotional elements so the issue is selecting the best answer. There is no accommodation by the manager. The manager explains (educates) and Smith agrees and embraces the idea of selling. This is more reflective of easy to modify cognitive biases.

6. **C**   Neither is necessary. Either would increase the investor's allocation to their primary capital and decrease holdings in their surplus capital. However, the investors primary capital in the home less mortgage plus savings plus stocks and bonds is $1.0 − 0.7 + 0.15 + 6.0 = \$6.45$ million, which is more than the primary capital needs of \$6.0 million.

7. **C**   The primary purpose is to shift taxation of future appreciation and taxes on that appreciation to someone other than the current owner. The other items are certainly appropriate goals and the estate tax freeze might well be structured to aid in meeting those goals, but they are not its primary intent. The freeze might well trigger some tax bill being due now but shift other taxes to someone else payable at a future date and perhaps at a lower rate.

8. **A**   A prepaid variable forward is equivalent to hedging the risky asset with a collar (buying a put and selling a call) plus borrowing the value of the hedged position. The other two choices are less appropriate comparisons. A protective put consists of owning the asset and buying a put. A covered call program consists of owning the asset and selling calls. They are only partial descriptions of a collar and, hence, less complete answers.

9. **B**   SFR 70,000 is received this period and taxed at 40% for a tax due of SFR 28,000. The SFR 100,000 paid increases the cost basis of the underlying asset. When the asset is sold (not this period), that reduces any gain taxed at 10% by SFR 100,000, a potential tax savings of SFR 10,000. This is describing a mismatch in tax character.

10. **A** With a public company, a public share price should be available to determine its value. With a private company, value is more difficult to determine and subject to the intended use of the buyer and other factors. Currency and tax issues would have to be analyzed in either situation. Taxation might be more straightforward in selling stock of a public company but determining value is the most significant, time consuming, and significant issue in valuing a private company.

11. **C** This is a sale, and any tax liability is due. The present value of the transaction is most likely the sale price. The sale part of the sale leaseback does give up control, but the leaseback then allows the businessowner to continue using the asset and restores a measure of control, subject to the terms of the lease. A nonrecourse mortgage can be viewed as the equivalent of a protective put and would generally not be taxed as a sale.

12 **A.**
   - The portfolio lacks diversification with $45 million (90%) in Steve's business.
   - A private business is generally high risk with substantial specific risk.
   - Steve could be misestimating the business's value. He talks about "no doubt" and shows evidence of naive extrapolation of past results into future growth.
   - Even if the value is correct, when Steve retires, he will no longer receive a salary and the company pays no dividend. He will need to generate cash flow for living.

   B. Sale to the financial buyer is the best of the three. It is the only one that meets Steve's objective of a clean break from the business and provides ample cash to build a diversified portfolio in excess of their $25 million need. After taxes they should net:

   tax = ($45 − 4)(0.20) = $8.2 million

   After tax, this is $36.8 million plus the $5.0 million in stocks for $41.8 million.

   Even if the business value estimate is too high, this is a considerable cushion.

   The employee buyout is partially funded by Steve and leaves him at risk of going back to running the company. The private equity firm would expect Steve to retain a stake and role in the business.

   C. A short sale against the box is a hedging technique that then allows a loan equal to most of the value of the company to be taken out. It requires borrowing and shorting the company stock. It is more suited to a company with public shares.

   An exchange fund would involve Steve joining with other individuals who have concentrated positions in other companies. With each investor contributing their shares to the fund, all investors now own a portion of the resulting diversified portfolio. No tax liabilities are realized on the initial contribution of shares.

   Neither option makes sense for the Peters because both options leave Steve responsible for running the business. Both are more typically done with public companies.

The following is a review of the Private Wealth Management principles designed to address the learning outcome statements set forth by CFA Institute. Cross-Reference to CFA Institute Assigned Reading #12.

RISK MANAGEMENT FOR INDIVIDUALS

Study Session 5

EXAM FOCUS

This is an old topic with a substantially revised and expanded reading as of 2017. Be sure you recognize insurance is a risk management and transfer mechanism that in aggregate reduces the expected wealth of the users. Its primary purpose is to protect against adverse financial consequences. Life insurance can insure against premature death and annuities against living too long. Hence, they are risk management tools for the total wealth of the user.

Not every risk warrants the use of insurance. If a risk can be reduced or avoided, that is often the simplest and least expensive way to deal with it. In other cases, it may be best to just accept the risk. If neither of those approaches is acceptable, it may be possible to purchase insurance that will provide monetary compensation if the risk occurs. An investment manager may be able to help clients determine the best approach to a given situation and advise how that solution can change over the client's stages of life.

TOTAL WEALTH

LOS 12.a: Compare the characteristics of human capital and financial capital as components of an individual's total wealth.

CFA® Program Curriculum, Volume 2, page 382

An investor's **total wealth** is composed of both human capital and financial capital. **Human capital (HC)** is the discounted present value of expected future labor income. **Financial capital (FC)** is the sum of all the other assets of an individual. This includes financial items such as stocks, bonds, and alternative investments as well as personal items such as a home, car, and other physical assets.

Expected defined benefit (DB) plan benefits for an individual have elements of both HC and FC. DB benefits are deferred labor income, which suggests treating them as HC, but they have already been earned and paid for with past labor to provide future cash flow. This is more analogous to buying a financial asset (FC) and receiving future cash flows. An individual's expected DB plan benefits are best considered as part of the individual's FC.

 Professor's Note: A deleted CFA reading categorized DB plan benefits as HC, but did not dwell on the issue. This current reading correctly acknowledges DB plan benefits have blended characteristics but chooses the FC classification. Stick with the current reading's classification of FC.

Human Capital

Valuing **human capital** is analogous to valuing a stock or bond. Value is the discounted PV of future cash flows. The discount rate applied to the future cash flows is related to the riskiness of the cash flows. Higher risk employment requires a higher discount rate and all else the same reduces the value of the HC. Examples include high yield bond managers and downhill ski racers. Lower risk employment is discounted at lower discount rates. Examples include union employment and tenured college professors.

While the valuation is simple in theory, HC can only be estimated. The estimate requires multiple assumptions: projected future earnings and their real rate of growth, mortality rates to determine the probability the earnings will be realized, real and nominal risk-free discount rates, plus appropriate risk premiums to add to the real discount rate. All of these variables are subject to change over time.

Example 1: Estimating HC

Alex Hamilton is 62 and expected to retire in 3 years. His current annual wage is 100,000 and expected to increase 4% per year. The risk-free discount rate is 3%, and his continued employment is considered very risky. A 10% risk premium is assumed. Using this information and the survival probabilities in the table, calculate his HC.

Increase earnings by 4% per year for the 3 years of employment, probability weight the earnings, and discount to the present value (PV) at 13% per year. 13% is the risk-free rate plus the risk premium.

Year	Probability of Life	Projected Wage	Probability Weighted	PV
1	98%	104,000	101,920	90,195
2	98%	108,160	105,997	83,011
3	97%	112,486	109,111	75,619
4	97%	0		
5	96%	0		
			HC =	248,825

Financial capital is the value of all other assets owned by the individual. It includes current assets such as money market assets that may be consumed within the next year, personal assets such as a car or furniture that are likely to be consumed over time, and investment assets that may appreciate over time. Some assets such as real estate may have both consumption and investment characteristics. Investment assets include both publicly traded marketable assets, which are relatively easy to value, and non-publicly traded. The later include:

- Real estate (other than publicly traded REITs). A home is often an individual's largest single asset and may also be highly leveraged. If leveraged with recourse, default on the loan allows the lender to claim other assets of the individual as well. On a non-recourse loan, the lender can only seize the mortgaged property.

- Annuities (see further discussion later) are economically equivalent to a private defined benefit plan in that they pay a continuing income stream. Their value should include some discount of future cash flows to reflect the potential the payer may default.
- Cash-value life insurance (see further discussion later) is life insurance with a provision to borrow or take some present value portion of the future payout prior to death (which reduces the ultimate payout).
- Business assets or private equity may represent a substantial portion of wealth for some self-employed individuals. This can lead to concentrated risk exposures in the investor's wealth.
- Collectables (such as paintings and book collections) often involve substantial transaction costs and can have elements of personal consumption and utility as well as investment value.
- Pensions can be a significant non-marketable financial asset for some. The pension could be from a private or government entity. The vested portion of the pension already belongs to the individual and can be valued as the discounted value of benefits to be received (PV). The discounting must also include a mortality projection if payments are contingent on the beneficiary being alive (which is typical). The discount rate will reflect the riskiness of the plan portfolio and sponsor as well as any other guarantees or insurance of payment. Future payments of the pension may be indexed for inflation. Typically government pensions will be less risky.

FINANCIAL STAGES OF LIFE

LOS 12.b: Discuss the relationships among human capital, financial capital, and net wealth.

CFA® Program Curriculum, Volume 2, page 386

Net wealth is the sum of the individual's FC and HC less any liabilities owed by the individual. A typical individual might start an employment career with high HC and low FC. As remaining work career decreases with age, HC generally declines over time while FC increases as the individual saves and invests.

LOS 12.c: Discuss the financial stages of life for an individual.

CFA® Program Curriculum, Volume 2, page 392

Education. The individual gains knowledge and skills through formal and informal education and apprenticeship. There is minimal emphasis on saving or risk management.

Early Career. The individual enters the workforce, often starts a family, and assumes other personal responsibilities. Saving may be difficult and life insurance may be needed to insure substantial HC against death and the cessation of work income to meet continuing financial obligations to the family.

Career Development. After becoming established in a career, job skills can continue to expand and upward mobility increases. Financial obligations often increase to fund the college education of children. Successful individuals generally build FC and retirement savings over time.

Peak Accumulation. FC accumulation is typically greatest in the decade before retirement. Earnings and the need to accumulate funds for retirement are high. Financial obligations to educate the children are ceasing. Investment risk may start being reduced in anticipation of retirement. Career risk can also be high as it can be more difficult to find equivalent employment in the event of unplanned job loss.

Preretirement. Emphasis continues to be on accumulating FC for retirement, beginning to reduce investment risk, and tax planning for retirement.

Early Retirement. Individuals adjust to a new lifestyle. For those with FC and good health, expenses could increase as they make use of the free time. The portfolio emphasis is on managing the portfolio so it will last for the remaining lifetime.

Late Retirement. This stage is highly unpredictable. Individuals face longevity risk (out living their assets), increasing health care expenses could be an issue, and cognitive functions used to make decisions can decline.

In all stages, there can be unpredicted needs for health care and/or to care for family members.

THE INDIVIDUAL'S BALANCE SHEET

LOS 12.d: Describe an economic (holistic) balance sheet.

CFA® Program Curriculum, Volume 2, page 394

The **economic (holistic) balance sheet** extends the traditional balance sheet assets to include HC. Liabilities are extended to include consumption and bequest goals. This more complete economic view allows better planning of resource consumption to meet remaining lifetime goals. Example 2 provides an example of an economic balance sheet. Note that a defined contribution plan balance with an explicit balance would likely have been included in the traditional balance sheet, but DB plan estimated PV likely would not.

Example 2: Holistic Balance Sheet

(The items in bold italics are those not found on a traditional balance sheet.)

Assets (in thousands):		Liabilities (in thousands):	
Financial		Short-term debt	175
Current assets	500	Home mortgage	500
Investment assets	1,500		
Non-marketable		*Primary capital to fund*	*3,500*
Home	750	*lifetime expenses*	
DC plan balance	1,450		
Private pension	*40*	*Planned bequests*	*1,000*
Government pension	*450*		
Human			
Future labor income	*250*		
Total Assets	4,940	Total Liabilities	5,175

Based only on the traditional balance sheet, the assets of 4,200,000 well exceed explicit debts of 675,000, while the holistic balance sheet shows negative net wealth of 235,000. This suggests consumption and bequest plans are unrealistic. However, it is generally more difficult to value the additional items on the economic balance sheet, and the negative net wealth could be an estimation error. There could also be missing economic assets such as expected inheritance that need to be included. If net wealth is actually negative, it indicates ultimate spending plans will eventually have to change. The relatively low amount of HC (not pension benefits) suggests the individual is near retirement.

For many individuals, total wealth (HC + FC) as well as FC will peak near retirement. Both will then be drawn down in retirement.

The composition of the balance sheet is likely to change over the individual's life cycle. HC is likely the dominant asset for younger individuals. Over time, HC will decline as remaining work life shortens. FC should increase as the individual saves and invests in FC. Net wealth can be positive or negative based on the adequacy of savings versus projected needs. Early in the life cycle assets such as real estate and other tangible assets may dominate the balance sheet. Other FC is then likely to increase in the later stages of life as funds are saved and invested. In early retirement, pension benefits are the dominant asset for many. For wealthier individuals pension benefits may be relatively smaller and FC may be relatively larger.

RISK EXPOSURES

Risk management for individuals requires:

- Specifying the objective, which is to maximize household welfare (utility).
- Identifying the risks to FC and HC.

- Evaluating and managing those risks through:
  - Risk avoidance: choose actions to avoid the chance of the loss occurring.
  - Risk reduction: choose actions that reduce the likelihood or amount of the loss.
  - Risk transfer: use insurance products to transfer the loss to others.
  - Risk retention (self-insurance): maintain sufficient assets to absorb the loss.
- Monitoring results and adjusting as needed.

LOS 12.e: Discuss risks (earnings, premature death, longevity, property, liability, and health risks) in relation to human and financial capital.

CFA® Program Curriculum, Volume 2, page 400

The typical risks for individuals include:

Earnings risk (insure with disability insurance) refers to loss in HC. Job loss and other career disruptions can reduce HC and may even lead to the need to consume FC prematurely. Some jobs are inherently more risky than others. A logger has a higher probability of death or injury and resulting loss of HC. A high risk security manager may have a higher risk of job termination. Other jobs are at risk of a location transfer, which could disrupt the HC of a spouse whose job is less mobile and reduce the household's total wealth. Other jobs are cyclical, and income for the self-employed can be less certain.

Premature death risk (insure with life insurance) can be a serious risk early in the career when substantial HC could be lost. In addition, it may cause unexpected expenses that consume limited FC of the survivors.

Longevity risk (insure with annuities) is the opposite of premature death risk as individuals who live too long are at risk of outliving their FC. The determination of how much capital is required for retirement is complicated and risky. A given individual's lifespan is highly uncertain. The return on portfolio assets, rate of inflation, the inclusion or exclusion of inflation adjustment in DB payouts, distribution needs, and other income sources must be estimated. Mortality tables and Monte Carlo simulations are generally used to quantify longevity risk.

Property risk (insure with property insurance) refers to sudden loss in value of physical property (FC). A house or car can be damaged or lost in a flood, a direct loss. This can also trigger unexpected needs such as temporary living or transportation expense or lost income such as rental income, leading to consumption of FC and reduction in total wealth. The loss of business property could reduce FC and also HC of the owner if the property is necessary to generate business income.

Liability risk (insure with liability insurance) refers to being legally responsible for damages and a reduction in FC. The driver of a car may be responsible for damages or loss of life caused by an accident.

Health risk (insure with health insurance) can lead to direct loss of FC to pay illness or injury related expenses. It can reduce HC through diminished or inability to work. It can also affect future expense needs and life expectancy. Coverage for health risk varies widely by country. Government and/or private insurance may provide for short-term but not for long-term care.

Basic Life Insurance Terminology

- Benefits or face amount. The future payout (e.g., $1,000,000). The terms may specify payout as a lump sum or an annuity.
- Premium. The cost of the insurance.
- Cash value. What the owner can withdraw before payout, which reduces or terminates final payout.
- Paid up. A date when the insurance is fully paid for and no additional premiums are required.
- Limitations. Restrictions on the payout of the insurance amount (e.g., misrepresentation of the health status of the insured leading to no payment).
- Contestability period. Time period for the insurance company to investigate or deny payment of the claim.
- Identity of the insured.
- Policy owner. Responsible for making premium payments, often the insured. If the owner is not the insured, he must have an insurable interest in the insured. In other words, the owner must have a vested interest in the continued life of the insured and not simply be speculating on the insured's death.
- Beneficiaries. Receivers of the payout.
- Premium schedule. Amount and frequency of payments.
- Riders. Additional provisions included in the policy.
- Modifications. Allowable changes that can be made to the policy.

LOS 12.f: Describe types of insurance relevant to personal financial planning.

CFA® Program Curriculum, Volume 2, page 405

Life insurance protects the survivors from the adverse financial consequences of the insured's premature death. The optimal amount of insurance depends on the cost of the insurance and the loss in value to the survivors caused by the death. The insurance can also provide liquidity to meet death and estate expenses. This is more important if the other estate assets are illiquid. Some life insurance provides tax benefits by accumulating cash value on a tax-sheltered basis.

Life insurance can be grouped in two main types: temporary and permanent. Both require continuing payment of premiums to remain in effect. The premium is often paid annually or on some other designated basis.

Professor's Note: Insurance terminology is not mutually exclusive. Think of term insurance as pure insurance. What is the cost to charge all members of a large group today such that the funds will cover the payout on those who die this year? In simple terms, if the group includes 100 people, probability of death for any one is 1%, and the payout on death is GBP100,000, charge each individual GBP1,000. For permanent insurance, start with a premium today (higher than GBP1,000) that, if held constant and invested, will for the life of the group provide sufficient funds to pay the death benefit for all members of the group. A 5-year level payment term policy will have some of the characteristics of permanent insurance, but the price will be closer to pure annual insurance. First we discuss the general differences in life insurance type and then we get further into the pricing issue.

Temporary (term) insurance covers only a designated period such as 1, 5, or 20 years. The cost can be fixed or increasing over the designated period. The policy then ceases at the end of the period unless it includes a provision to renew the policy. Term insurance is less costly than permanent insurance because the mortality risk is lower for the insurance company as the individual's risk of dying increases later in life (after the insurance ceases). The mortality risk also means term insurance for younger individuals and for shorter time periods will cost less than for older individuals and longer periods, all other factors the same.

Permanent insurance is more costly and lasts for the life of the insured. The premium (cost) per period is usually fixed, and the policy builds value as the premium exceeds the pure cost of insurance in the initial years. In later years, this built up value covers the increasing cost that would be paid for pure (term) insurance. Permanent insurance can be categorized as whole life or universal insurance.

Whole life typically has a fixed annual premium payment. The policy continues and the policy cannot be canceled by the insurance company as long as premiums are paid. The non-cancelability makes purchase at a young age more desirable as new insurance may be unavailable or much more expensive if the insured person's health deteriorates. The policy may also reach a fully paid status in later years and require no further premiums. Participating whole life shares in company profits and may increase in value more quickly.

Universal life is similar in concept but with more flexibility. The premium payment can be increased or decreased to increase or decrease the amount of insurance and/or the rate at which cash value grows. There may be investment choices for where the premiums are invested. Premium payments can be discontinued and the insurance continues (a non-forfeiture clause) as long as the cash value and earnings on the cash value are sufficient to pay the pure (term) cost of insurance each period.

Life insurance policies can include riders, which provide additional benefits. Accidental death and dismemberment (AD&D) increases the payout if the insured dies or is dismembered in an accident. Accelerated death benefits (ADB) pay part or all of the insurance amount if the insured is terminally ill. A viatical settlement allows the sale of the policy to a third party. This provides immediate funds to the beneficiaries. The third party becomes the policy beneficiary and is responsible for future premium payments. Guaranteed insurability allows the purchase of more insurance regardless of future health. Waiver of premium keeps the insurance in force without premium payments if the insured becomes disabled.

LOS 12.g: Describe the basic elements of a life insurance policy and how insurers price a life insurance policy.

CFA® Program Curriculum, Volume 2, page 405

Life insurance pricing is simple in concept but complex in application. It is a large time value of money problem. The insurance company must charge sufficient premiums such that the money after investing the premiums is sufficient to pay the policy benefits, cover the company's costs, and leave a profit. The company is applying the law of large numbers. The remaining term of life for any one individual is highly uncertain, but predictable in aggregate for a large group. The pricing model can be broken down into three issues:

Mortality estimates. Mortality tables are built to reflect past experience and future projections of mortality. Probability of death (1 – probability of life) can be refined and based on age, health, gender, and lifestyle choices. An 80-year-old male smoker in poor health who sky dives will pay more than a 40-year-old healthy woman with safer hobbies. The insurance company will gather information regarding the insurability of the applicant and may employ third party investigators and medical professionals to assess the risk factors. The company's goal is to avoid adverse selection and undercharging for the risks assumed.

Net premium. Based on the assumed mortality rates, the company estimates the net premiums to charge for insurance based on an assumed discount rate. The discount rate is also the assumed rate of return on investing the premiums. At that discount rate, the premiums must be sufficient such that the PV of the premiums and payouts are equal (i.e., the premiums must be sufficient to pay future benefits).

Load. The load plus net premium is the **gross premium** charged for the insurance. The load must cover the company's operating cost and expenses for writing the policy. This can include a sales commission to sell the policy and cost of any medical tests to determine insurability. Stock companies are owned by shareholders and must include a planned profit to provide a return to shareholders. Mutual companies are owned by the policyholders but must also charge more than the net premium to cover risk. If costs are eventually less than expected, some policies allow the policyholders to receive a dividend (which is technically a return of premium).

For a simple one-year term insurance policy, the application is relatively simple. Risk is limited as only one year of variables must be considered to estimate the net premium for pure insurance. Load will also be fairly simple to estimate. If the policy is renewed the following year, a new gross premium will be calculated. For a level payment multi-year term policy, the process is slightly more complex. The level premium will be higher than the year 1 and less than the year 5 premium for annual term. The premium is conceptually a weighted average of five sequential one-year term premiums. In reality, it should be higher as the company is at greater risk; it must project the relevant variables for the five-year period and cannot change the premium each year. See Figures 1 and 2.

Figure 1: Annual Term Insurance for $100,000

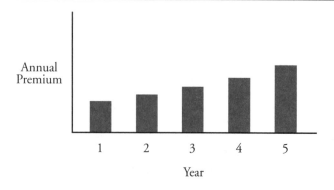

Figure 2: 5-Year Term Insurance for $100,000

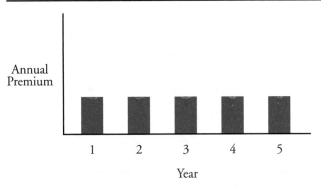

Permanent insurance pricing extends the same concepts, but with more uncertainty as the ultimate life expectancy of the insured individual has to be considered. The longer time period puts the insurance company at greater risk in correctly estimating mortality rate, discount rate (return on invested premiums), and expenses. These factors will make the initial premium higher. In addition, many such policies include a buildup of cash value that the policyholder can access before policy payout. The cash buildup is created by charging an even higher premium. Such policies typically include a paid up date when return on cash value is sufficient to pay future costs of insurance and premiums cease. See Figure 3.

Figure 3: Insurance Versus Cash Value in Permanent Insurance for $100,000

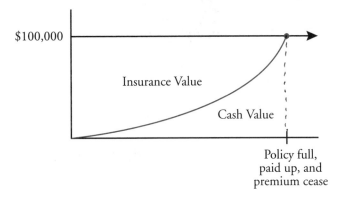

Comparing cost between insurance policies becomes more difficult as policy complexity increases. For annual term, when all else is the same, the lowest premium is lowest cost. For permanent insurance, the number of variables makes comparison complex as it is highly unlikely any two policies will be the same. Two common approaches are the **net payment cost index** and **net surrender cost index**. Both require an assumed age of death for the insured and a discount rate. The second also requires a cash value projection.

Professor's Note: There is no direct LOS for these methods. However, they are a direct application of time value of money concepts. They are not unreasonable questions. You should also be able to reason through implications if a case clearly favors one policy over another, such as lower premium payment and higher dividend payment, or a lower index value.

To illustrate the issues, assume a 25-year time horizon till death and a 5% discount rate on a $100,000 insurance policy.

- Policy XX has annual beginning of year premiums of $2,000 and an assumed annual end of year dividend (return of premium) of $500. Terminal 25 year cash value projected (by the insurance company) to be $25,000.
- Policy YY has annual beginning of year premiums of $2,200 and an assumed annual end of year dividend (increase in cash value) of $550. Terminal 25 year cash value projected (by the insurance company) to be $27,500.

*Professor's Note: **Be careful with the following calculations.** Some steps require use of the **ordinary annuity (payments at end of period)** settings for your calculator. Other steps require the **annuity due (payments at start of period)** setting. If you do not use the proper setting at each step, your answer will be wrong.*

Most CFA calculations use ordinary annuity. I keep my calculator set on ordinary annuity and only reset it to annuity due if required for a specific calculation. Then I reset it back to ordinary annuity. Many calculators show a small note on the screen of "beg" or "end" to show the mode.

Net payment cost index assumes the individual dies at the end of the horizon and cash value is not considered. It is often used if the insurance is projected to be paid up at that point:

Step 1: Compute the FV of the premiums paid, an annuity due (premiums paid at start of year).

XX: 2,000 PMT, 5 i_p, 25 n, FV = 100,227

YY: 2,200 PMT, 5 i_p, 25 n, FV = 110,250

Step 2: Compute the FV of the dividends, an ordinary annuity (dividends at end of year).

XX: 500 PMT, 5 i_p, 25 n, FV = 23,864

YY: 550 PMT, 5 i_p, 25 n, FV = 26,250

Step 3: The 25-year FV cost of insurance is Step 1 – Step 2.

XX: 100,227 – 23,864 = 76,363

YY: 110,250 – 26,250 = 84,000

Step 4: Annuitize this FV difference for the annual cost. Use an annuity due to match the requirement to pay premiums at the start of the year.

XX: 76,363 FV, 5 i_p, 25 n, PMT = 1,524

YY: 84,000 FV, 5 i_p, 25 n, PMT = 1,676

Step 5: Divide by $1,000 of insurance policy amount to index the annual cost ($100,000 / $1,000 = 100 units of insurance).

XX: $1,524 / 100 = $15.24 per $1,000 of insurance per year.

YY: $1,676 / 100 = $16.76 per $1,000 of insurance per year.

Net surrender cost index assumes the individual terminates the policy (insurance ceases) at the end of the horizon and the cash value is received. Step 1 and Step 2 are the same. Step 3 will be different and have consequences for Step 4 and Step 5.

Step 1: Compute the FV of the premiums paid, an annuity due (premiums paid at start of year).

XX: 2,000 PMT, 5 i_p, 25 n, FV = 100,227

YY: 2,200 PMT, 5 i_p, 25 n, FV = 110,250

Step 2: Compute the FV of the dividends, an ordinary annuity (dividends at end of year).

XX: 500 PMT, 5 i_p, 25 n, FV = 23,864

YY: 550 PMT, 5 i_p, 25 n, FV = 26,250

Step 3: The 25-year FV cost of insurance is Step 1 – Step 2 less the projected cash value.

XX: 100,227 – 23,864 – 25,000 = 51,363

YY: 110,250 – 26,250 – 27,500 = 56,500

Step 4: Annuitize this FV difference for the annual cost. Use an annuity due to match the requirement to pay premiums at start of year.

XX: 51,363 FV, 5 i_p, 25 n, PMT = 1,025

YY: 56,500 FV, 5 i_p, 25 n, PMT = 1,127

Step 5: Divide by $1,000 of insurance policy amount to index the annual cost ($100,000 / $1,000 = 100 units of insurance).

XX: $1,025 / 100 = $10.25 per $1,000 of insurance per year.

YY: $1,127 / 100 = $11.27 per $1,000 of insurance per year.

Professor's Note: Many insurance regulators require companies to provide such standardize cost comparisons. Even then, the estimate of true cost depends on the assumptions. Of course, if you can precisely plan when you will die, this would be easier, but that's not a very practical solution.

Estimating the amount of insurance needed is another task. The starting point is estimating the remaining HC (PV of future earnings) of the insured plus expenses associated with the death and the PV of any other legacy goals (financial objectives that would have been met in the absence of premature death). The need may be lower as only expenses of the survivors, not the insured, are relevant.

Other Types of Insurance:

- **Disability income insurance** provides partial replacement of the insured's job income if the job is lost.
- **Property insurance** provides compensation for losses in value of real property. **Homeowners insurance** covers the home, and **automobile insurance** covers the car.
- **Health and medical insurance** covers health care expense.
- **Liability insurance** covers losses if the insured is found legally responsible for damages to another.

ANNUITIES

A basic annuity is a one-time premium payout in exchange for fixed payouts received for the life of the annuitant. The initial premium is the investment. When the annuity ends, the payouts cease. The initial investment is not returned at the end. The overly simple analogy is to a level payout amortizing mortgage, the payouts are interest and a return of principal. The complication in an annuity is how long the insured's life will last. Basic terminology includes:

- The **insurer** collects the premium and makes the future payouts. (The insurer is often an insurance company, the company.)
- The **annuitant** receives the **annuity payouts** in the future.
- The contract **owner** pays the premium to purchase the annuity and is usually the annuitant.
- The **beneficiary** receives any remaining value of the contract at death of the annuitant. In many cases, there is no beneficiary as payouts cease at death of the annuitant.
- The **premium**, which is normally paid once at purchase, could also be referred to as the value of the contract. **The premium paid to the company is the price of the annuity.** However, the convention is to keep the premium constant and adjust the stated annual payout. This means that a **lower/higher quoted payout to the annuitant is equivalent to a higher/lower price for the annuity.**

LOS 12.h: Discuss the use of annuities in personal financial planning.

CFA® Program Curriculum, Volume 2, page 422

Annuities are the economic opposite of life insurance: for life insurance, pay an annual premium and receive one payoff at death to insure against premature death; for annuities, pay once and receive payouts back for life to insure against longevity risk. Both products spread the risk of when any one individual will die across a large pool of individuals.

Annuities take many forms. A DB pension plan from a private company or government that pays for the life of the retiree is a form of annuity. Annuities can also be purchased and used to supplement or replace DB plan payouts. While the potential permutations and features are not limited, annuities can generally be classified as deferred versus immediate and fixed versus variable. Usually, the annuity is illiquid once purchased, though it is possible there can be provisions to liquidate early or sell the future payout stream to a third party.

In a **deferred annuity**, the annual receipts start at a deferred future date. **Deferred variable annuities** are common and allow the owner to select from a list of investment options. Higher/lower investment returns will increase/decrease the future payouts to be received. While often compared to mutual funds, the investment choices are more limited and expenses are high. The annuity can also include an insurance feature with a guarantee of some minimum payouts received back. Otherwise, the payouts would just cease at death of the recipient. The investor may also be able to cash out the value and terminate the annuity at a future date (subject to a surrender charge that reduces what they receive). Unless the individual pays for additional features, the variable annuity does not guarantee any minimum future payouts.

Deferred fixed annuities pay a fixed benefit for life that starts at a defined future date. The longer the delay between initial premium paid and start of payouts received, all else the same, the lower the cost of the annuity, as the company can invest and increase the funds available before making payouts on the annuity.

An **advanced life deferred annuity** is a relatively lower cost way to hedge the longevity risk of the annuitants outliving their other assets. Like most fixed and variable annuities, they require an immediate premium payout at purchase. Like deferred fixed annuities, the payouts are fixed, but the delay period before they start is long, often age 80 or 85 for the annuitant. The low premium reflects three factors. First, the long delay before payouts begin allows the company a longer period to invest and grow the premium's value. Second, the period of payouts will be shorter as the life expectancy of the older annuitant will be shorter when payouts do begin. Third, a greater proportion of the annuitants will die before they receive any payouts.

Immediate variable annuities start payouts immediately, but the amount of the future payouts is indexed to the performance of some reference asset, such as a stock index. As the reference asset increases/decreases, the payouts increase/decrease. **Immediate fixed annuities** begin payout immediately and the payout amount does not change.

The features of the annuity and the annuitant's status will affect the payout. Typical features include:

- Life annuity with payouts for the life of the annuitant.
- Period certain annuity with payouts for a specified time period.
- Life annuity and period certain with payouts for the longer of the two periods.
  - Life annuity with refund is similar in concept but specifies a refund amount if a specified minimum payout amount has not been received before death of the annuitant.
- Joint life annuity specifies payout continues as long as at least one of the annuitants is alive.

Consider an initial $100,000 investment in (premium paid for) an annuity.

- A 60-year-old female might receive 5,900 per year for life on an immediate fixed annuity, while a 60-year-old male might receive 6,300. The higher payout for the male reflects the statistical probability he will not live as long, and total payouts made by the company will be less.
- Annual payouts for an 80-year-old female or male will be higher, say 14,300 and 15,200 respectively. This reflects that their remaining life expectancy is shorter, reducing the number of payouts the insurance company is likely to make.
- A rider specifying payouts be made for at least 10 years reduces the annual payout, reflecting higher cost to the insurance company. It no longer benefits from cessation of payouts to annuitants that live less than 10 years.
- A joint life provision that payouts continue as long as either member of a couple is alive will lower the annual payout on any of the previous annuities. Statistically, this increases the total number of payouts as the company pays as long as at least one member is alive.
- Adding a, or increasing the deferral period until start of payouts would increase the annual payout, as the company can keep the premium invested longer and it reduces the number of payouts excepted to be made.
- Generally, in any of the above policies, the initial annual payout on a variable annuity will be lower than a fixed annuity, but the expected total payout amount can be higher for the variable annuity based on the performance of the reference asset. Of course, there is no guarantee of this; it depends on the performance of the reference asset.

Professor's Note: It should be occurring to you that the number and combination of features on insurance products is infinite. Why would that surprise you? Think product proliferation. The companies have every incentive to offer a vast menu of options to attract customers. Do not imagine the CFA material can produce a comprehensive analysis model. It does not exist. That does not mean a question cannot be written that can be solved by applying the basic economic and time value of money concepts being discussed; just think the case facts through logically.

LOS 12.i: Discuss the relative advantages and disadvantages of fixed and variable annuities.

CFA® Program Curriculum, Volume 2, page 422

The **volatility** of future benefits is obviously different. Lower risk investors may prefer the certainty of fixed payouts, and higher risk investors may prefer the potential for increasing variable payouts.

Flexibility often differs. Fixed annuities are generally irrevocable and payouts cannot be changed. In variable annuities the future value of the annuity and payouts are linked to the performance of a reference asset. Variable annuities are more likely to allow withdrawal of the funds at subsequent market value (after surrender fees for withdrawal).

Future market expectations will affect the choice. Payouts on a fixed annuity are largely determined by initial bond market interest rates. If rates are expected to increase, delay in purchase can lead to higher payouts on annuities purchased later.

However, the choice is not so simple and requires a consideration of **mortality credits**. Some individuals will die before, and some after, their expected lifespan. Annuitants who die earlier collect fewer payouts, effectively subsidizing those who die later. That is why insurance is called risk sharing or transfer. This concept is called mortality credits. All other factors the same, mortality credits make annuities less costly to purchase at a younger age. (Think of it as the annuitants who live longer earn a mortality credit paid by those who do not live as long and collect fewer payouts). However, the effect of mortality credits is difficult to see directly because other factors are also often changing.

As a simple example, consider a 60 year old who pays $100,000 for a lifetime annual payout of $5,000. Waiting to age 65 for the purchase might produce an annual payout of $6,000. Waiting appears to be economically beneficial, but this is deceptive. If market conditions are unchanged, the payout amount is reduced by mortality credits but increased by the fact the older individual who waits to purchase will statistically receive fewer payouts.

An easier way to see the effect of the mortality credit is to look at a deferred annuity for the 60 year old, which would start payouts at age 65. The initial payout could be $6,450. This is clearly better than if the individual waits until age 65 to purchase and immediately start receiving $6,000. It is the same individual, so the total payouts to be made are the same. Even here, two factors are at work. The annual payout amount, if purchased at age 60 to start payouts at age 65, is higher because the company can invest the premium for 5 years before making payouts at 65, and it is also higher because some of the annuitants will not live to age 65 to collect anything. Those who die earlier have subsidized and paid a mortality credit to those who live longer than age 65 and collect payouts.

> *Professor's Note: While the effect of mortality credits can be difficult to see directly, the concept is fundamental to insurance risk sharing and pricing.*
>
>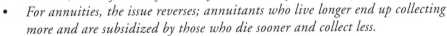
>
> - *Just remember that for life insurance the ultimate cost is lower if you die and the beneficiaries collect the one-time fixed payout sooner, while those who live longer end up paying more for the same payout. Admittedly, who wants to die sooner! (Be careful that your beneficiaries want you around for a long time.)*
> - *For annuities, the issue reverses; annuitants who live longer end up collecting more and are subsidized by those who die sooner and collect less.*
>
> *While this is a bit morbid, rest assured the insurance company is not stupid and fully understands all the implications of mortality tables, future payouts, and how they affect insurance pricing. The industry invented mortality tables.*

Market expectations also affect variable annuity versus fixed annuity payouts because variable annuities shift risk to the annuitant from the company. The payout is based on the future performance of the risky reference asset. The annuitant earns both a mortality credit and a risk premium. The net effect is the total expected value of the payouts is higher, reflecting the higher expected return on the reference asset (although the initial annual payout is generally lower). The variable annuity is also more likely to allow cashing out, but at a value linked to the reference asset. There is a downside; **fees** for variable annuities tend to be higher. Variable annuities are also more complex and difficult to analyze. This difficulty tends to reduce price competition and further increase the price of variable annuities (i.e., lowers the annual payout received for premium invested compared to fixed annuities).

Inflation is also a factor. Variable annuities that link payout to an appreciating asset like the stock market are more likely to provide long-term inflation protection. Conventional fixed annuities that pay a constant nominal amount offer no inflation protection. (In contrast many DB plan benefits are indexed to inflation.) A fixed annuity with a rider to increase payments with inflation can be purchased, but at a higher cost. Alternatively, fixed annuities can be designed with payments that increase by predetermined amounts for some inflation protection. The prespecified increases may or may not match actual inflation.

Taxes are a factor, but they are complex and vary by jurisdiction. Consult a qualified advisor before making decisions. Typically, increases in value of an insurance product are not taxed before payouts. At payout, tax may or may not be due on the increase in value.

> *Professor's Note: This tax comment is more cautionary than comments in some other Level III insurance readings. The bottom line in all the readings is taxation of insurance products is complex, you need more than the CFA curriculum will provide, and there can be some tax advantages. Do not send emails saying the statements in the different readings are not identical. The bottom line is consistent among readings.*

The alternative to purchase of an annuity is to **self-insure** longevity risk. In other words, invest in financial assets and set a withdrawal amount that lasts to an assumed life expectancy. The life expectancy should be high because the alternative is running out of money. The decision is complex because the annuity payment reflects three components:

- Return of the principal (premium).
- Interest on the principal.
- Mortality credits as annuitants who die sooner are subsidizing (receiving fewer payouts) the annuitants who live longer (receive more payouts).

Self-insurance can earn the first two, but not the third. This favors use of the annuity. However, use of annuities reduces aggregate wealth of the users as the insurance companies invest rather conservatively and must cover costs plus profit (which is just the cost of invested capital). The decision becomes how much risk for the retiree to take versus cost. Factors that favor use of annuities rather than self-insurance include:

- A longer than average life expectancy.
- A desire for lifetime income.
- Less desire to leave an estate for the benefit of others.
- Conservative investors (high risk aversion).
- An absence of other guaranteed income sources such as pensions.

RISK MANAGEMENT

LOS 12.j: Analyze and critique an insurance program.

CFA® Program Curriculum, Volume 2, page 433

 Professor's Note: This LOS is typical of Level III. A question can describe facts and ask for an answer that may draw on any of the relevant material covered in the readings. Don't panic, the case facts and taught material will provide the answer; just keep your cool and think it through.

Risk management involves multiple techniques. Some risks can be avoided (risk avoidance) (e.g., don't own expensive cars that are costly to repair). Avoiding the risk is a pure form of loss control. Loss prevention involves reducing the probability of the loss (e.g., keep the car in secure storage). Loss reduction involves taking actions to reduce the amount of the loss [e.g., installing fire suppression devices (the fire may still occur, but the likely damages are reduced)]. Risk management also involves risk transfer (buying insurance) and risk retention (self-insurance).

One approach to risk management involves categorizing the severity and frequency of the loss. Severity refers to the size of the loss in relationship to the financial resources of the individual. A $50,000 loss could be trivial to some but devastating to others. Likewise, if the loss is infrequent, it is less burdensome than if it occurs frequently. The matrix classification in Figure 4 can indicate the appropriate risk management technique to use.

Figure 4: Risk Management Decision Matrix

Characteristic of the loss:	Occurs regularly	Infrequent
Very severe	Risk avoidance	Risk transfer
Not severe	Risk reduction	Risk retention

Example: Analyze an Individual's Insurance Program

Case facts:

- A couple in their early 40s has 3 dependent children.
- The husband earns $200,000 annually and is employed in a low risk profession. The employer provides life insurance equal to 2 years of salary. The health insurance plan is generous and covers the family. The employer provides short-term disability insurance to cover 75% of the earnings of the husband, but the benefits last for only 3 months.
- The wife works part time and earns $10,000. Her primary responsibility is care of the children and home. She expects to return to the workforce in the next few years. Her job skills are current, in high demand, and highly compensated.
- Their home was purchased a few years ago at the bottom of a severe real estate collapse and has appreciated 150%. The original loan balance was 90% of purchase price has been only slightly reduced. The couple has been collecting valuable antiques to furnish the home. Property insurance on the home and contents has not been changed since the purchase.
- The couple has a $2,000,000 investment portfolio. A wealthy friend of the couple recently suffered a severe financial loss due to her negligence when she caused a car accident. Her auto insurance only covered liability claims up to $50,000. The couple has a similar auto policy.
- The wife's mother died recently and her 65-year-old father is still alive. The father is in average health and has a large, secure, inflation indexed pension. The father's parents and both sets of grandparents died at relatively young ages.

A. **Discuss** the insurance needs of the couple with regard to life, health, long-term disability, auto, other property, and liability insurance.

B. **Comment** on factors that may increase and decrease their ability to self-insure.

C. **Discuss** two reasons why the wife's father is likely a poor candidate for purchase of an advanced life deferred annuity that would begin payment at age 85.

Answer:

A.

- It is unlikely life insurance equal to 2 years of the husband's salary would cover the family's loss in value if he dies. He needs more life insurance. While the wife's current income is low, her HC is high and she provides substantial value to the family now. Her services would be costly to replace. Some life insurance is needed on her to protect the family's standard of living.
- Employer health insurance is good and covers the family.
- Long-term disability is needed as the family is at risk if the husband cannot work for an extended period of time. This is mitigated by the potential for the wife to return to work.
- Auto insurance and or liability insurance need to be increased. The couple has substantial assets that are at risk if they were responsible for damages to another.
- Property insurance on the home and contents needs to be increased to match their current value.

B. They have substantial assets that increase their ability to absorb losses and self-insure. It is also likely they have substantial explicit liabilities in the form of a mortgage and implicit liabilities in the need to care for the children. These decrease their net wealth and ability to self-insure.

C.

- With a family history of below average life expectancy, the cost versus benefit is relatively low as the father may end up collecting no or only a small number of payments.
- With a large, secure, inflation indexed pension, the father will have less need for increased additional payments from an annuity starting in the future.

HUMAN CAPITAL AND THE IMPLICATIONS FOR ASSET ALLOCATION

LOS 12.k: Discuss how asset allocation policy may be influenced by the risk characteristics of human capital.

CFA® Program Curriculum, Volume 2, page 440

Asset allocation should consider the investor's total economic wealth, FC and HC. The characteristics of the HC are relatively hard to change, so the adjustment is likely to be in the FC. The nature of the HC may affect both the overall risk taken in the FC, and the assets and asset classes selected. For example, an individual employed in a high-risk profession would, all else the same, choose lower risk FC. If the HC is positively correlated with the stock market, then it will be best to select asset classes other than equity for any risky assets that are used. Of course, the individual should try and avoid FC tied directly to her employer.

Example: Asset Allocation

Sally is an MBA with high-risk HC that is 90% stock like. Her sister, Hellen, is a tenured college professor with HC that is 10% stock like. Based on these and all other considerations, they have both selected a 70/30 asset allocation (stock to bond) of total wealth. Sally has HC of 1.9 million and FC of 2.5 million. Hellen's HC and FC are 0.8 and 1.1 million respectively. Based only on this information, **calculate** the target equity amount that each would hold in her FC.

Sally:

- Total desired equity amount = $(1.9 + 2.5) \times 0.7 = 3.08$ million.
- Equity exposure from HC = $1.9 \times 0.9 = 1.71$ million.
- For her 2.5 million FC, she should allocate 1.37 million to equity.

Hellen:

- Total desired equity amount = $(0.8 + 1.1) \times 0.7 = 1.33$ million.
- Equity exposure from HC = $0.8 \times 0.1 = 0.08$ million.
- For her 1.1 million FC, she would have to allocate 1.25 million to equity to reach her total wealth allocation goal. Most likely she will allocate all 1.1 million and be somewhat below her desired total allocation goal for equity.

The characteristics of HC can be complex. For example:

- For a couple, the HC of each member is not likely to be perfectly correlated (+1) with the other, making the couple's HC in aggregate less risky. Likewise, if both are employed, the couple's HC is less risky than if the same amount were earned but only by one member of the couple.
- If one member of the couple has less geographically mobile career skills, the couple's HC is at risk if the other member must move.
- If one member of the couple is not working but could return to work if needed, that lowers the risk of the couple's HC.
- Generally, HC is less risky than many forms of FC, and, all else the same, the asset allocation in FC is tilted toward riskier assets.

LOS 12.l: Recommend and justify appropriate strategies for asset allocation and risk reduction when given an investor profile of key inputs.

CFA® Program Curriculum, Volume 2, page 443

> *Professor's Note: Another cumulative LOS that can lead to a question and facts that draw on any of the relevant material covered in the readings.*

 The reading terms idiosyncratic *and* systematic risk *are analogous to more general terms in portfolio theory. Idiosyncratic is specific or diversifiable risk that can be reduced through diversification or use of insurance products. Insurance is just a pooling and diversification of risk through the insured group. For example, life insurance pools the risk of those who die sooner and later than expected. Systematic risk is market risk for which the holder should be compensated. More/ less risk tolerant individuals may choose more/less systematic risk.*

Risk management strategies include:

- Determining and taking the appropriate amount of systematic (market) risk through an asset allocation of total wealth.
- Reducing where appropriate idiosyncratic (non-market) risks:
  - Through asset diversification.
  - Use of insurance to transfer risks.

For example:

- A young MBA with large debts and high expenses may skip saving for retirement in the early years of her career. If there is any need for life insurance, it should be low-cost, temporary insurance. Security portfolio diversification is relatively unimportant while HC dominates FC.
- A financially well off couple nearing retirement must be more concerned with FC diversification. Outliving the FC becomes of greater concern and longevity risk can be hedged with annuities. HC shrinks and the need for life and disability insurance diminishes or ceases. Health, long-term care, and liability insurance are more important priorities. The more affluent may choose to self-insure as long as it does not imperil standard of living.

Conclusion

The risk management process for individuals is complex and must consider risk and return to total wealth. At different stages of life, the relative importance of and risks to human and financial capital will shift. Market risks to FC can be largely addressed with standard portfolio tools. Adding insurance tools provides more comprehensive risk management of HC and total wealth.

KEY CONCEPTS

LOS 12.a

Total wealth is composed of both human capital and financial capital. Human capital (HC) is the discounted present value of expected future labor income. Estimation includes the future amount, the probability the individual will be alive to earn it, and a discount rate related to the riskiness of the amounts. Financial capital (FC) is the sum of all the other assets of an individual.

LOS 12.b

Net wealth is the sum of the individual's FC and HC less any liabilities owed by the individual. A typical individual might start an employment career with high HC and low FC. As the individual's remaining work career decreases with age, HC generally declines over time while FC increases as the individual saves and invests.

LOS 12.c

Generally, HC is highest in early career and declines until retirement. FC is likely to peak at retirement. The life stages are Education, Early Career, Career Development, Peak Accumulation, Preretirement, Early Retirement, and Late Retirement.

In all stages, there can be unpredicted needs for health care and/or to care for family.

LOS 12.d

The economic (holistic) balance sheet extends the traditional balance sheet assets to include HC. Liabilities are extended to include consumption and bequest goals. This more complete economic view allows better planning of resource consumption to meet remaining lifetime goals.

LOS 12.e

- Earnings risk. Job loss and other career disruptions can reduce HC and may even lead to the need to consume FC prematurely.
- Premature death risk. Can be a serious risk early in the career when substantial HC could be lost and cause unexpected expenses that consume limited FC.
- Longevity risk. Individuals who live too long are at risk of outliving their FC.
- Property risk. Loss in value of physical property (FC).
- Liability risk. If legally responsible for damages, leading to a reduction in FC.
- Health risk. Direct loss of FC to pay illness or injury related expenses and may reduce HC through diminished or inability to work.

LOS 12.f

- Life insurance protects the survivors from the adverse financial consequences of the insured's premature death.
- Disability income insurance provides partial replacement of the insured's job income if the job is lost.
- Property insurance provides compensation for losses in value of real property. Homeowners insurance covers the home and automobile insurance covers the car.
- Health and medical insurance covers health care expense.
- Liability insurance covers losses if the insured is found legally responsible for damages to another.

LOS 12.g

Temporary life insurance is for a set period of time. **Permanent insurance** builds up value sufficient to pay for insuring the remaining lifetime of the insured. Pricing reflects **mortality estimates** that determine how many in the group are expected to die during the insurance period and allow calculating the **net premium** to charge to make those payouts. **Load** is an estimate of company expenses and profit that is added to determine the **gross premium** charged for the insurance.

LOS 12.h

Annuities are the economic opposite of life insurance, pay once and receive payouts back for remaining life to insure against longevity risk. **Immediate annuities** begin payout immediately and **deferred** at a future time. **Fixed annuity** payouts do not change in amount, and **variable** payouts are linked to change in a reference asset.

LOS 12.i

Fixed versus variable annuities:

- Fixed provide a known future payout, while variable have a better chance of keeping up with inflation.
- Fixed will be priced to reflect bond market rates at the time of purchase, while variable will perform in line with changes in the reference asset and are more likely to allow withdrawals.
- Fees for variable are generally higher.
- Both may be subject to some taxes.
- Both earn a mortality credit:
  - For life insurance, the ultimate cost is lower if you die and the one-time fixed payout occurs sooner, while those who live longer end up paying more for the same payout.
  - For annuities, the issue reverses; annuitants who live longer end up collecting more and are subsidized by those who die sooner and collect less.

LOS 12.j

A cumulative LOS, expect questions that draw on the entire reading.

Characteristic of the loss:	Occurs regularly	Infrequent
Very severe	Risk avoidance	Risk transfer
Not severe	Risk reduction	Risk retention

LOS 12.k

Asset allocation should consider the investor's total economic wealth, FC and HC. For example, an individual employed in a high-risk profession would, all else the same, choose lower risk FC. If the HC is positively correlated with the stock market, then it will be best to select asset classes other than equity for any risky assets that are used. Of course, the individual should try and avoid FC tied directly to her employer.

LOS 12.1
A cumulative LOS, expect questions that draw on the entire reading.
- Determine and take the appropriate amount of systematic (market) risk through an asset allocation of total wealth.
- Reduce where appropriate idiosyncratic (non-market) risks:
  - Through asset diversification.
  - Use of insurance to transfer risks.

CONCEPT CHECKERS

1. An individual's present value of future defined benefit payments will *most likely* be classified as:
    A. financial capital.
    B. human capital.
    C. financial capital and total wealth.

2. Financial capital is *least likely* to peak at retirement for:
    A. the very wealthy.
    B. those with a pension.
    C. those who purchase an annuity.

3. Individuals are *most likely* to need substantial amounts of life insurance in which stage of life?
    A. Education.
    B. Career development.
    C. Early retirement.

4. An individual with negative net worth on a traditional balance sheet:
    A. should reduce expenses.
    B. should increase risk in their investment portfolio.
    C. may have positive net wealth.

5. An individual with a large alternative investment holding in art work is *most likely* to need:
    A. property insurance.
    B. life insurance.
    C. liability insurance.

6. Insured individuals who live longer than the statistical average are *most likely* to earn a positive (benefit from the) mortality credit with:
    A. life insurance.
    B. an annuity.
    C. both life insurance and an annuity.

7. In which of the following situations would an individual be *most likely* to purchase a variable rather that a fixed annuity?
    A. They need a more certain income stream.
    B. They want to avoid higher fees.
    C. They want the flexibility to redeem the annuity in the future.

8. An individual should *most likely* purchase insurance for a risk that:
    A. poses high standard of living risk and is infrequent.
    B. poses high standard of living risk and is frequent.
    C. is smaller in amount and infrequent.

9.	An individual in a high-risk job will *most likely*:
	A.	increase their allocation to industries that are highly correlated with their wage income.
	B.	increase their allocation to risk-free assets.
	C.	reduce their savings.

10.	The need for retirement savings is *most likely* higher for:
	A.	a recent college graduate with very young children.
	B.	a young couple who has recently received a large inheritance.
	C.	an older couple in their peak earnings years but employed in a declining industry.

11.	An individual is about to retire. She will receive her first annual pension payment of $25,000 immediately upon retirement and immediately spend it on a lavish vacation. Then, one year later, she will receive another payment. Each payment will increase by 5% from the previous payment amount. Given her life expectancy, she expects to receive a total of 11 payments.

	The risk-free discount rate is 3%, and the risk premium for the pension is 8%. Ignoring the first payment, which she will immediately spend, the pension asset of 10 payments to include on the individual's holistic balance sheet is *closest* to:
	A.	170,000.
	B.	185,000.
	C.	200,000.

For more questions related to this topic review, log in to your Schweser online account and launch SchweserPro™ QBank; and for video instruction covering each LOS in this topic review, log in to your Schweser online account and launch the OnDemand video lectures, if you have purchased these products.

ANSWERS – CONCEPT CHECKERS

1. **C** While DB plan benefits have elements of both FC and HC, they are best categorized as FC. They are also part of total wealth, making C the best answer.

2. **A** The very wealthy may spend less than the total return earned on their assets and see FC increase over time. All others are more likely to spend more than their return and see FC decline. The value of both pensions and annuities is the PV of expected future payments and so declines with age and the reduction in number of future payments.

3. **B** HC and the need for life insurance is likely at its peak in the early career stage, followed by the career development stage when the expected work career and HC remain high.

4. **C** Making changes based only on the traditional balance sheet analysis would be premature because it fails to consider all economic variables affecting the individual. The holistic balance sheet with all variables included could show positive net wealth. On the traditional balance sheet, negative balance may mean little. Individuals who are early in their career with college debt could have negative net worth. Even if both balance sheets show a negative balance, it does not mean immediate changes must be made, only that long-term plans may need revision.

5. **A** While it is true they may be wealthy and may also need the other two, the direct need is for property insurance.

6. **B** With a long life, the individual will collect more payouts than the average annuitant and benefit(earning the positive mortality credit). In contrast, the payout on life insurance will be further in the future, and they are effectively subsidizing (earning a negative credit) those with a shorter life whose beneficiaries are paid the policy amount sooner.

7. **C** Variable annuities are more likely to allow cashing out (at the market value with surrender fees). Fixed annuities have more certain income and generally lower fees but are generally not redeemable.

8. **A** This is the most likely situation to use insurance. It will be difficult to recover if the risk is realized, and because it is infrequent, the cost of insurance will be relatively lower. B is something to avoid, and C is a good case for self-insurance (risk retention).

9. **B** Higher risk HC will, all else the same, reduce the allocation in FC to risky assets in favor of lower risk assets. The risky job makes savings more important and investing in assets with positive correlation to HC should generally be avoided in order to provide diversification within total wealth.

10. **C** This is typically the period of maximum savings for retirement, and the risk of early job loss makes this even more important. While it is always good to start saving for retirement, the other two likely have more immediate needs. Answer choice A probably needs low-cost term life insurance and liquidity. B is likely in good financial shape and could benefit from advice on what to do with the inheritance. B can certainly consider retirement savings, but C has the greatest need.

11. **B** The first pension receipt is offset by a liability, a planned expenditure, so it has zero value in our calculations.

The long (and unrealistic under exam conditions) way to solve this question is to set up a spreadsheet to project the payments at end of years 1 to 10, with the first payment on the spreadsheet being 5% higher than the $25,000 and all subsequent payments increasing by 5% annually. Each FV payment would be discounted to PV at 3% + 8% = 11%. The more realistic way to solve the question is to realize the starting $25,000 is growing 5% each year and is then discounted at 11%. This can be reduced to a net discount rate (including the effect of growth) each year of [1 + (0.03 + 0.08)] / 1.05 − 1 = 5.7%.

The question is then an ordinary annuity calculation of 10 payments: 10 n, 25,000 PMT, 5.7 ip, PV = 186,646.

Variations on this calculation, such as [(1.03)(1.08)] / 1.05 − 1 or 3 + 8 − 5, are also likely to be acceptable, but they are less consistent with the CFA text.

SELF-TEST: PRIVATE WEALTH MANAGEMENT

Use the following information for Questions 1 through 6.

Chen Wang and his wife, Tao, have been married for nearly 30 years, during which time they have enjoyed enormous business success. The Chens started their marriage as small shopkeepers and grew their business rapidly. They turned their first shop into a successful chain of retail stores. From that base, they expanded into global trading. Eventually, they began to manufacture a variety of items for sale in both their own stores and for export.

After diversifying their business geographically and integrating vertically, the Chens broadened their business interests into real estate. Their holdings expanded beyond their initial investment in residential apartments into large commercial spaces and office buildings. Ultimately, they parlayed their first small business into a large conglomerate, incorporating several industries on both sides of the Pacific. Even though Chen Wang is 61 and his wife is 58, they remain very active in running their businesses.

In addition to their varied business interests, the Chens have a substantial portfolio of marketable securities. Although they have historically managed their securities portfolio themselves, they decided to bring in a professional adviser once the portfolio exceeded 100 million Hong Kong dollars (HKD).

They are now consulting Park Jung Hee, CFA, about the asset allocation and security selection in their investment portfolio.

The Chens tell Park, "We have two grandchildren, and we would like to be able to leave each one 100 million HKD in today's dollars (i.e., in real value) of marketable securities in our estate." Park reminds the Chens that they could expect to enjoy long lives, but Chen Wang responds, "Kindly plan our investments so the portfolio reaches the target by the time I am 75." Park points out that the current value of the portfolio is already 102 million HKD, so that goal should be reachable, especially because the Chens are not subject to income taxes on portfolio income or capital gains.

The Chens would also like to fund some charitable activities. "If the portfolio can afford it, we would also like to give 1 million HKD per year to various organizations," Chen Tao tells Park. "And we would like to increase that figure every year for inflation," adds Chen Wang. Park and the Chens agree to plan for an inflation rate of 1% per year.

Park reviews the current holdings in the portfolio with the Chens. He notes that the portfolio contains nearly 20 million HKD of equity in the Golden Flower Trading Company (GFTC). The Chens have had GFTC in their portfolio for several years because they consider it a good company. Park advises them, however, to sell some of the position in order to diversify their portfolio. Chen Wang points out to Park that GFTC has fallen 15% from its high, reached several months ago. "We don't want to lose money, so please wait to sell until it comes back."

Chen Tao has also expressed some reservations about leaving the grandchildren such large sums of money and asks for recommendations for a cost effective way to provide the benefits of the money over an extended period of time to the grandchildren. Park promises to get back to the Chens with some suggestions.

1. Based on the Chens' situation, their *least likely* need for insurance is to manage:
   A. property risk.
   B. longevity risk.
   C. liability risk.

2. Which of the following is *least likely* to be included in the five main classes of investment constraints?
   A. Regulatory and legal constraints.
   B. Risk tolerance.
   C. Time horizon.

3. The return objective on the portfolio necessary for the Chens to reach their investment goals is *closest* to:
   A. 4.5%.
   B. 5.5%.
   C. 6.5%.

4. Chen Wang's reluctance to sell GFTC until it returns to its earlier high is *best* described as:
   A. regret.
   B. anchoring.
   C. myopic loss aversion.

5. Park suggests to Chen Wang that derivatives can be used as an alternative to an immediate sale as a way to reduce the risk in GFTC. In order to retain all of the security upside and minimize initial cost, Park would recommend:
   A. a collar.
   B. an at-the-money protective put.
   C. buying an OTM put and selling a further OTM put.

6. Based on Chen Tao's objectives, Park is *most likely* to recommend:
   A. a discretionary trust with the grandchildren as the beneficiaries.
   B. term life insurance on the grandchildren.
   C. a deferred start annuity with the grandchildren as the annuitants.

ANSWERS – SELF-TEST: PRIVATE WEALTH MANAGEMENT

1. **B** With extensive property and complex global business interests, they are likely to have substantial property and potential legal/liability risk that warrant insurance. Given their apparent wealth and bequest plans, the risk that they will have insufficient funds for living expenses is most likely low.

2. **B** Although risk tolerance is a critical aspect of an IPS, it is not considered an investment constraint. The five main categories of investment constraints are liquidity, time horizon, legal and regulatory concerns, tax considerations, and unique circumstances.

3. **C** Because Chen Wang is currently 61 years old and wants the portfolio to reach 200 million HKD by the time he is 75, the time horizon for the portfolio is 14 years. The goals are 200 million in real HKD and annual real distributions of 1 million HKD. The inflation estimate is 1%. Using the TVM keys: –102 million = PV, 200 million = FV, 1 million = PMT, 14 = N, CPT → I/Y = 5.66% + 1% inflation = 6.66%.

4. **A** The Chens are attempting to avoid the feeling of regret associated with not selling GFTC at its historical high. This is a stereotypical case of trying to avoid a feeling of *if only*. If they sold the stock now, they would say, "*If only* we had sold GFTC when it was at $X, we would have realized much more on the investment." In other words, they would have to admit that they were unable to recognize and take advantage of the historical high. Anchoring refers to locking onto the first information received and is more common in a forecasting setting. The Chens are showing loss aversion, but myopic loss aversion is something else. It refers to loss aversion that leads to distortions in the market equity risk premium for equity and is not relevant here.

5. **C** Only one choice meets all the objectives of reducing the risk, retaining all upside, and reducing initial cost. Purchase and sale of the puts won't eliminate all risk, but it does eliminate risk between the two strike prices. All upside is retained, and sale of the lower strike price put reduces initial cost. A collar gives away all upside above the call strike price. The ATM put is the most expensive strategy and does nothing to reduce initial cost.

6. **A** Chen Tao can set the terms of the trust to direct the trustee in what she wants to achieve but then leave the trustee discretion in determining how best to respond to changing circumstances. Term insurance that pays when the grandchildren die meets none of the objectives. A deferred start annuity meets some of the objectives by making payouts to the grandchildren over time rather than all at once, and it could even be set up to start payments coincident with the anticipated date of the estate. But costs are high for such annuities, and given the size of the funds, self-insurance (i.e., putting the money in a trust and investing the funds) would be more likely to increase family wealth.

MANAGING INSTITUTIONAL INVESTOR PORTFOLIOS

EXAM FOCUS

It is important to read the Notes for Study Sessions 4, 5, and 6 in order. They cover the basic framework, structure, construction, and uses of the investment policy statement (IPS). This study session for institutional investors builds on the concepts covered for individual investors. Collectively these study sessions have been the most tested topic areas for the Level III exam. LOS 13. i, j, k, and n are cumulative and apply to the entire reading. You should be prepared to write and use an IPS in situations presented as specific cases using anything covered in this reading.

WARM-UP: PENSION PLAN TERMS

General Pension Definitions

- *Funded status* refers to the difference between the present values of the pension plan's assets and liabilities.
- *Plan surplus* is calculated as the the value of plan assets minus the value of plan liabilities. When plan surplus is positive the plan is *overfunded* and when it is negative the plan is *underfunded*.
- *Fully funded* refers to a plan where the values of plan assets and liabilities are approximately equal.
- *Accumulated benefit obligation* (ABO) is the total present value of pension liabilities to date, assuming no further accumulation of benefits. It is the relevant measure of liabilities for a terminated plan. [terminated]
- *Projected benefit obligation* (PBO) is the ABO plus the present value of the additional liability from projected future employee compensation increases and is the value used in calculating funded status for ongoing (not terminating) plans. [ongoing]
- *Total future liability* is more comprehensive and is the PBO plus the present value of the expected increase in the benefit due current employees in the future from their service to the company between now and retirement. This is not an accounting term and has no precise definition. It could include such items as possible future changes in the benefit formula that are not part of the PBO. Some plans may consider it as supplemental information in setting objectives.
- *Retired lives* is the number of plan participants currently receiving benefits from the plan (retirees).
- *Active lives* is the number of currently employed plan participants who are not currently receiving pension benefits.

©2017 Kaplan, Inc.

DEFINED-BENEFIT PLANS AND DEFINED-CONTRIBUTION PLANS

LOS 13.a: Contrast a defined-benefit plan to a defined-contribution plan and discuss the advantages and disadvantages of each from the perspectives of the employee and the employer.

CFA® Program Curriculum, Volume 2, page 463

In a **defined-benefit** (DB) retirement plan, the sponsor company agrees to make payments to employees after retirement based on criteria (e.g., average salary, number of years worked) spelled out in the plan. As future benefits are accrued by employees, the employer accrues a liability equal to the present value of the expected future payments. This liability is offset by plan assets which are the plan assets funded by the employer's contributions over time. A plan with assets greater (less) than liabilities is termed overfunded (underfunded). The employer bears the investment risk and must increase funding to the plan when the investment results are poor.

In a **defined-contribution** (DC) plan, the company agrees to make contributions of a certain amount as they are earned by employees (e.g., 1% of salary each month) into a retirement account owned by the participant. While there may be vesting rules, generally an employee legally owns his account assets and can move the funds if he leaves prior to retirement. For this reason we say that the plan has **portability**. At retirement, the employee can access the funds but there is no guarantee of the amount. In a *participant directed* DC plan, the employee makes the investment decisions and in a *sponsor directed* DC plan, the sponsor chooses the investments. In either case, the employee bears the investment risk and the amount available at retirement is uncertain in a DC plan. The firm has no future financial liability. This is the key difference between a DC plan and a DB plan. In a DB plan, the sponsor has the investment risk because a certain future benefit has been promised and the firm has a liability as a result. A firm with a DC plan has no liability beyond making the agreed upon contributions.

A **cash balance plan** is a type of DB plan in which individual account balances (accrued benefit) are recorded so they can be portable. A **profit sharing plan** is a type of DC plan where the employer contribution is based on the profits of the company. A variety of plans funded by an individual for his own benefit, grow tax deferred, and can be withdrawn at retirement (e.g., individual retirement accounts or IRAs) are also considered defined contribution accounts.

LOS 13.b: Discuss investment objectives and constraints for defined-benefit plans.

CFA® Program Curriculum, Volume 2, page 464

The objectives and constraints in the IPS for a defined-benefit plan are the standard ones you have learned. The objectives of risk and return are jointly determined. The constraints can be separated into the plan's time horizon, tax and regulatory status, liquidity needs, legal and regulatory constraints, and unique circumstances of the plan that would constrain investment options.

Analysis of these objectives and constraints, along with a discussion of the relevant considerations in establishing them, is covered in the next two LOS.

LOS 13.c: Evaluate pension fund risk tolerance when risk is considered from the perspective of the 1) plan surplus, 2) sponsor financial status and profitability, 3) sponsor and pension fund common risk exposures, 4) plan features, and 5) workforce characteristics.

CFA® Program Curriculum, Volume 2, page 465

Several factors affect the risk tolerance for a defined benefit plan.

1. **Plan surplus.** The greater the plan surplus, the greater the ability of the fund to withstand poor/negative investment results without increases in funding. Thus a positive surplus allows a higher risk tolerance and a negative surplus reduces risk tolerance. A negative surplus might well increase the desire of the sponsor to take risk in the hope that higher returns would reduce the need to make contributions. This is not acceptable. Both the sponsor and manager have an obligation to manage the plan assets for the benefit of the plan beneficiaries. Compared to foundations and endowments, which may be managed aggressively, DB plans will range from low to moderately above-average risk tolerance. A negative surplus may increase the willingness of the sponsor to take risk, but this willingness does not change or outweigh the fact that the plan is underfunded and the fund risk tolerance is lowered by a negative surplus.

2. **Financial status and profitability.** Indicators such as debt to equity and profit margins indicate the financial strength and profitability of the sponsor. The greater the strength of the sponsor, the greater the plan's risk tolerance. Both lower debt and higher profitability indicate an ability to increase plan contributions if investment results are poor.

3. **Sponsor and pension fund common risk exposures.** The higher the correlation between firm profitability and the value of plan assets, the less the plan's risk tolerance. With high correlation, the fund's value may fall at the same time that the firm's profitability falls and it is least able to increase contributions.

4. **Plan features.** Provisions for early retirement or for lump-sum withdrawals decrease the duration of the plan liabilities and, other things equal, decrease the plan's risk tolerance. Any provisions that increase liquidity needs or reduce time horizon reduce risk tolerance.

5. **Workforce characteristics.** The lower the average age of the workforce, the longer the time horizon and, other things equal, this increases the plan's risk tolerance. The higher the ratio of retirees drawing benefits to currently working plan participants, the greater the liquidity requirements and the lower the fund's risk tolerance. Conversely, when the ratio of active lives to retired lives is higher the plan's risk tolerance is higher.

LOS 13.d: Prepare an investment policy statement for a defined-benefit plan.

CFA® Program Curriculum, Volume 2, page 467

The objectives for risk and return are jointly determined with the risk objective limiting the return objective. The factors affecting risk tolerance discussed for the previous LOS should be considered in determining the risk tolerance objective included in an IPS for a defined benefit plan fund.

While these factors determine the relative risk tolerance for plan assets, they do not address the issue of how risk should be measured for a DB plan and the form that a risk objective should take. As already noted, from a firm risk standpoint the correlation of operating results and plan results is important. If operating results and pension results are positively correlated, the firm will find it necessary to increase plan contributions just when it is most difficult or costly to do so.

The primary objective of a DB plan is to meet its obligation to provide promised retirement benefits to plan participants. The risk of not meeting this objective is best addressed using an **asset/liability management** (ALM) framework. Under ALM, risk is measured by the variability (standard deviation) of plan surplus. Alternatively, many plans still look at risk from the perspective of assets only and focus on the more traditional standard deviation of asset returns.

> **For the Exam:** ALM is a major topic in the Level III material. Expect it to occur on the exam, perhaps more than once. This section does not discuss it in any detail but it will be covered elsewhere. In a general IPS question on any portfolio with definable liabilities, it is appropriate to mention the desirability of looking at return in terms of maintaining or growing the surplus and risk as variability of surplus.

Another approach to setting a risk objective for a DB plan focuses on its **shortfall risk** (the probability that the plan asset value will be below some specific level or have returns below some specific level) over a given time horizon. Shortfall risk may be estimated for a status at some future date of fully funded (relative to the PBO), fully funded with respect to the total future liability, funded status that would avoid reporting a liability (negative surplus position) on the firm's balance sheet, or funded status that would require additional contribution requirements of regulators or additional premium payments to a pension fund guarantor. Alternative or supplemental risk objectives may be included to minimize the volatility of plan contributions or, in the case of a fully or over-funded plan, minimizing the probability of having to make future plan contributions.

DB Plan Return Objective

The ultimate goal of a pension plan is to have pension assets generate return sufficient to cover pension liabilities. The specific return requirement will depend on the plan's risk tolerance and constraints. At a minimum the return objective is the discount rate used to compute the present value of the future benefits. If a plan were fully funded, earns the discount rate, and the actuarial assumptions are correct, the fully funded status will remain stable. It is acceptable to aim for a somewhat higher return that would grow the surplus and eventually allow smaller contributions by the sponsor. These are legitimate plan objectives if not taken to excess, but ultimately the return objective is limited by the appropriate level of risk for the plan participants and pension plans should not take high risk.

DB Plan Constraints

Liquidity. The pension plan receives contributions from the plan sponsor and makes payments to beneficiaries. Any net outflow represents a liquidity need. Liquidity requirements will be affected by:

- *The number of retired lives.* The greater the number of retirees receiving benefits relative to active participants, the greater the liquidity that must be provided.
- *The amount of sponsor contributions.* The smaller the corporate contributions relative to retirement payments, the greater the liquidity needed.
- *Plan features.* Early retirement or lump-sum payment options increase liquidity requirements.

Time horizon. The time horizon of a defined-benefit plan is mainly determined by two factors:

1. If the plan is terminating, the time horizon is the termination date.

2. For an ongoing plan, the relevant time horizon depends on characteristics of the plan participants.

    The time horizon for a going concern defined-benefit plan is often long term. Legally it may have an infinite life. However, the management of the current plan assets and the relevant time horizon of the portfolio depend on the characteristics of the current plan participants and when distributions are expected to be made. Some sponsors and managers view going concern plans as a multistage time horizon, one for active lives and one for retired lives, essentially viewing the portfolio as two sub portfolios. The active lives portion of the plan will have a time horizon associated with expected term to retirement. The retired lives portion will have a time horizon as a function of life expectancy for those currently receiving benefits.

Taxes. Most retirement plans are tax exempt and this should be stated. There are exceptions in some countries or some portions of return are taxed, but others are not. If any portions are taxed, this should be stated in the constraint and considered when selecting assets.

Legal and regulatory factors. In the United States, the Employee Retirement Income Security Act (ERISA) regulates the implementation of defined-benefit plans. The requirements of ERISA are consistent with the CFA program and modern portfolio theory in regard to placing the plan participants first and viewing the overall portfolio after considering diversification effects. Most countries have applicable laws and regulations governing pension investment activity. The key point to remember is that when formulating an IPS for a pension plan, the adviser must incorporate the regulatory framework existing within the jurisdiction where the plan operates. Consultation with appropriate legal experts is required if complex issues arise. A pension plan trustee is a **fiduciary** and as such must act solely in the best interests of the plan participants. A manager hired to manage assets for the plan takes on that responsibility as well.

Unique circumstances. There are no unique issues to generalize about. Possible issues include:

- A small plan may have limited staff and resources for managing the plan or overseeing outside managers. This could be a larger challenge with complex alternative investments that require considerable due diligence.
- Some plans self impose restrictions on asset classes or industries. This is more common in government or union-related plans.

LOS 13.e: Evaluate the risk management considerations in investing pension plan assets.

CFA® Program Curriculum, Volume 2, page 477

Another dimension of DB plan risk is its affect on the sponsor. These plans can be large with the potential to affect the sponsoring company's financial health. The company needs to consider two factors.

1. *Pension investment returns in relation to the operating returns of the company.* This is the issue of correlation of sponsor business and plan assets considered earlier, now viewed from the company's perspective. The company should also favor low correlation to minimize the need for increasing contributions during periods of poor performance. The plan should avoid investing in the sponsor company (which is often illegal) and in securities in the same industry or otherwise highly correlated with the company.

2. *Coordinating pension investments with pension liabilities.* This is the ALM issue. By focusing on managing the surplus and stability of surplus, the company minimizes the probability of unexpected increases in required contributions.

> *Professor's Note: This will be discussed in great detail elsewhere. At its simplest this means matching the plan asset and liability durations using fixed-income investments. In a more sophisticated fashion, a closer match may be achieved by using real rate bonds and equity as a portion of the assets. ALM will also lead to a surplus efficient frontier and a minimum variance surplus portfolio. For now just realize the Level III material is highly integrated and questions normally draw from multiple LOS and study sessions—keep studying.*

LOS 13.f: Prepare an investment policy statement for a participant directed defined-contribution plan.

CFA® Program Curriculum, Volume 2, page 479

Constructing the IPS for a sponsor-directed DC plan is similar to that for other DB plans, but simpler. Here we will distinguish between the IPS for a DB plan and the IPS for a participant directed DC plan. With a participant directed DC plan, there is no one set of objectives and constraints to be considered since they may be different over time and across participant accounts. The IPS for this type of plan deals with the sponsor's obligation to provide investment choices (at least three under ERISA) that allow for diversification and to provide for the free movement of funds among the choices offered. Additionally, the sponsor should provide some guidance and education for plan participants so they can determine their risk tolerance, return objectives, and the allocation of their funds among the various investment choices offered. When the sponsor offers a choice of company stock, the IPS should provide limits on this as a portfolio choice to maintain adequate diversification (think Enron).

So overall the IPS for a participant directed DC plan does not relate to any individual participant or circumstance, but outlines the policies and procedures for offering the choices, diversification, and education to participants that they need to address their own objectives of risk and return, as well as their liquidity and time horizon constraints. The management of the individual participant balances and setting their objectives and constraints in the participant directed plan would be handled like any other O&C for an individual.

In contrast, a sponsor-directed DC plan would be treated like a DB plan. However, there is no specified future liability to consider in setting the objectives and constraints. Otherwise, the analysis process would be similar to a DB plan.

HYBRID PLANS AND ESOPS

LOS 13.g: Discuss hybrid pension plans (e.g., cash balance plans) and employee stock ownership plans.

CFA® Program Curriculum, Volume 2, page 483

Cash balance plan. A cash balance plan is a type of defined-benefit plan that defines the benefit in terms of an account balance. In a typical cash balance plan, a participant's account is credited each year with a pay credit and an interest credit. The pay credit is usually based upon the beneficiary's age, salary, and/or length of employment, while the interest credit is based upon a benchmark such as U.S. Treasuries. These features are similar to DC plans.

However, and more like DB plans, the sponsor bears all the investment risk because increases and decreases in the value of the plan's investments (due to investment decisions, interest rates, etc.) do not affect the benefit amounts promised to participants. At retirement, the beneficiary can usually elect to receive a lump-sum distribution, which can be rolled into another qualified plan, or receive a lifetime annuity.

Employee stock ownership plans (ESOPs). An ESOP is a type of defined-contribution plan that allows employees to purchase the company stock, sometimes at a discount from market price. The purchase can be with before- or after-tax dollars. The final balance in the beneficiary's account reflects the increase in the value of the firm's stock as well as contributions during employment. ESOPs receive varying amounts of regulation in different countries.

At times the ESOP may purchase a large block of the firm's stock directly from a large stockholder, such as a founding proprietor or partner who wants to liquidate a holding. An ESOP is an exception to the general aversion to holding the sponsor's securities in a retirement plan. It does expose the participant to a high correlation between plan return and future job income.

FOUNDATIONS

LOS 13.h: Distinguish among various types of foundations, with respect to their description, purpose, and source of funds.

CFA® Program Curriculum, Volume 2, page 466

We will discuss foundations and endowments separately as done in the CFA text. But realize the way they are managed and the issues to consider are overwhelmingly consistent between the two. Read both sections together and then apply what is taught. In general, **foundations** are grant-making entities funded by gifts. **Endowments** are long-term funds owned by a non-profit institution (and supporting that institution). Both are not for profit, serve a social purpose, generally are not taxed if they meet certain conditions, are often perpetual, and unlike pension plans may well and should pursue aggressive objectives.

Figure 1 contains a summary of the characteristics of the four basic types of foundations.[1]

Professor's Note: Caution, this table is based on U.S.-only generalizations. The table illustrates that a variety of rules exist and they are not uniform. What is given in the case facts should always take precedence over generalizations from the table.

---

1. Based upon Exhibit 2, "Managing Institutional Investor Portfolios," by R. Charles Tschampion, CFA, Laurence B. Siegel, Dean J. Takahashi, and John L. Maginn, CFA, from *Managing Investment Portfolios: A Dynamic Process*, 3rd edition, 2007 (CFA Institute, 2018 Level III Curriculum, Reading 13, Vol. 2, p. 485).

Figure 1: Types of Foundations and Their Important Characteristics

Type of Foundation	Description	Purpose	Source of Funds	Annual Spending Requirement
Independent	Private or family	Grants to charities, educational institutions, social organizations, etc.	Typically an individual or family, but can be a group of interested individuals	5% of assets; expenses cannot be counted in the spending amount
Company sponsored	Closely tied to the sponsoring corporation	Same as independent; grants can be used to further the corporate sponsor's business interests	Corporate sponsor	Same as independent foundations
Operating	Established for the sole purpose of funding an organization (e.g., a museum, zoo, public library) or some ongoing research/medical initiative		Same as independent	Must spend at least 85% of dividend and interest income for its own operations; may also be subject to spending 3.33% of assets
Community	Publicly sponsored grant-awarding organization	Fund social, educational, religious, etc. purposes	General public, including large donors	None

LOS 13.i: Compare the investment objectives and constraints of foundations, endowments, insurance companies, and banks.

LOS 13.k: Prepare an investment policy statement for a foundation, an endowment, an insurance company, and a bank.

CFA® Program Curriculum, Volume 2, pages 484 and 486

Foundation Objectives

Risk. Because there are no contractually defined liability requirements, foundations may be more aggressive than pensions on the risk tolerance scale. If successful in earning higher returns the foundation can increase its social funding in the future. If unsuccessful the foundation suffers and can fund less in the future. In either case the benefit and risk are symmetrically borne. The board of the foundation (and manager) will generally consider the time horizon and other circumstances of the foundation in setting the risk tolerance.

Return. Time horizon is an important factor. If the foundation was created to provide perpetual support, the preservation of real purchasing power is important. One useful guideline is to set a minimum return equal to the required payout plus expected inflation and fund expenses. This might be done by either adding or compounding the return elements. (Note: this issue is discussed under endowments).

Foundation Constraints

Time horizon. Except for special foundations required to spend down their portfolio within a set period, most foundations have infinite time horizons. Hence, they can usually tolerate above-average risk and choose securities that tend to offer high returns as well as preservation of purchasing power.

Liquidity. A foundation's anticipated spending requirement is termed its **spending rate**. Many countries specify a minimum spending rate, and failure to meet this will trigger penalties. For instance the United States has a 5% rule to spend 5% of previous year assets. Other situations may follow a **smoothing rule** to average out distributions.

For ongoing foundations there is generally a need to also earn the inflation rate to maintain real value of the portfolio and distributions. Earning the required distribution and inflation can be challenging with conflicting interpretations for risk. It may argue for high risk to meet the return target or less risk to avoid the downside of disappointing returns.

Many organizations find it appropriate to maintain a fraction of the annual spending as a cash reserve in the portfolio.

Tax considerations. Except for the fact that investment income of private foundations is currently taxed at 1% in the United States, foundations are not taxable entities. One potential concern relates to *unrelated business income*, which is taxable at the regular corporate rate. On average, tax considerations are not a major concern for foundations.

Legal and regulatory. Rules vary by country and even by type of foundation. In the United States most states have adopted the Uniform Management Institutional Funds Act (UMIFA) as the prevailing regulatory framework. Most other regulations concern the tax-exempt status of the foundation. Beyond these basics, foundations are free to pursue the objectives they deem appropriate.

ENDOWMENTS AND SPENDING RULES

Endowments are legal entities that have been funded for the expressed purpose of *permanently* funding the endowment's institutional sponsor (a not for profit that will receive the benefits of the portfolio). The intent is to preserve asset principal value in perpetuity and to use the income generated for budgetary support of specific activities. Universities, hospitals, museums, and charitable organizations often receive a substantial portion of their funding from endowments. Spending from endowments is usually earmarked for specific purposes and spending fluctuations can create disruptions in the institutional recipient's operating budget.

Most endowments (and foundations) have spending rules. In the United States, foundations have a minimum required spending rule but endowments can decide their spending rate, change it, or just fail to meet it.

Three forms of spending rule are as follows:

- **Simple spending rule.**

  The most straightforward spending rule is spending to equal the specified spending rate multiplied by the beginning period market value of endowment assets:

  $$spending_t = S(market\ value_{t-1})$$

  where:
  S = the specified spending rate

- **Rolling 3-year average spending rule.**

  This modification to the simple spending rule generates a spending amount that equals the spending rate multiplied by an average of the three previous years' market value of endowment assets. The idea is to reduce the volatility of what the portfolio must distribute and of what the sponsor will receive and can spend:

  $$spending_t = \left(spending\ rate\right)\left(\frac{market\ value_{t-1} + market\ value_{t-2} + market\ value_{t-3}}{3}\right)$$

- **Geometric spending rule.**

  The rolling 3-year rule can occasionally produce unfortunate consequences. Consider a case of dramatic, steady decline in market value for three years. It would require a high distribution in relation to current market value. The geometric spending rule gives some smoothing but less weight to older periods. It weights the prior year's spending level adjusted for inflation by a smoothing rate, which is usually between 0.6 and 0.8, as well as the previous year's beginning-of-period portfolio value:

  $$spending_t = (R)(spending_{t-1})(1 + I_{t-1}) + (1 - R)(S)(market\ value_{t-1})$$

  where:
  R = smoothing rate
  I = rate of inflation
  S = spending rate

Endowment Objectives

Risk: Risk tolerance for endowments (and foundations) can be quite high. Risk tolerance should be set at a level to meet long-term objectives and distribution needs. Factors that affect risk tolerance include:

- If there is no smoothing rule to dampen the effect of market value volatility on distribution amounts, risk tolerance is reduced. However, this does not automatically mean less volatile assets are appropriate or will reduce long-term risk. Less volatile assets will likely lower return and may reduce the probability of meeting long-term objectives.
- If the institution funded by the endowment is heavily dependent on the distributions from the endowment, risk tolerance is reduced. In contrast, if the receiver has other income sources, it allows the endowment to take more risk.
- Poor recent performance that reduces portfolio value combined with a smoothing rule decreases short-term ability to take risk as the required distribution amount in relation to current market value will increase (i.e., a larger percentage of the portfolio must be distributed).
- Higher return objectives may indicate a higher willingness to take risk as the objectives can only be met through higher risk. On the other hand, if the endowment board expresses serious concerns over short-term market declines, this may indicate lower willingness to take risk.

Return. As previously indicated, one of the goals of creating an endowment is to provide a permanent asset base for funding specific activities. Attention to preserving the real purchasing power of the asset base is paramount.

A total return approach is typical. The form of return, income, realized, or unrealized price change is not important. If the return objective is achieved, in the long run the distributions will be covered. It is not necessary in any one year that the amount earned equal the distribution. However the long-term nature also requires the inflation rate be covered (earned as well). The inflation rate used is not necessarily the general inflation rate but should be the rate reflecting the inflation rate relevant to what the endowment spends. For example if the spending for health care is the objective and health care inflation is 6%, use 6%.

While it is typical to add the spending rate, relevant inflation rate, and an expense rate if specified, others argue for using the higher compound calculation. Monte Carlo simulation can analyze path dependency and multiple time periods to shed some light on this issue. For example if the asset value declines and the spending amount is fixed, the distribution disproportionately reduces the size of the portfolio available. This suggests the return target be set somewhat higher than is conventionally done.

Endowment Constraints

Time horizon. Because the purpose of most endowment funds is to provide a permanent source of funding, the time horizon for endowment funds is typically perpetual.

Liquidity requirements. The liquidity requirements of an endowment are usually low. Only emergency needs and current spending require liquidity. However, large outlays (e.g., capital improvements) may require higher levels of liquidity.

Tax considerations. Endowments are generally tax exempt. There are exceptions and these might occur and be described in a given situation. In the United States, some assets generate unrelated business income. In that case, Unrelated Business Income Tax (UBIT) may have to be paid. If a case does include details on taxation, note this as a tax constraint and consider the after-tax return of that asset.

Legal and regulatory considerations. Regulation is limited. Foundations and endowments have broad latitude to set and pursue their objectives. In the United States, 501(c)(3) tax regulations require earnings from tax-exempt entities not be used for private individuals. Most states have adopted the Uniform Management Institutional Fund Act (UMIFA) of 1972 as the governing regulation for endowments. If no specific legal considerations are stated in the case, for U.S. entities, state UMIFA applies. Other countries may have other laws.

Unique circumstances. Due to their diversity, endowment funds have many unique circumstances. Social issues (e.g., defense policies and racial biases) are typically taken into consideration when deciding upon asset allocation. The long-term nature of endowments and many foundations have lead to significant use of alternative investments. The cost and complexity of these assets should be considered. They generally require active management expertise.

INSURANCE COMPANIES

Insurance companies sell policies that promise a payment to the policyholder if a covered event occurs during the life (term, period of coverage) of the policy. With life insurance that event would be the death of the beneficiary. With automobile insurance that might be an accident to the automobile. In exchange for insurance coverage the policyholder pays the insurer a payment (premium). Those funds are invested till needed for payouts and to earn a return for the company.

Historically there were **stock companies** owned by shareholders seeking to earn a profit for the shareholders and **mutuals** owned by the policyholder and operated only for the benefit of the policyholders. In recent years many mutuals have been **demutualized** and become stock companies.

LIFE INSURANCE COMPANIES

Life insurance companies sell insurance policies that provide a death benefit to those designated on the policy when the covered individual dies. A variety of types of life insurance exist that may have different time horizons and liquidity needs. It is common to segregate the investment portfolio by type of policy (line of business) and invest to match the needs of that product. Some of the important policy types and implications for portfolio management include:

- **Whole life or ordinary life** generally requires a level payment of premiums over multiple years to the company and provides a fixed payoff amount at the death of the policyholder. These policies often include a cash value allowing the policyholder to terminate the policy and receive that cash value. Alternatively the policyholder may be able to borrow the cash value. The cash value builds up over the life of the policy at a **crediting rate**.

There are portfolio implications to these features. The company faces competitive pressure to offer higher crediting rates to attract customers, which creates a need for higher return on the portfolio. In addition, **disintermediation risk** occurs during periods of high interest rates when policyholders are more likely to withdraw cash value causing increased demand for liquidity from the portfolio. High rates are also likely to be associated with depressed market values in the portfolio. While duration of whole life is usually long, the combination of policy features and volatile interest rates makes the duration and time horizon of the liabilities more difficult to predict. Overall, competitive market factors and volatile interest rates have led to shortening the time horizon and duration of the investment portfolio.

- **Term life** insurance usually provides insurance coverage on a year by year basis leading to very short duration assets to fund the short duration liability.
- **Variable life**, **universal life**, and **variable universal life** usually include a cash value build up and insurance (like whole life), but the cash value buildup is linked to investment returns. The features are less likely to trigger early cash withdrawals but increase the need to earn competitive returns on the portfolio to retain and attract new customers.

Life Insurance Company Objectives

Risk. Public policy views insurance company investment portfolios as *quasi-trust funds*. Having the ability to pay death benefits when due is a critical concern. The National Association of Insurance Commissioners (NAIC) directs life insurance companies to maintain an asset valuation reserve (AVR) as a cushion against substantial losses of portfolio value or investment income. Worldwide the movement is towards risk-based capital, which requires the company to have more capital (and less financial leverage) the riskier the assets in the portfolio.

- **Valuation risk** and ALM will figure prominently in any discussion of risk, and interest rate risk will be the prime issue. Any mismatch between duration of assets and of liabilities will make the surplus highly volatile as the change in value of the assets will not track the change in value of liabilities when rates change. The result is the duration of assets will be closely tied to the duration of liabilities.
- **Reinvestment risk** will be important for some products. For example, annuity products (sometimes called guaranteed investment contracts or GICS) pay a fixed amount at a maturity date. (Effectively they are like a zero-coupon bond issued by the company.) The company must invest the premium and build sufficient value to pay off at maturity. As most assets in the portfolio will be coupon-bearing securities, the accumulated value in the portfolio will also depend on the reinvestment rate as the coupon cash flow comes into the portfolio.

ALM is the prime tool for controlling both of these risks. The risk objective will typically state the need to match asset and liability duration or closely control any mismatch.

Other risk issues are:

- **Cash flow volatility.** Life insurance companies have a low tolerance for any loss of income or delays in collecting income from investment activities. Reinvesting interest on cash flow coming in is a major component of return over long periods. Most companies seek investments that offer minimum cash flow volatility.
- **Credit risk.** Credit quality is associated with the ability of the issuers of debt to pay interest and principal when due. Credit analysis is required to gauge potential losses of investment income and has been one of the industry's strong points. Controlling credit risk is a major concern for life insurance companies and is often managed through a broadly diversified portfolio.

Traditionally life insurance company portfolios were conservatively invested but business competition increases the pressure to find higher returns.

Return. Traditionally insurance companies focused on a minimum return equal to the actuaries' assumed rate of growth in policyholder reserves. This is essentially the growth rate needed to meet projected policy payouts. Earn less and the surplus will decline. More desirable is to earn a **net interest spread**, a return higher than the actuarial assumption. Consistent higher returns would grow the surplus and give the company competitive advantage in offering products to the market at a lower price (i.e., lower premiums).

While it is theoretically desirable to look at total return it can be difficult to do in the insurance industry. Regulation generally requires liabilities to be shown at some version of book value. Valuing assets at market value but liabilities at book value can create unintended consequences.

The general thrust is to segment the investment portfolio by significant line of business and set objectives by the characteristics of that line of business. The investments are heavily fixed-income oriented with an exception. The surplus may pursue more aggressive objectives such as stock, real estate, and private equity.

Life Insurance Company Constraints

Liquidity. Volatility and changes in the marketplace have increased the attention life insurance companies pay to liquidity issues. There are two key issues:

- Companies must consider **disintermediation risk** as previously discussed. This has led to shorter durations, higher liquidity reserves, and closer ALM matching. Duration and disintermediation issues can be interrelated. Consider a company with asset duration exceeding liability duration. If interest rates rise, asset value will decline faster than liability value. If the company needs to sell assets to fund payouts it would be doing so at relatively low values and likely a loss on the asset sale. A mismatch of duration compounds the problem of disintermediation.
- **Asset marketability risk** has also become a larger consideration. Traditionally life insurance companies held relatively large portions of the portfolio in illiquid assets. The increased liquidity demands on the portfolios have lead to greater emphasis on liquid assets.

The growth of derivatives has lead many companies to look for derivative-based risk management solutions.

Time horizon. Traditionally long at 20–40 years, it has become shorter for all the reasons discussed previously. Segmentation and duration matching by line of business is the norm.

Tax considerations. Life insurance companies are taxable entities. Laws vary by country but often the return up to the actuarial assumed rate is tax free and above that is taxed. The reality is quite complex and tax laws are changing. Ultimately after-tax return is the objective.

Professor's Note: Again remember the CFA exam does not presume you are a tax or legal expert. Only state what you are taught and remember if a case brings up complex issues to state the need to seek qualified advice. <u>Candidates are expected to know when to seek help, not to know what the advice will be.</u>

Legal and regulatory constraints. Life insurance companies are heavily regulated. In the United States, it is primarily at the state level. These regulations are very complex and may not be consistent by regulator. Regulations often address the following:

- **Eligible investments** by asset class are defined and percentage limits on holdings are generally stated. Criteria such as the minimum interest coverage ratio on corporate bonds are frequently specified.
- In the United States, the **prudent investor rule** has been adopted by some states. This replaces the list of eligible investments approach discussed in the bullet above in favor of portfolio risk versus return. (Essentially modern portfolio theory as the risk is portfolio risk including correlation effects).
- Valuations methods are commonly specified (and are some version of book value accounting). Because the regulators do consider these valuations, it limits the ability to focus on market value and total return of the portfolio.

These regulatory issues do significantly affect the eligible investment for and the asset allocation of the portfolio.

Unique circumstances. Concentration of product offerings, company size, and level of surplus are some of the most common factors impacting each company.

NON-LIFE INSURANCE COMPANIES

Professor's Note: Non-life companies include a variety of insurance types. The reading is specifically discussing property and casualty companies.

Non-life insurance is very similar to life insurance. ALM is crucial to both. It differs from life insurance in a several areas:

- While policies are written for a specific time period (usually a year or less) and the liability duration is short, there is often a **long tail** to the policy. A claim could be filed and take years to process before payout. Think of a contentious claim that is litigated for years before payout.

- Many non-life policies have **inflation risk**. The company may insure replacement value of the insured item creating less certain and higher payoffs on claims. In contrast life insurance policies are typically for a stated face value.
- Life insurance payouts are generally very predictable in amount but harder to predict in timing. Non-life is hard to predict in both amount and timing.
- Non-life business risk can be very concentrated geographically or with regard to specific events.

The conclusion will be that the operating results for non-life insurance companies are more volatile than for life insurance companies, duration is shorter, liquidity needs are both larger and less predictable.

Non-Life Insurance Company Objectives

Risk. Like life companies, non-life companies have a quasi-fiduciary requirement and must be invested to meet policy claims. However, the payoffs on claims are less predictable. For example a company that insures property in a specific area that is then hit with severe weather can experience sudden high claims and payouts. Also there is inflation risk if the payout is based on replacement cost of the insured item. Key considerations are:

1. The *cash flow characteristics* of non-life companies are often erratic and unpredictable. Hence, risk tolerance, as it pertains to loss of principal and declining investment income, is low.

2. The *common stock-to-surplus ratio* has been changing. Traditionally the surplus might have been invested in stock. Poor stock market returns in the 1970s and regulator concerns lead to reduced stock holdings. Bull markets in the 1990s only partially reversed this trend.

> *Professor's Note: The underlying issue about to be discussed is that the non-life business is both cyclical and erratic in profitability and cash flow. The investment portfolio seeks to smooth profitability and provide for unpredictable liquidity needs. Unfortunately there is no obvious way to do this. This reading will only make you aware of some complexities. It will not make you an insurance portfolio expert.*

Return. Historically and irrationally, non-life companies often ignored the expected return on the investment portfolio when deciding how to price their insurance policies. This is irrational because the premiums received from selling policies provide the funds to invest and the investment returns partially cover future payouts on the policies. That is changing, but in this highly competitive and cyclical business, setting a long-term portfolio return objective is difficult. The key factors include:

- Competitive product pricing: When policy prices are low, there is pressure to set high investment return targets to balance the low premiums received from selling policies.

- Profitability: Profits can swing from positive (in which case taxes are owed and the tax rate is positive) to losses (in which case no taxes are owed and the tax rate is effectively zero). Over the course of this profitability cycle, the objective is to earn a sufficient return on the portfolio to provide an attractive return on capital.
- Grow the surplus: Higher investment returns allow the value of assets to grow faster than that of liabilities. This has two beneficial effects. With a higher surplus (which means increased capital), the company can sell more insurance and grow the business faster. Second, with a higher surplus, the investment portfolio can take more risk and increase the allocation to securities such as common stock, convertible securities, and alternative investments with a higher expected return.
- Tax issues: As profits swing from negative and an effective tax rate of 0 to positive and a non-zero tax rate, the portfolio may swing from taxable bonds to tax exempt bonds (in the United States where such bonds exist).
- Total return approach: These companies generally focus more on total return (no distinctions between income earned, realized, and unrealized gains and losses) compared to life insurance.

These factors interact to produce an **underwriting** or **profitability cycle**. When profitable, companies will pay taxes and may find it attractive to shift investments out of taxable bonds and into tax-exempt bonds. While tax-exempt bonds have a lower yield, the untaxed return is higher than an after-tax return on taxable bonds. However, the tax-exempt yield curve tends to be relatively steeper than the yield curve for taxable bonds. This creates an inducement to buy longer tax-exempt bonds and increase asset duration for higher expected return.

The positive profitably may also lead companies to lower policy premiums (the prices charged on policies) to attract business. Then, as claims on these policies are made, profits turn to losses. At the same time, there are increased demands to liquidate portfolio assets to meet policyholder claims and with no taxes owed, taxable bonds become more attractive than tax-exempt bonds. The less steep yield curve for taxable bonds provides less incentive to extend asset duration, and asset duration is likely to decline. To restore profitability, the company increases premiums charged. As profits are restored, liquidity demands decline, the effective tax rate increases, and the incentive to hold tax-exempt bonds increases again.

All of this makes setting asset duration more complex than just matching liability duration. Companies model multiple scenarios of the underwriting/profit cycle, liability duration in each product line, and liquidity needs. Asset duration shifts with these variables.

Non-Life Insurance Company Constraints

Compared to life insurance companies:

- **Time horizon** is shorter due to shorter liability duration but with a **long tail** for policyholder payouts.
- **Liquidity** needs are higher and less predictable. There are typically large holdings of marketable, money market type assets. Marketable government bonds are used to match liability characteristics and specific, identifiable cash flow needs.
- The **underwriting cycle** can lead to shifts in allocation between taxable and tax exempt bonds.

Legal and regulatory constraints. Regulatory considerations are less onerous for non-life insurance companies than for life insurance companies. An asset valuation reserve (AVR) is not required, but risk-based capital (RBC) requirements have been established. Non-life companies are given more leeway in choosing investments compared to life insurance companies.

Unique circumstances. There are no generalizations to make.

Conclusion

Despite this attempt to make general comments, the investment approach and results of non-life companies are divergent. There is wide variation in what particular regulators allow. Types of insurance products and resulting liability duration vary. Tax situations differ. Some companies may favor income return versus price change. Company financial strength and surplus position vary.

BANKS

> **For the Exam:** A bank IPS is somewhat unique. It is driven by the fundamentals of the banking business and derives from the role of the investment portfolio in that business.

The objectives and constraints of a bank's securities portfolio derive from its place in the overall asset liability structure of the bank. Banks are in business to take in deposits (liabilities), make loans (assets), and make a profit primarily from a spread off the interest earned on assets less paid on liabilities. A potential problem exists in the relationship between a bank's assets and liabilities. Liabilities are mostly in the form of short-term deposits, while assets (loans) can be fairly long term in nature and illiquid. The loans also generally offer returns that are higher and more risky than can be earned on the securities in which banks invest. This leads to a significant mismatch in asset-liability durations, liquidity, and quality.

The bank's security (investment) portfolio is a **residual use of funds** (i.e., excess funds that have not been loaned out or are required to be held as reserves against deposits). While it is desirable to earn an attractive return on the portfolio, the primary purposes of the securities portfolio in order of importance are:

1. Manage total balance sheet interest rate risk by adjusting the duration of assets to more closely match the duration of liabilities.

2. Maintain adequate liquidity to compensate for the less liquid loan assets. In general, the bank investment portfolio is heavily or exclusively short-term government securities.

3. Contribute to bank income with interest earned.

4. Manage overall credit risk, normally by holding very high quality securities to balance the higher risk of loan assets.

Managing Interest Rate Risk

It is generally easier and timelier to adjust the characteristics of the investment portfolio than it is to adjust the characteristics of the liabilities or of the other assets (the loans). Generally the investment portfolio manager adjusts the bank's investment portfolio duration such that overall **asset duration** is kept in the desired relationship to **liability duration**.

In theory if a manager forecasts increasing interest rates, she can decrease the duration of the portfolio to set the overall asset duration below the liability duration. If the interest rate prediction is correct, the assets will decline less than the liabilities for an economic gain. The reality is this is very risky and is not done or done in very limited fashion for banks. Bank leverage is very high with very low equity capital to assets. Thus the primary goal is to adjust the duration of the portfolio such that overall duration of assets matches liability duration.

Bank Risk Measures

Professor's Note: Banks are heavily regulated and the regulators define various reporting measures for the bank. Following is a brief discussion of some of them. VAR is discussed extensively in other parts of the curriculum and is a common source of questions.

Leverage adjusted duration gap (LADG) receives only a passing comment in the CFA text and no math is covered. It is just duration of assets versus liabilities taking into account that they will not be of equal size. LADG is just a specialized application of ALM used by some bank regulators.

Both assets and liabilities are sensitive to changing interest rates. Banks continually monitor their interest rate risk. Value at risk (VAR) is one commonly used tool. Regulators often define and specify calculation methodology, set minimum target levels, and impose restrictions if targets are not met.

Leverage-adjusted duration gap is another regulatory tool. It is defined as the duration of the bank's assets less the *leveraged* duration of the bank's liabilities:

$$LADG = D_{assets} - \left(\frac{L}{A}\right) D_{liabilities}$$

where:
$LADG$ = leverage adjusted duration gap
D_{assets} = duration of the bank's assets
$D_{liabilities}$ = duration of the bank's liabilities
$\frac{L}{A}$ = leverage measure (market value of liabilities over market value of assets)

If LADG is:

- Zero, equity should be unaffected by interest rate changes.
- Positive, equity change is inverse to rates (e.g., rates up equity down).
- Negative, equity value moves in the same direction as rates.

THE BANK IPS

Bank Objectives

Risk. The acceptable risk should be set in an ALM framework based on the effect on the overall bank balance sheet. Banks usually have a below-average risk tolerance because they cannot let losses in the security portfolio interfere with their ability to meet their liabilities.

Return. The return objective for the bank securities portfolio is to earn a positive interest spread. The interest spread is the difference between the bank's cost of funds and the interest earned on loans and other investments.

Bank Constraints

Liquidity. A bank's liquidity needs are driven by deposit withdrawals and demand for loans as well as regulation. The resulting portfolio is generally short and liquid.

Time horizon. The time horizon is short and linked to the duration of the liabilities.

Taxes. Banks are taxable entities. After-tax return is the objective.

Legal and regulatory. Banks in industrialized nations are highly regulated. Risk-based capital (RBC) guidelines require banks to establish RBC reserves against assets; the riskier the asset, the higher the required capital. This tilts the portfolio towards high-quality, short-term, liquid assets.

Unique. There are no particular general issues.

ASSET/LIABILITY MANAGEMENT FOR INSTITUTIONAL INVESTORS

LOS 13.m: Compare the asset/liability management needs of pension funds, foundations, endowments, insurance companies, and banks.

CFA® Program Curriculum, Volume 2, page 467

ALM is the preferred framework for evaluation portfolios with definable, measurable liabilities. Focusing on asset return and risk is not sufficient. The focus should be on surplus and surplus volatility. At a minimum, asset and liability duration should be matched to stabilize surplus. Depending on risk tolerance, active management through defined deviations in asset and liability duration might be used to exploit expected changes in interest rates.

Hint: this is discussed in multiple study sessions and perhaps best covered in fixed income with numeric calculations.

➡ DB pension plans, insurance companies, and banks are the most suited to the ALM approach.

INVESTMENT COMPANIES

LOS 13.l: Contrast investment companies, commodity pools, and hedge funds to other types of institutional investors.

CFA® Program Curriculum, Volume 2, page 526

The institutional portfolios discussed up to now manage money for a particular entity (e.g., a bank or an insurance company). Categorizing by group offers useful insights. All DB plans have similarities in their objectives and share common issues of analysis. In contrast, **investment companies**, **commodity pools**, and **hedge funds** are institutional investors but are just intermediaries that pool and invest money for groups of investors and pass the returns through to those investors. Unlike other institutional investors it is not possible to generalize about their policy statements.

- **Investment companies** are **mutual funds** and invest in accord with their prospectus. There are mutual funds, for example, to fit just about any equity or fixed-income investment style, from small-cap growth funds to large-cap value funds to funds that invest exclusively in one of a variety of sectors or industries.
- **Commodity pools** invest in commodity-related futures, options contracts, and related instruments.
- **Hedge funds** are highly diverse. Grouping all hedge fund types under the same general heading explains virtually nothing about what each fund does. Hedge funds gather money from institutional and wealthy individual investors and construct various investment strategies aimed at identifying and capitalizing on mispriced securities.

☾ All three of these pool money from a group of investors and pursue the stated objective of the portfolio.

INVESTMENT POLICIES OF INSTITUTIONAL INVESTORS

LOS 13.i: Compare the investment objectives and constraints of foundations, endowments, insurance companies, and banks. (Cont.)

LOS 13.j: Discuss the factors that determine investment policy for pension funds, foundations, endowments, life and non-life insurance companies, and banks.

LOS 13.k: Prepare an investment policy statement for a foundation, an endowment, an insurance company, and a bank. (Cont.)

LOS 13.n: Compare the investment objectives and constraints of institutional investors given relevant data, such as descriptions of their financial circumstances and attitudes toward risk.

CFA® Program Curriculum, Volume 2, pages 484, 486, and 465

The following tables provide a general summary of some key differences. Answers to questions should be based on the specifics of each case. All portfolios, both individual and institutional, should be presumed to follow a total return perspective unless the case facts direct otherwise. Total return does not distinguish between the sources of return; whether they be income, unrealized, or realized price change.

Figure 2: Summary of Risk and Return Issues

	Return	Risk
Defined benefit plans	The plan liability discount rate is normally the minimum return target though many plans aim for a percent or two higher. ALM is the focus.	Determined by plan and sponsor characteristics. Risk tolerance is decreased by a negative surplus, weak financial status of sponsor, strong + correlation of plan and sponsor results, and plan or workforce characteristics that reduce time horizon and increase liquidity needs. Generally moderate or lower compared to foundations and endowments.
Foundations and endowments	Typically the multiplicative combination of target distribution, relevant future inflation, and expense rates. Asset-only is the focus.	Often the most aggressive of institutions. May be reduced when the receiver is more dependent on the fund distributions.
Insurance	Generally the actuarial assumed return needed to meet liabilities or higher. Segmenting the portfolio by line of business is common. Higher risk equity type return is generally limited to the surplus. ALM is the focus.	Typically conservative (except for the surplus). It is not unusual for non-life companies to reset the return objective during the course of the underwriting cycle. Often considered to be quasi-fiduciaries.
Banks	Contribute to interest earnings but the securities portfolio is primarily managed as a residual to adjust bank asset to liability duration and provide liquidity. ALM is the focus.	Conservative, fixed income, and mostly government securities.

Figure 3: Summary of Constraints

	Time Horizon	*Liquidity*
Defined benefit plans	Primarily determine by the characteristics of the plan participants (i.e., the duration of the plan liabilities).	As required to meet payout needs.
Foundations and endowments	Often perpetual.	Varies and based on case specifics. A smoothing rule makes distributions more predictable, less dependent on a single ending market value, and may therefore increase risk tolerance.
Insurance	Generally the duration of the liabilities. Life insurance is often longer and non-life shorter though non-life can face a long tail related to litigation of claims.	Life insurance aggregate liquidity needs are generally predictable though some policies include provisions that create disintermediation risk. Non-life needs are generally higher, less predictable, and some policies insure replacement value (linking future payouts to inflation).
Banks	Short and linked to liability duration.	Emphasis on highly liquid securities.

Figure 4: Summary of Constraints, continued

	Taxes	Legal/Regulatory	Unique
Defined benefit plans	Generally tax exempt.	Generally a prudent expert standard*, ERISA in the United States, managed solely for the plan beneficiaries.	None in particular, a small plan may not have the financial resources for appropriate due diligence on complex investments.
Foundations and endowments	Generally tax exempt, but watch out for case-specific exceptions.	Generally a prudent investor standard*, lightly regulated, UMIFA in the United States.	Watch for concentrated single asset positions, restrictions on sale of assets, and SRI.
Insurance	Generally taxable.	Heavily and subject to multiple levels of regulation. There may be restrictions on allowable assets and capital requirements. Non-life is somewhat less regulated.	None in particular.
Banks	Generally taxable.	Heavily regulated. There may be restrictions on allowable assets and capital requirements.	None in particular.

*For prudent expert (different than the prudent investor), the manager is presumed to be trained and to know what she is doing. It generally presumes a need to diversify. A prudent investor is not presumed to have the same investment training but would operate as an ordinary business person.

KEY CONCEPTS

LOS 13.a

For DB plans, the sponsor promises a future benefit. This creates a pension liability and the sponsor bears the investment risk (i.e., defined future benefits are promised).

For DC plans, the sponsor promises a current contribution and the employees bear the investment risk (i.e., no specific future benefit is promised).

DB plans create early termination risk that the plan will be terminated or the employee will leave before vesting (owning the promised benefit).

For DC plans, the employee generally owns the contribution and subsequent return as soon as they occur. The benefits are generally portable.

DC plans can be sponsor directed where the sponsor makes the investment decision on behalf of the participants or participant directed where participants select from among a set of investment alternatives offered by the sponsor.

LOS 13.b

The two objectives are:
- Risk.
- Return.

The five constraints are:
- Time horizon.
- Taxes.
- Liquidity.
- Legal and regulatory factors.
- Unique circumstances.

In determining the investment objectives, it is helpful to first determine the plan sponsor's risk tolerance before the determination of the return objective. Pension plans are typically tax exempt.

LOS 13.c

Pension fund risk tolerance is increased (decreased) by:
- Positive (negative) surplus.
- Stronger (weaker) financial status and profitability of the plan sponsor.
- Lower (higher) correlation of plan asset returns and the sponsor's business.
- Plan features and workforce characteristics that increase (decrease) time horizon and lower (increase) liquidity needs.

LOS 13.d
IPS for Defined-Benefit Plan

Return: The actuarial discount rate or somewhat higher.

Risk: Determined by plan and sponsor characteristics. Factors reducing risk tolerance include shorter time horizon, higher liquidity needs, weak sponsor, and positive correlation of sponsor results with plan asset returns.

Time horizon: Linked to liability duration.

Taxes: Generally untaxed.

Legal/regulatory: A prudent expert managing the assets for the benefit of plan participants.

Liquidity: Linked to needs for plan payouts.

Unique: Watch for small plans with inadequate resources to complete proper due diligence.

LOS 13.e
High (positive) correlation of plan asset returns to sponsor operating results reduces risk tolerance because when asset returns are poor and additional contributions may be required, the sponsor is least able to make those contributions and meet the pension liabilities.

ALM is superior to asset only management because it explicitly manages the expected return and volatility of the surplus. It is the size of the surplus that directly affects the future burden of the plan on the sponsor and the sponsor's ability to meet the pension liabilities.

LOS 13.f
In a defined-contribution plan, the plan employer does not establish the investment goals and constraints; rather, the employee decides her own risk and return objectives. Therefore, the employee bears the risk of the investment results. Consequently, the investment policy statement (IPS) for a defined-contribution plan describes the investment alternatives available to the plan participants. This IPS becomes a document of governing principles instead of an IPS for an individual. Some of the issues addressed in the IPS would be:

- Making a distinction between the responsibilities of the plan participants, the fund managers, and the plan sponsor.
- Providing descriptions of the investment alternatives available to the plan participants.
- Providing criteria for monitoring and evaluation of the performance of the investment choices.
- Providing criteria for selection, termination, and replacement of investment choices.
- Establishing effective communication between the fund managers, plan participants, and the plan sponsor.

LOS 13.g

A cash balance plan is a defined-benefit plan that defines the benefit in terms of an account balance, which the beneficiary can take as an annuity at retirement or as a lump sum to roll into another plan. In a typical cash balance plan, a participant's account is credited each year with a pay credit and an interest credit. The pay credit is typically based upon the beneficiary's age, salary, and/or length of employment, and the interest credit is based upon a benchmark such as U.S. Treasuries. Rather than an actual account with a balance, the cash balance is a paper balance only and represents a future liability for the company.

An employee stock ownership plan (ESOP) is a type of defined-contribution benefit plan that allows employees to purchase the company stock. The purchase can be with before- or after-tax dollars and the final balance in the beneficiary's account reflects the increase in the value of the firm's stock as well as contributions during employment.

LOS 13.h

Foundations

Type of Foundation	Description	Purpose	Source of Funds	Annual Spending Requirement
Independent	Private or family	Grants to public groups	Individual or family	5% of assets
Company sponsored	By a corporation	Public and company grants	Corporate sponsor	5% of assets
Operating	Established to fund an organization (e.g., museum, zoo, or some ongoing research/medical initiative)		Individual or family	At least 85% of dividend and interest income for operations
Community	Publicly sponsored	Grants to public groups	General public	None

LOS 13.i, j, k, n

Defined Benefit Plans

Return: The actuarial discount rate or somewhat higher.

Risk: Determined by plan and sponsor characteristics. Factors reducing risk tolerance include shorter time horizon, higher liquidity needs, weak sponsor, and positive correlation of sponsor results with plan asset returns.

Time horizon: Linked to liability duration.

Taxes: Generally untaxed.

Legal/regulatory: A prudent expert managing the assets for the benefit of plan participants.

Liquidity: Linked to needs for plan payouts.

Unique: Watch for small plans with inadequate resources to complete proper due diligence.

Foundations and Endowments

Return: Geometric link of distribution, relevant inflation, and expense rates.

Risk: Often higher, may be diminished if the beneficiary is heavily dependent on the distributions.

Time horizon: Often perpetual.

Taxes: Generally untaxed, but watch out for specifically taxed income sources.

Legal/regulatory: Relatively unregulated.

Liquidity: Situation specific.

Unique: Watch for concentrated positions, restrictions on sale, and SRI.

Insurance

Return: At minimum the return assumed by the actuaries, may be set by line of business.

Risk: Generally conservative though the surplus may be invested more aggressively.

Time horizon: Related to duration of the liabilities, non-life tends to be shorter but with a long tail related to claims litigation.

Taxes: Generally taxable.

Legal/regulatory: Heavily regulated at multiple levels. Non-life is generally less regulated.

Liquidity: Situation specific. Life is generally more predictable than non-life. Some life policies introduce disintermediation risk. Non-life may also insure replacement value making liquidity needs dependent on inflation.

Unique: None in particular.

Banks

Return: Contribute to interest earnings, but the securities portfolio is primarily a residual used to manage overall asset duration and provide liquidity.

Risk: Heavily regulated and conservative.

Time horizon: Related to duration of the liabilities, generally shorter.

Taxes: Generally taxable.

Legal/regulatory: Heavily regulated at multiple levels. Subject to numerous asset and capital limits.

Liquidity: Emphasis on highly liquid securities, mainly government securities.

Unique: None in particular.

LOS 13.l

Investment companies, **commodity pools**, and **hedge funds** are intermediaries which gather and invest funds. Funds are invested according to the specific rules of the portfolio making generalizations about investment characteristics impossible.

LOS 13.m

ALM (management of surplus) is more appropriate than asset-only management when there are definable future liabilities. Thus, ALM is more appropriate for DB plans, insurance companies, and banks (but not for foundations and endowments).

Total return management (as opposed to specifying sources of return: income, realized, and unrealized price change) is appropriate for all portfolios unless otherwise specified.

CONCEPT CHECKERS

1. Alexander Ellington, President of Ellington Foods, has contacted your firm to discuss the company's defined-benefit pension plan. He has provided the following information about the company and its pension plan:

   - Ellington Foods has annual sales of $300 million.
   - The annual payroll is about $100 million.
   - The average age of the workforce is 43 years.
   - 30% of the plan participants are now retired.
   - Company profits last year were $10 million and have been growing at 10% annually. The Ellington Foods pension plan has $80 million in assets and is currently overfunded by 10%.
   - The duration of the plan's liabilities is 15 years.
   - The discount rate applied to liabilities is 6%.
   - Fund trustees wish to maintain 5% of plan assets in cash.

   Ellington would like to achieve a rate of return of 7% on its pension fund (which is less than the 9% that the fund has historically achieved). Ellington would like to be able to reduce contributions to the pension fund and possibly increase employee benefits.

   Formulate and **justify** investment policy objectives for the Ellington Foods pension plan in the following three areas:

   i.   Return objective.

   ii. Risk tolerance.

   iii. Time horizon.

2. Ellington appreciated your advice but decided to handle the situation "in house." Assume ten years have passed and Ellington has returned to you for advice. The average age of the workforce is now 51 years. Sixty percent of the plan participants are now retired. The duration of the plan's liabilities is four years. The fund is currently underfunded by 20%. The discount rate applied to the liabilities is 9%. Company profits have been in decline for the past two years but are expected to turn around in the upcoming year. Given the updated information:

    Discuss and **justify** how investment policy objectives for the Ellington Foods Pension Plan in the following three areas have changed from 10 years ago.

    i. Return objective.

    ii. Risk tolerance.

    iii. Time horizon.

3. **Describe** how a defined contribution (DC) plan most likely differs from a defined benefit (DB) plan in relation to:

    i.   Who makes the contributions.

    ii. Investment risk.

    iii. Who makes investment decisions.

4.   Aid to the Homeless is a nonprofit organization that provides funding throughout the Washington D.C. area to run shelters for the homeless. The Cassidy Endowment Fund provides a large portion of the Aid to the Homeless's operating budget. The endowment fund was set up by the Cassidy family as a way to leave a legacy to their father. He was a wealthy entrepreneur throughout his lifetime but suffered from dementia in old age and consequently lived out his last days wandering the streets of D.C. as a homeless person. The fund has assets totaling $5 million, and directors of the endowment anticipate a spending rate of 6%. Inflation is expected to be 3% annually.

A. i.   **Calculate** the return objective for the fund. Show your work.

ii.   **Explain** one factor that increases and one factor that decreases the fund's risk objective. Each factor must be based directly on the information provided. Then draw an overall conclusion for the risk objective.

iii.   **State** the time horizon for the fund.

B. From the following asset allocations, **select** the one allocation that best
serves the needs of the Endowment Fund and **justify** its selection by
discussing return objective, diversification, and efficiency.

Asset Classes	Expected Total Return	Cash Flow Yield	Portfolios			
			A	B	C	D
U.S. stocks	12%	2.0%	20%	40%	35%	20%
Non-U.S. stocks	15%	1.5%	15%	20%	15%	0%
U.S. corporate bonds	8%	8.0%	20%	0%	25%	40%
U.S. Treasury bonds	7%	7.0%	5%	0%	20%	35%
Real estate	10%	4.0%	10%	20%	0%	0%
U.S. Treasury bills	4%	4.0%	30%	20%	5%	5%
Expected total return			8.8%	10.6%	10.1%	8.3%
Expected yield (cash flow)			4.2%	2.7%	4.5%	6.3%
Sharpe measure			0.20	0.21	0.26	0.27

5. U.S.-based Liles Insurance Company has recently decided to segment its portfolio into those assets used to meet liabilities and those assets considered surplus. George Baxter, CFO, has drafted his proposal for the asset allocation for the surplus portfolio, which appears below. He has contacted your firm to establish an IPS and to review the proposed asset allocation for its surplus portfolio. The surplus portfolio contains $75 million of the firm's $800 million in total assets. The goal of the surplus portfolio is to increase the firm's competitive advantage while the non-surplus portfolio is duration matched to the liability duration of 15.

Proposed Allocation—Liles Life Insurance Surplus Portfolio

Asset Class	Proposed Allocation (%)	Expected Return (%)
Cash	10	4
U.S. intermediate bonds (5-year duration)	5	6
U.S. long-term bonds (20-year duration)	45	7
U.S. equities	25	12
Developed market equities	15	13
Equity REITs	0	14
Venture capital	0	22

A. For each of the following objectives and constraints, **state** whether and **explain** why it is likely to be higher or lower in the surplus portfolio than in the non-surplus portfolio.

   i. Return objective.

   ii. Risk tolerance.

   iii. Liquidity requirements.

B. For the surplus portfolio and each asset class listed below, **state** and **explain** whether it should most likely be increased, decreased, or unchanged from the current allocation, and **explain** why. Each decision should be independent of the others; if you increase one it does not automatically mean you must decrease another.

    i. Cash

    ii. U.S. long-term bonds

    iii. U.S equity

6.   The asset-liability management committee (ALCO) for First Southern Piedmont Bank (FSPB) is discussing recent changes in the bank's balance sheet due to an acquisition of another bank. FSPB expects that (1) loan demand will increase substantially, (2) borrower credit quality will decline, and (3) loans will shift toward floating rate rather than long-term fixed rate. **Discuss** the three most likely instructions the ALCO will issue to the bank's portfolio manager in light of these three anticipated balance sheet changes.

For more questions related to this topic review, log in to your Schweser online account and launch SchweserPro™ QBank; and for video instruction covering each LOS in this topic review, log in to your Schweser online account and launch the OnDemand video lectures, if you have purchased these products.

ANSWERS – CONCEPT CHECKERS

1. i. *Return objective.* The minimum return is the discount rate of 6% with a higher desired return of 7%.

   ii. *Risk tolerance.* The fund has an above-average ability to tolerate risk. First, the time horizon is relatively long with an average employee age of 43 and liability duration of 15. Second, the plan is 30% retired lives versus 70% active lives, which suggest higher contributions (inflows) to benefit payments (outflows) and reduced liquidity needs. Third, the plan is overfunded by 10%.

   iii. *Time horizon.* Long term with liability duration of 15.

   Professor's Note: The exam is generally shifting to more structured questions such as, "Give three reasons that increase the plan's risk tolerance." Less frequently, the exam requires you to label a factor as average, above average, or below average. If required to label, look at how all the relevant factors line up and see which way they tilt. If labeling is not requested, you do not have to, though if you are familiar with the cases presented in the curriculum, you can often make a reasonable judgment and can do so.

2. i. *Return objective.* Required return has increased to the new discount rate of 9%. The ability to aim for a higher desired return has been diminished as the ability to take risk has declined.

   ii. *Risk tolerance has decreased.* The surplus is now a deficit. Retired lives have increased to 60%. Liability duration has declined to 4 and workforce age has increased to 51.

   iii. *Time horizon.* The time horizon has decreased due to the shortening of the duration of the plan's liabilities.

3. i. The sponsor typically funds a DB plan, while DC plans are often a combination of employee contributions with employer matches.

   ii. For DC plans, the sponsor risk is primarily limited to making the contributions, while for a DB plan, the sponsor remains at risk to fund a promised payout at retirement. Overall DC plans shift the investment risk to the employees.

   iii. For DB the sponsor. For DC each employee typically selects investments from a list of choices, although there are sponsor-directed DC plans where the sponsor selects the investments.

4. A.

   i. Earn the distribution rate and future inflation:

   $(1.06)(1.03) - 1 = 9.18\%$

   Candidate Discussion: An additive return of 9% is usually accepted but multiplicative is preferred for foundations and endowments.

        ii.   • The fund provides a "large portion" of the endowment's operating budget, which reduces risk tolerance as the receiver is more dependent on the distributions.
               • Endowments are generally perpetual and that long time horizon increases risk tolerance because time tends to average out the volatility of returns.
               • Overall risk tolerance is average compared to other endowments.

        iii. Perpetual

    B. Select C.
        • It meets the return objective of 9.18%.
        • It is well diversified with 50% stock and 50% fixed income. The stock also includes international diversification.
        • It is efficient with the second-best Sharpe of 0.26 (the highest Sharpe ratio, is Portfolio D and D is unacceptable with a below acceptable return).

> Candidate Discussion: Only C is acceptable following the process of elimination. A and D have insufficient return. B is inefficient with a low Sharpe ratio, likely due to excessive cash drag of 20% T-bills. Once C is selected, then the conclusions to support it are listed. The 50/50 equity/fixed allocation is a bit low, but C is still the only acceptable choice. Discussion of current yield is irrelevant as total return is the normal perspective; if the return is sufficient, funds for distribution can be generated.

5. A. i. Higher in the surplus portfolio to meet the objective of using the surplus portfolio to increase competitive advantage. Higher return will directly increase profit margins and indirectly grow the surplus to support expanding the business to gain market share.

        ii. Higher in the surplus portfolio. Insurance companies are allowed to take more risk with the surplus.

        iii. Lower in the surplus portfolio. Liquidity needs to fund payouts are covered by the non-surplus portfolio.

    B. i. Decrease, liquidity needs are met by the non-surplus portfolio. The cash in the surplus just creates cash drag and lower return.

        ii. Decrease, liability duration matching is done in the non-surplus portfolio allowing the surplus to be invested in higher return, non-fixed income assets.

        iii. Increase to increase expected return, grow the surplus, and meet the objective of increasing competitive advantage.

6.   • Emphasize liquid securities in anticipation of reducing the size of the investment portfolio in order to meet increased loan demand.
     • Emphasize higher quality assets to offset higher credit risk in the loans.
     • Lengthen securities portfolio duration to offset declining loan portfolio duration.

> Candidate Discussion: This is a test of the residual theory of the bank portfolio. Recall that a bank's assets are primarily the loan and securities portfolios. For each anticipated change in the loan portfolio, the securities portfolio would be expected to make an offsetting change to compensate. When answering these questions, do not make unsupported assumptions that might lead to different conclusions [e.g., do not assume that the bank's deposit (liability) duration is also shifting and, therefore, a different action is required for the securities portfolio]. While not asked, the net result is likely to be an increase in the allocation to longer term, government securities.

                                ©2017 Kaplan, Inc.

Use the following information for Questions 1 through 6.

Rob Baker, an investment manager at Welker Auto Parts, is responsible for managing his company's defined-benefit pension plan. The plan has been underfunded for several months and Baker is meeting today with Gary Thompson, the company's CFO, to discuss possible ways to erase this liability funding shortfall.

During the meeting, Baker and Thompson make a number of comments:

Comment 1:   Baker proposes that the plan should increase the value of its pension assets by investing in riskier securities. Currently, the plan invests a majority of its funds in investment-grade corporate bonds and large-cap equities. Baker is confident that investments in small-cap equities will help bring the fund back to fully funded status.

Comment 2:   Thompson is not confident that shifting to riskier securities will guarantee an increase in pension asset values and points to the company's high debt ratio as an indication of a need to take a more risk-averse stance.

Comment 3:   Baker notifies Thompson of the high correlation of pension asset returns with the firm's operations and states that the high correlation increases the ability to take risk by increasing predictability and diversification.

Comment 4:   Thompson disagrees, suggesting that a firm's high ratio of active to retired lives diminishes the ability to take on more risk.

Baker and Thompson then turn to a list of additional discussion items:

Item 1:   Add an option to the plan that will allow participants to retire five years earlier than currently permitted at a 15% reduction in the value of the benefit payout.

Item 2:   Adopt an asset-only perspective to manage the pension plan, allowing for increased risk tolerance and a higher rate of return as compared to an asset/liability management perspective.

Item 3:   Freeze the plan. All new employees will participate in a new defined contribution plan where employees can select from a list of investment alternatives that will range from more conservative to more aggressive than the defined benefit plan.

Each item is independent and is to be considered in isolation, as if it is adopted and no other changes are made.

As they are leaving the meeting, Thompson mentions to Baker that the company founder is starting a perpetual foundation to fund technical studies at a local community college. Thompson has been asked to serve on the foundation's board.

1. Regarding Baker's comment 1 and Thompson's comment 2, which of the following *best* describes the appropriateness or inappropriateness of their views?

	Baker	Thompson
A.	Inappropriate	Appropriate
B.	Appropriate	Inappropriate
C.	Inappropriate	Inappropriate

2. Regarding Baker's comment 3 and Thompson's comment 4, which is *most likely* correct and incorrect?

	Baker	Thompson
A.	Incorrect	Correct
B.	Correct	Incorrect
C.	Incorrect	ncorrect

3. If the plan adopts the early retirement provision in item 1, what is the *most likely* immediate effect on the plan's liquidity needs and surplus?

	Liquidity needs	Surplus
A.	Increase	Increase
B.	Increase	Decrease
C.	Decrease	No change

4. Which of the following statements regarding item 2 is *most* correct? Item 2 is:
   A. correct; an asset-only perspective allows for an increased risk tolerance and return objective.
   B. correct; an asset-only perspective is an accepted method of managing plan assets in a defined benefit plan.
   C. incorrect; the plan is currently underfunded, which reduces its risk tolerance, and thus the plan sponsor should make additional payments into the plan, bringing it up to fully funded status.

5. Assuming item 3 is adopted and that most plan participants choose more aggressive assets than those in the pension plan portfolio, risk for the sponsor (Welker Auto Parts) will *most likely*:
   A. increase.
   B. decrease.
   C. be unchanged.

6. In contrast to a typical defined benefit plan, a foundation's risk and return objectives are likely to be:

	Risk tolerance	Return objective
A.	Higher	Higher
B.	Lower	Higher
C.	Lower	Lower

ANSWERS – SELF-TEST: PORTFOLIO MANAGEMENT FOR INSTITUTIONAL INVESTORS

1. **A** Baker's views are inappropriate. Despite the willingness to take greater risk by investing in small-cap equities, the plan's underfunded status has decreased the ability to take risk. Therefore, taking greater risk is inappropriate. Thompson's views are appropriate. A high debt ratio would indicate a decreased capability of making contributions and meeting plan liabilities.

2. **C** Baker's statement is incorrect. A high correlation of pension asset returns with a firm's operations reduces the ability to take risk. For example, the ability of the firm to make contributions will be low at the same time that the plan is underfunded. Thompson's statement is also incorrect. A high ratio of active to retired lives usually indicates an increased ability to take risk because it lowers liquidity needs and increases the time horizon.

3. **A** The early retirement option will increase liquidity needs. While the payments made to a given individual will be discounted by 15%, that individual can start taking money sooner, and disbursements from the plan will increase immediately. Liquidity refers to disbursement needs now, not the final amount of total payments made over time. If the early payout were done at full value of the payout, the cash disbursed (reducing PVA) would equal the reduction in PVL. However, with the 15% discount applied to the distribution's value, PVA will decline less than PVL and surplus will improve.

4. **C** The pension plan is currently underfunded, which reduces the plan's risk tolerance. Thus, the best option is for the plan sponsor to increase payments into the plan, thereby increasing plan assets and bringing the plan up to fully funded status. A pension plan could be managed from an asset-only perspective, but this is not the correct way to manage the pension plan assets in this instance because the plan is underfunded and the primary objective of a defined benefit plan is to meet its future obligations to plan participants.

5. **B** The risk of the plan for the plan sponsor will decrease regardless of the investment choices made by each participant. In a defined contribution plan, each participant bears the investment risk, not the sponsor.

6. **A** While specific situations can vary, a perpetual foundation may be very aggressive in their risk and return objectives in order to meet the intergenerational needs of the foundation.

Formulas

annual accrual taxation: $\text{FVIF}_{AT} = [1 + r(1 - t_i)]^n$

deferred capital gains taxation: $\text{FVIF}_{AT} = (1 + r)^n(1 - t_{cg}) + t_{cg}B$

$\qquad\qquad\qquad\qquad$ B = cost basis / asset value at start of period n

annual wealth taxation: $\text{FVIF}_{AT} = [(1 + r)(1 - t_w)]^n$

blended taxation:

$\quad$ weighted annual realized tax rate: $\text{wartr} = p_i t_i + p_d t_d + p_{cg} t_{cg}$

$\quad$ return after realized taxes: $r^* = r[1 - (p_i t_i + p_d t_d + p_{cg} t_{cg})] = r(1 - \text{wartr})$

$\quad$ effective capital gains tax rate: $T^* = t_{cg}[p_{deferred\ cg} / (1 - \text{wartr})]$

$\quad$ future value of the investment: $\text{FVIF}_{AT} = (1 + r^*)^n(1 - T^*) + T^* - (1 - B)t_{cg}$

future value interest factor for a tax-deferred account (TDA): $\text{FVIF}_{AT} = (1 + r)^n(1 - t_n)$

future value interest factor for a tax-exempt account: $\text{FVIF}_{AT} = (1 + r)^n$

after tax return: $r_{AT} = r(1 - t)$

after tax standard deviation: $\sigma_{AT} = \sigma(1 - t)$

relative after-tax value:

$$RV_{\text{tax-free gift}} = \frac{FV_{\text{tax-free gift}}}{FV_{\text{bequest}}} = \frac{\left[1 + r_g\left(1 - t_{ig}\right)\right]^n}{\left[1 + r_e\left(1 - t_{ie}\right)\right]^n \left(1 - T_e\right)}$$

$$RV_{\text{taxable gift}} = \frac{FV_{\text{taxable gift}}}{FV_{\text{bequest}}} = \frac{\left[\left(1 - T_g\right)\right]\left[1 + r_g\left(1 - t_{ig}\right)\right]^n}{\left[1 + r_e\left(1 - t_{ie}\right)\right]^n \left(1 - T_e\right)} \quad \text{If the receiver pays the gift tax}$$

$$RV_{\text{taxable gift}} = \frac{\left(1 - T_g + T_g T_e\right)\left[1 + r_g\left(1 - t_{ig}\right)\right]^n}{\left[1 + r_e\left(1 - t_{ie}\right)\right]^n \left(1 - T_e\right)} \quad \text{(donor pays gift taxes)}$$

$$RV_{\text{charitable donation}} = \frac{FV_{\text{charitable gift}}}{FV_{\text{bequest}}} = \frac{\left(1+r_g\right)^n + T_{oi}\left[1+r_e\left(1-t_{ie}\right)\right]^n\left(1-T_e\right)}{\left[1+r_e\left(1-t_{ie}\right)\right]^n\left(1-T_e\right)}$$

generation skipping:

$$FV_{\text{no skipping}} = PV[(1+r)^{n1}(1-t)][(1+r)^{n2}(1-t)]$$

$$FV_{\text{skipping}} = PV[(1+r)^N(1-T_e)] \qquad\qquad [N = n1 + n2]$$

endowment spending rules:

$$\text{spending}_t = S\left(\text{market value}_{t-1}\right)$$

$$\text{spending}_t = \left(\text{spending rate}\right)\left(\frac{\text{market value}_{t-1} + \text{market value}_{t-2} + \text{market value}_{t-3}}{3}\right)$$

$$\text{spending}_t = \left(R\right)\left(\text{spending}_{t-1}\right)\left(1+I_{t-1}\right)+\left(1-R\right)\left(S\right)\left(\text{market value}_{t-1}\right)$$

leverage-adjusted duration gap: $LADG = D_{\text{Assets}} - \left(\frac{L}{A}\right)D_{\text{Liabilities}}$

Index

Symbols

Notes

Notes

Notes

Notes

Notes

Notes

Notes

Notes

Notes

Notes

Notes